Theodore C. Rose, James F. Burke

Proceedings of the Tenth Republican National Convention

held in the city of Minneapolis, Minn., June 7, 8, 9 and 10, 1892

Theodore C. Rose, James F. Burke

Proceedings of the Tenth Republican National Convention
held in the city of Minneapolis, Minn., June 7, 8, 9 and 10, 1892

ISBN/EAN: 9783337291280

Printed in Europe, USA, Canada, Australia, Japan

Cover: Foto ©Suzi / pixelio.de

More available books at **www.hansebooks.com**

OF THE

TENTH

Republican National Convention

HELD IN THE CITY OF

Minneapolis, Minn., June 7. 8. 9 and 10, 1892.

RESULTING IN THE NOMINATION OF

BENJAMIN HARRISON, OF INDIANA, FOR PRESIDENT,

AND

WHITELAW REID, OF NEW YORK, FOR VICE-PRESIDENT.

REPORTED BY

THEODORE C. ROSE, of New York, and
JAMES F. BURKE, of Pennsylvania,

Official Stenographers.

THE PROCEEDINGS.

THESE proceedings are published under the authority of the following resolution:

Resolved, That the Secretary of the Convention prepare a full report of the Republican National Conventions of 1856, 1860 and 1864, and cause them to be sold at the cost of printing, and a similar arrangement shall also be made for the publication of the Proceedings of this Convention.

Adopted, June 10, 1892.

CHAS. W. JOHNSON,
Secretary.

MINNEAPOLIS, MINN.:
HARRISON & SMITH, PRINTERS.
1892.

OFFICERS:

Temporary Chairman:
>HON. JACOB SLOAT FASSETT,
>>of New York.

Permanent Chairman:
>HON. WILLIAM McKINLEY, JR.,
>>of Ohio.

Secretary:
>CHARLES W. JOHNSON,
>>of Minnesota.

Sergeant-at-Arms:
>CHANNING F. MEEK,
>>of Colorado.

THE LOCAL COMMITTEE AND ITS WORK.

BY H. C. CHAPIN.

The idea that Minneapolis could and should be the place for holding a National Political Convention dates back as far as 1886. It came in connection with the erection of the great Exposition building—one argument used in behalf of that enterprise being that it would provide a place for such a national gathering. The following year, as the time approached for selecting the place for holding the Republican Convention of 1888, Minneapolis stepped into the arena as a contestant for the honor. Quite a large delegation went to Washington in December and urged the claims of the city at the Falls. Minneapolis received a comparatively small vote, but the entering wedge was driven and this city had taken its place on the list of possible convention cities.

In 1891, Minneapolis was one of the first in the field. The fact that Chicago would have the World's Fair on its hands, suggested the possibility that she would be willing to waive her claims to the National Convention. This would certainly give Minneapolis a good fighting chance. The various organizations of the city took hold of the movement and appointed committees to attend a general conference. At a meeting of the Exposition directors, May 20th, plans for fitting up a Convention hall in the building were discussed.

William Henry Eustis, who had been one of the most enthusiastic agitators, presided at the general meeting held in the rooms of the Union League, at which it was decided that a systematic effort be made to raise a guarantee fund of $50,000. Throughout the campaign that followed, leading Democrats co-operated with the Republicans cordially, notwithstanding the fact that one of the principal arguments used to get the Convention was that it would be a potent factor in keeping the Northwestern States within the Republican fold. Mayor P. B. Winston, a Democrat, accepted the Chairmanship of the Committee to raise the proposed fund, and many business men put their devotion to their city ahead of that to their party and contributed liberally of their time and money.

Various interruptions, notably the great Harvest Festival, delayed the final announcement that the fund had been raised. This was made at a meeting held Sept. 27th. Frequent meetings were held thereafter, but the responsibility was thrown upon an Executive committee, consisting of W. D. Washburn, W. S. King, Thomas Lowry, Gilbert A. Pierce, C. W. Johnson, Geo. A. Brackett, S. P. Snider, Wm. McCrory, A. R. McGill, John Goodnow, Eugene Hay, H. F. Brown, Wm. H. Eustis and S. E. Olson.

Hon. Gilbert A. Pierce was Chairman, William McCrory, Secretary, and E. J. Phelps, Treasurer, of this Committee. Secretary

McCrory and his assistant, E. A. Henderson, flooded the country with literature, and hundreds of letters were written by individuals to friends and acquaintances. Successful overtures were made securing the co-operation of citizens of St. Paul. Other overtures were made to secure a pledge from Chicago that no effort would be made to get the Convention to that city, and the announcement was soon published that Chicago was out of the race. While this raised Minneapolis' hopes high, it also roused the hopes and encouraged the efforts of many other cities. New York, Omaha, San Francisco and Cincinnati were each determined to become the Convention city, and Detroit, Pittsburgh and San Francisco were also advocated.

November 18th a special train whirled Washingtonward bearing a delegation of half a hundred representative citizens of Minneapolis and St. Paul. At the Capital their ranks were swelled by a large number of Northwestern men, all enthusiastic in the common cause of Minneapolis. There was a lively preliminary skirmish preceding the formal session of the Committee, that was conducted in a dignified, forceful way by the friends of Minneapolis, which was now generally recognized as a leading contestant.

At the formal hearing the spokesmen for Minneapolis had pitted against them such distinguished men as M. H. DeYoung, of California, Ex-Senator Palmer, of Michigan, Senator Hiscock, of New York, Senator Hawley, of Connecticut, Hon. J. S. Fassett, of New York. Those pleading for Minneapolis were Senator W. D. Washburn, Governor W. R. Merriam, Charles W. Johnson, Senator Casey and Representative Johnson, of North Dakota. All spoke earnestly and forcefully. An elaborate argument was made by C. W. Johnson, who had been chosen to present formally "the case" of Minneapolis. The major part of it was devoted to a presentation of the political phase. The influence of the presence and eloquence of the great men of the party would be felt far and wide over the territory of which the Convention city was a center and type. He went back to the early days of the party, pointing out how the holding of the Convention in Chicago and the rallying of the Western States around the Republican standards were co-incident—and it was more than a co-incidence. He argued that the doubtful States are now to be found in the West and Northwest, owing to the flocking in of the foreign population and the growth of the Alliance movement. There was a political chaos. A National Convention at Minneapolis would be one of the best ways to restore order in that great region. He figured that there were fourteen States west of Minneapolis that might be called doubtful—at least it would be risky to assume that they are safe. More briefly he showed that Minneapolis is a great railroad center and easily accessible from all directions; that it could furnish the finest hall in the country; that its hotel and street car facilities were ample; that the climate was in its favor. He told how the city had entertained the Christian Endeavor crowd, and as a final argument called attention to the character and standing of the men who pledged that Minneapolis would take the best of care of the Convention.

The other speakers enlarged upon some of these latter lines of argument and the North Dakota gentlemen assured the Committee that the Northwest was solid for Minneapolis and needed the Convention to make it solidly Republican. Senator Washburn urged strongly the political importance of having the Convention in the heart of the doubtful districts.

The story of the balloting is told quickest and best in the following summary of the eight votes required to settle the question:

CITIES.	1st.	2d.	3d.	4th.	5th.	6th.	7th.
Minneapolis.....................	13	14	13	13	13	17	20	29
New York.......................	9	10	11	10	7	7	5	3
Omaha..........................	5	3	4	4	4	3	4	0
Cincinnati	4	8	12	13	15	15	15	15
San Francisco...................	8	6	2	7	8	5	3	....
Detroit.........................	1	1	....	....	....	....	....	....
Pittsburgh......................	2	1	....	....	....	....	....	....
St. Louis.......................	1	0	....	....	....	....	....	....
Chattanooga	4	4	....	....	....	....	....	....
Totals......................	47	47	42	47	47	47	47	47

NOTE—The first ballot was informal.

The news reached Minneapolis late on the night of November 23d; the necessity that zeal should materialize in hard work was manifest soon after. The Citizens' Committee reorganized with George A. Brackett as Chairman, William McCrory, Secretary and E. J. Phelps, Treasurer. It was decided that the Executive Committee should be supplemented by a large number of subcommittees, to attend to the vast amount of detail work to be done. The following is the complete roster of the local committes that attended to the work of preparation for the Convention:

Citizens' Executive Committee—George A. Brackett, chairman; E. J. Phelps, treasurer; William McCrory, secretary; Gilbert A. Pierce, W. D. Washburn, C. S. Brackett, John Goodnow, J. S. McLain, H. F. Brown, S. E. Olson, C. W. Johnson, W. E. Steele, S. P. Snider, A. J. Blethen, R. G. Evans, Thomas Lowry, R. B. Langdon, A. R. McGill, Eugene G. Hay, William H. Eustis, W. D. Hale, George W. Marchant, D. Morrison, J. W. Nash, W. S. King, W. E. Haskell and Lucian Swift, Jr.

Committee on Finance—R. B. Langdon, chairman; H. F. Brown, Charles S. Brackett, D. M. Clough, A. C. Haugan, William H. Eustis, Thomas Lowry, C. A. Pillsbury and George Huhn.

Committee on Halls—W. D. Hale, chairman; Theodore Hays, A. R. McGill, J. F. Conklin and S. B. Lovejoy.

Committee on Hotels—George A. Brackett, chairman; H. F. Brown, R. B. Langdon, C. S. Brackett and J. F. Force.

Committee on Transportation—John Goodnow, chairman; W. J. C. Kenyon, George H. Heafford, C. B. Hibbard, W. A. Carpenter, J. C. Pond, F. H. Lord, T. W. Teasdale, C. M. Pratt, F. I. Whitney, C. S. Fee and George W. Bull.

Committee on Music—J. W. Nash, chairman; A. M. Shuey, James P. Moore, H. C. Chapin and A. D. S. Johnston.

Committee on Decorations—George W. Marchant, chairman; William Butters, Wyman Elliott, J. A. Fillmore and William Donaldson.

Committee on Telegraph—W. S. King, chairman; H. A. Tuttle, L. D. Parker, I. McMichael and E. A. Henderson.

Committee on State Headquarters—Eugene Hay, chairman; C. P. Lovell, H. Doerr, N. O. Werner, Robert Jamison and Charles F. Haney.

Committee on Press—G. A. Pierce, chairman; L. Swift, Jr., chairman pro tem; J. Newton Nind and H. S. Harris, secretaries; A. J. Blethen, T. Guldbransen, Luther Jaeger, Lewis Baker, H. P. Hall, James Gray, George W. Thompson, Fred Driscoll and C. H Lienau.

Committee on Building and Hall—R. B. Langdon, chairman; W. M. Brackett, D. M. Clough, E. G. Potter and C. L. Travis.

Auditing Committee—G. A. Pierce, C. S. Brackett and H. F. Brown.

Committee on Accommodations—W. E. Steele, chairman; E. M. Conant, secretary; J. F. Blaine, W. K. Hicks, H. W. Foote, Paul Blackmar, William . Regan, W. F. Brooks, J. A. Peterson, Henry Downs, J. G. Robb, W. R. Morris, Franc B. Daniels and Willis McDonald.

Committee on Reception—D. Morrison, chairman; J. S. Pillsbury, W. D. Washburn, W. R. Merriam, H. Mattson, J. W. Dunjee, J. S. Bell, Anthony Kelly, C. Morrison, R. A. Smith, W. H. Sanborn, F. C. Stevens, Albert Scheffer, J. E. Bradley, C. R. McKenney, G. A. Pillsbury, T. B. Walker, Isaac Atwater, D. F. Morgan, J. P. Rea, S. Listoe, P. B. Winston, C. K. Davis, E. C. Babb, R. T. Gray, M. Falk Gjertsen, Titus Mareck, Cyrus Northrop, Thomas Lowry, Bishop Ireland, W. J. Freaney, F. G. Ingersoll, A. H. Wilder, George R. Newell, J. H. Rolfe, S. P. Snider, S. Oftedahl, L. F. Menage, R. D. Russell, J. Q. Adams and George McNeir.

Committee on Entertainment—William H. Eustis, chairman; W. E. Haskell, C. M. Foote, L. Fletcher, Samuel Hill, O. C. Merriman, John De Laittre, F. G. Winston, George Huhn, Nelson Williams, Jasper Gibbs, F. H. Peavey, C. R. Cooley, A. T. Rand T. H. Shevlin, John D. Smith, E. B. Zier and O. J. Breda.

Ladies' Reception Committee—Mrs. H. F. Brown, chairman; Mesdames T. B. Walker, D. Morrison, R. B. Langdon, A. J. Blethen, P. B. Winston, W. E. Haskell, Samuel Hill, G. H. Christian, C. J. Martin, S. T. McKnight, H. H. Kimball. H. Harrison, A. H. Linton, Thomas Lowry, S. H. Knight, S. P. Snider, J. S. Pillsbury, F. L. Greenleaf, W. D. Washburn, E. G. Hay, F. C. Pillsbury, W. H. Hinkle, S. S. Brown, William Wolford and Miss Barton.

There was a determination to fulfill every pledge to the letter. Neither time, trouble nor money were to be spared. The $50,000 guarantee fund was nearly doubled. A suite of rooms in the Bank of Commerce Building was made Convention Headquarters and here Chairman Brackett and Secretary McCrory worked week after week, month after month.

The Washington delegation had made large promises as to a Convention Hall. The Committee on Hall, with the aid of Architect W. H. Hayes, got an early start and had the great auditorium ready to turn over to the Committee on Decoration, weeks before the date of the Convention. The interior of the building had been completely transformed and brilliantly decorated, and a hall was ready for the gathering hosts which almost defied criticism, so excellently was every appointment adapted to the purpose in view. Its seating capacity was something over 11,000, and from every seat seeing and hearing were easily possible.

The Press Committee secured the use of the New York Life Insurance Company's great 12-story office building, much of which was not as yet occupied, as press headquarters. This was transformed into a temporary hotel and provided with every convenience, so that the correspondents might sleep, eat and work here, with nothing to disturb their equanimity. Secretaries Nind and Harris did splendid service.

How should the multitude be lodged and fed, was the problem confronting the Sub-Committee on Hotels and Accommodations. So while the Hotel Committee was trying to please all the different delegations and adjust conflicting interests in the parceling out of the hotel quarters, the Accommodations Committee went to work to provide places for everyone who might come. Secretary Conant had the advantage of a valuable experience. Applicants for board or rooms had a list to select from and it was estimated that 50,000 people might have found comfortable quarters through this agency. This Committee had its headquarters in the heart of the business center and was at the bidding of any comer, day or night, during Convention week. To help feed the crowds many temporary restaurants and the lumber camp were established.

The testimonials that have poured in of congratulations are ample to confirm the claim that Minneapolis is emphatically a successful National Convention City.

Proceedings of the National Committee.

The Republican National Committee met at the Arlington Hotel in the city of Washington, D. C., on the 21st day of November, 1891, and after listening to the claims of several cities as to their availability, concluded to call the Republican National Convention to be held on the 7th day of June, 1892, in the city of Minneapolis, Minnesota.

The preliminary arrangements were entrusted to the Executive Committee of the National Committee to perfect. The Executive Committee authorized Chairman Clarkson to appoint a sub-committee to take entire charge of all arrangements necessary to the holding of the Convention.

Chairman CLARKSON appointed as such Committee, Hon. A. L. Conger, of Ohio; Hon. Samuel Fessenden, of Connecticut; Hon. Henry C. Payne, of Wisconsin; Hon. Henry S. Hyde, of Massachusetts; Hon. Powell Clayton, of Arkansas; Hon. Chauncey I. Filley, of Missouri, and Hon. Robert G. Evans, of Minnesota. Chairman Clarkson and Secretary Fassett were made *ex officio* members of the Committee.

COL. CHANNING F. MEEK was elected Sergeant-at-Arms of the Convention; and to him was entrusted the duty of superintending the printing of tickets, and the organization of a necessary force of assistant Sergeants-at-Arms, Ushers, Pages and assistants to seat the people, and to maintain order during the sessions of the Convention.

PROCEEDINGS

OF THE

REPUBLICAN NATIONAL CONVENTION

AT MINNEAPOLIS.

FIRST DAY.

TUESDAY, June 7th, 1892.

The TENTH REPUBLICAN NATIONAL CONVENTION was called to order, in Convention Hall, Industrial Exposition Building, Minneapolis, Minn., at 12:37 P. M., Tuesday, June 7th, 1892, by Hon. JAMES S. CLARKSON, Chairman of the Republican National Committee, who said:

Gentlemen of the Convention: Our proceedings will be opened with prayer by the Rev. Dr. WILLIAM BRUSH, Chancellor of the University of Dakota.

The Convention rose.

Dr. BRUSH:

O, Thou, that rulest the universe, and dost preside over the destinies of nations and of men, we invoke Thy gracious presence as we now approach Thee in prayer. Thou art the source of all our blessings. Thou art infinite, and we are finite, and in view of the disparity between Thee and ourselves, we are emboldened to approach the Throne of Grace and ask for the blessings that we need. O God, regard us graciously as we now present ourselves as worshippers preparatory to the opening of the business of this representative body. Command Thy blessing to rest upon

all here assembled. Bless those in official relations. Bless the
constituencies they represent. O God, grant that this body may
be loyal to the principles of Thy word; loyal to nationality. May
all partisanship be held in abeyance in the presence of greater
good. O Lord, may there be such a disposition to surrender
local prejudices and preferences as to be unified in one grand
principle and policy to conserve the greatest good of this great
nation. Thou hast been with this nation in all its past career;
in its incipiency, in the successful processes of evolution.
O God, Thou hast been with it in dark crises and periods, and
Thou hast preserved the nation amid perils, and we thank Thee
that Thou hast preserved it as the representative nation of all the
nations of this globe.

We thank Thee, O Lord, as we pause on the threshold of this
representative body and occasion, to vouchsafe grace to every
individual, and may the greatest harmony be evolved from seem-
ing antagonisms and discords, and may the greatest good of the
nation be subserved. We ask Thee that party and platform may
be subordinated to the principles of Thy Word. May we recognize the great universal law that Righteousness exalteth a nation,
and that sin is a reproach to any people. O God, it is the change-
less law, it is the irreversible decree that Thou wilt preserve a
nation which is loyal to Thee and the principles of Thy word.

Guide us in our deliberations. May the best results be evolved.
Be with us and guide us and our nation in its future pathway as
in the past, and make it even more glorious.

We ask it in the name of Christ, our Redeemer. Amen.

THE CALL.

Chairman CLARKSON: The Secretary will read the call under
which the Convention has assembled.

The call was read by Hon. M. H. DE YOUNG, of California, acting
Secretary, as follows:

> HEADQUARTERS REPUBLICAN NATIONAL COMMITTEE, }
>   PLAZA HOTEL, NEW YORK, January 20, 1892. }

DEAR SIR: At a meeting of the National Committee in Washington, held November 24, 1891, the following call was formulated,
and the Secretary was authorized to promulgate the same, to-wit:
To the Republican Electors of the United States:

In accordance with usage and the instructions of the Republican
National Convention of 1888, a National Convention of delegated
representatives of the Republican party will be held at the city
of Minneapolis, Minnesota, on Tuesday, the 7th day of June, 1892,
at 12 o'clock noon, for the purpose of nominating candidates for
President and Vice-President, to be supported at the next National
Election, and for the transaction of such other and further busi-

ness as may be brought before it. The Republican electors in
the several States and Territories, and voters without regard to
past political affiliations who believe in Republican principles
and endorse the Republican policy, are cordially invited to unite
under this call in the formation of a National Ticket.

Each State will be entitled to four delegates at large, and for
each Representative in Congress at large, two delegates, and each
Congressional District, each Territory and the District of Columbia, to two delegates. The delegates at large shall be chosen by
popular State Conventions, called on not less than twenty days'
published notice, and not less than thirty days before the meeting
of the National Convention. The Congressional District delegates shall be chosen at conventions called by the Congressional
Committee of each such district, in the same manner as the
nomination for a Representative in Congress is made in said
district; *Provided,* That in any Congressional District where
there is no Republican Congressional Committee, owing to re-
districting the State under the new Congressional apportionment,
the Republican State Committee shall appoint from the residents
of such district a committee for the purpose of calling a District
Convention to elect district delegates. The Territorial delegates
shall be chosen in the same manner as the nomination of a Delegate in Congress is made. The delegates from the District of
Columbia shall be chosen at a convention constituted of members
elected in primary district assemblies, held under the call and
direction of the Republican Central Committee of the District of
Columbia, which said committee shall be chosen one from each
assembly district on the first Tuesday of January, 1892, at the
hour of 7 o'clock P. M., at a place of meeting in each assembly
district to be designated by a joint call, with not less than ten
days' notice, signed by the member of the National Committee for
the District of Columbia and the chairman of the Republican
Central Committee of said District.

An alternate delegate for each delegate to the National Convention, to act in case of the absence of the delegate, shall be elected
in the same manner and at the same time as the delegate is
elected.

All notices of contests must be filed with the National Committee in writing, accompanied by printed statements of the
grounds of contest, which shall be made public. Preference in
the order of hearing and determining contests will be given by
the Convention in accordance with the dates of filing such notices
and statements with the National Committee.

JAMES S. CLARKSON, Chairman.

JACOB SLOAT FASSETT, Secretary.

Chairman CLARKSON. *Gentlemen of the Convention:* I am
instructed by the Republican National Committee to recommend
for your temporary Chairman, the Hon. J. Sloat Fassett, of New
York. [Applause.]

A vote being taken, Mr. Fassett was declared unanimously
elected, and on taking the Chair, was greeted with great applause. He spoke as follows:

Mr. FASSETT. *Gentlemen of the Convention:* For the distinguished honor which you have conferred upon me, I am very grateful. I assume the duties of presiding officer over this Convention with extreme diffidence, and am sustained only by a reliance upon your generous forbearance and co-operation in the discharge of those duties, during the short time that I am to occupy this position.

It is very appropriate that a Republican National Convention should be called together in a temple erected for, and devoted to, the exhibition of the products of protected American industries, [great applause] and in this beautiful city of Minneapolis [applause] at once the joy and the pride of the great Republican Northwest. This city, which just about equals in age the Republican party, presents on every street corner, and on every hand superb object lessons of genuine Republicanism. [Applause.] The smoking chimneys of factories; the busy hum of work shops and mills, speak louder and teach clearer than any words of mine could do, the wisdom of Republican doctrine when epitomized in facts.

As I look about this hall and note among its decorations sheaves of wheat and other products of the soil, I am reminded of a kind of Republican reciprocity which does not depend upon commercial considerations for its reward—a reciprocity of generosity and good will which could not be discouraged nor restrained by the narrow economy of a Democratic Congress, which refused to transport the food furnished out of the abundant supply of a protected nation, for the relief of starving brethren in a distant land. [Applause.]

We are met here to discharge one of the highest duties and to exercise one of the highest privileges of our citizenship. We are here as the trustees of seven millions of Republicans gathered from all the States and Territories of the Union. It becomes our duty to formulate for the inspection of the people the beliefs and purposes of our party relative to all the living political questions of national importance and to choose that man for leader under whose guidance we feel we shall be most sure of establishing this belief, in the form of laws. We are not here as warring factions, seeking supremacy by strife, under favorite leaders, but we are here as members of one great party seeking to select from the shining roll of our honored great men, the type of statesman who shall be regarded as the soundest and completest embodiment of the cardinal doctrines of the Republican party. I do not know a Republican in this Convention whose heart is not consumed with ardor for victory in the coming campaign. Our party is greater than any man in the party. [Loud applause.] We all desire the success of our party. We are here to make the preliminary arrangements for success, and we will see to it that they are made in the right way, and in the right spirit. [Applause.] If there is ever a time when it is proper that Republicans should differ, that time is now, and the occasion is here. We are here for the express purpose of comparing divergent views and divergent opinions, meaning out of the clash and conflict of opinions to arrive at ultimate unity. [Applause.]

In the delicate and wide-sweeping questions growing out of the selection of standard bearers for a great party, there has always been, and always will be, a wide opportunity for differences of opinion among honest and independent men, [applause] and the more earnest the men, the more honest the opinions, the more vigorous and determined will be the conflict, and the more complete the unification ultimately reached. [Applause.] The air is always sweeter and purer after a storm, and indicates a brighter to-morrow, as we have discovered in our short stay in Minneapolis. It is our right to differ to-day, but when the work of this Convention shall have concluded, it will be our duty to unite to-morrow. [Great applause.] When we leave this Convention Hall we will leave our contentions behind us. After we have finished our labors there will be but one choice, and they the nominees of this Convention. [Applause.] There will be but one purpose, and that their election. [Applause.] A campaign is not finished by a nomination. A nomination only begins a campaign. The campaign that is to follow the work of this Convention is not to be a campaign of candidates, by the candidates and for the candidates, but a campaign of the party, by the party, for the party, in the interests of the whole people. [Applause.] With malice towards none, but with affection and respect towards all, each of us, according to his light, as God gives him to see the light, should subordinate all merely local and personal considerations to an earnest endeavor to secure the best interests of the Republican party throughout the entire sisterhood of States.

None of our conspicuous leaders are weak men. They are all strong men. [Applause.] Some may be stronger than others; our duty is to select the strongest. [Applause.] If, as each delegate views the field, there is some man who seems to him larger than the others, whose stature is higher, whose fame and following more commanding, whose name is more inspiring than that of any other man, then the pathway of such delegate should be broad and easy. [Applause.]

The eyes of all the Republicans at home, and the eyes of our adversaries everywhere are intently fixed upon this Convention. We are not by ourselves, and we cannot hide our actions. A nation is watching us; our enemies eager to criticise, and our friends anxious to applaud. The duty and responsibility, touching as it does all interests of all the people, is enormous. It would be almost overwhelming, but for the fact that we are cheered by the recollection that the Republican party has never yet made a mistake in the selection of its candidates. [Applause.] You will not make a mistake at this time. You will subordinate personal preferences to wise judgment, and when your choice is announced, the cannons are already waiting to boom, the bonfires are set ready to be lighted, and the bells are waiting to ring out, and all our friends are waiting to proclaim their approval and ratification of our choice. [Applause.]

The history of our party since 1856 is the history of our country. There is not a single page which does not shine with greater lustre, because of some word, or some deed of some great Republican inscribed thereon. [Applause.] Count me over our chosen heroes, the men whom you and I are teaching our children to love, emulate and revere, and they shall be Republicans everyone. [Applause.] Lincoln [applause], Seward [applause], Grant [great applause]. When the spirit of Republicanism fills a man, it seems to have the power of transfiguration. These men are great. These men will always remain great, because of their growth in the line of devotion to Republican doctrine and Republican principles. [Applause.]

Sherman [applause], Garfield [great applause], Logan [applause], Harrison and Blaine [long continued applause]: these are a few only of our jewels, and we may proudly turn upon our Democratic friends and utter the defiant challenge, *Match them!!* [Applause.] Of all the vast array of Democratic orators and men who have spoken against these men, as each, one by one, rose higher and higher in public esteem, there is not one who would not give his sword arm if he could name one of them as a Democrat [applause]; only one.

Name me over the great master pieces of constructive and progressive legislation enacted since the civil war, and you shall find the author and finisher of each to be a Republican. [Applause.] From the measures of re-construction, to the measures of modified protection and reciprocity, each name along down the list belongs to us. He is of the household of our faith.

I have not the time even to catalogue the long list of good works undertaken and performed, nor have you the patience to listen to the long story of Republican achievements. You are all familiar with its history. The irrepressible conflict undertaken and concluded; slavery abolished; public credit re-established; the Constitution and the Union restored and re-constructed; the

old flag washed clean of every stain by the blood of half a million
heroes, and additional stars added to its glory [applause]; the
great west thrown open to easy access and settlement; the policy
of protection to American industry and American labor established, developed and vindicated; and the markets of the world
opened by the bright, persuasive logic of reciprocity, to the
products of the American farm, as well as of the American workshop, until to-day the nations of the earth are paying tribute to
the sagacity of our legislation and diplomacy, in millions of dollars of increased annual purchases.   Lord Salisbury has been
driven to the significant confession that even in England free
trade has proved a disappointment. [Applause.]   Rivers and
harbors have been opened to commerce; the white hulls of our
new navy are plowing the waters of every sea; peace has been
maintained at home, and our honor sustained abroad. [Applause.]
Our political adversaries, though perpetually opposing every
new measure of our Republican policy, have always in the end
been brought to the necessity of confessing their mistake and
admitting that we have been right. [Applause.]   They have just
about exhausted one congressional year in vain assaults upon
three items in a tariff bill, containing over 2,500 items, and if their
party should be continued in power it will take them, to complete
their reform tariff, on lines satisfactory to themselves, at their
present rate of progress, about eight hundred years. [Applause.]
In contrast with that record of imbecility and folly, consider the
work of the preceding Congress under the iron will and strong
arm of Thomas B. Reed. [Long continued applause and cheering.]   Your reception of this name shows that fearless aggressive
Republicanism appeals to every Republican.   His strong arm
brought order out of chaos, and established the doctrine that
representatives in Congress are there to transact business; and
under his rules that Congress accomplished more affirmative,
constructive legislation in fourteen months of its sessions, than
our Democratic friends accomplished in the preceding fourteen
years. [Applause.]

But I am here to preside and not to prophesy.   We cannot hope
to win simply by a recital of our past achievements, no matter
how brilliant, any more than our adversaries can hope to succeed
upon platforms of glittering promises.   The past is chiefly useful
to us in so far as it demonstrates the fidelity of the party in redeem-
ing its pledges, and its ability to govern in a broad and enlightened way a free and progressive people.   Our pledges have been
kept, all save one, and I greatly mistake the temper of the Republican party if it will ever be contented until that pledge is made
good.   Our manhood and our honor are pledged to continue the

contest for a free and honest ballot until this vexed question is settled in the right, and our pledges are made good. Be not deceived, God is not mocked. As a nation sows so shall it also reap. That a free people should cast a free vote and have it honestly counted and returned is the dream and the determination of the Republican party, and the despair and nightmare of the Democracy. It is the pride of the Republican party that it never yet has committed an assault upon the freedom of the ballot. The entire vocabulary of words which describe political crimes has been created to describe Democratic assaults upon the freedom of the ballot. [Applause.] Unless the votes of all men are safe, the vote of no man is safe. [Applause.] A nation that cannot protect to the uttermost the weakest, fails in its obligations to the strongest. How dare any American, looking at that flag and remembering what it has cost to make it the flag of the free, rest in peace or comfort until every guaranty of our Constitution is enforced and vindicated. [Applause.]

It seems to me this ought not to be Republican doctrine alone. It ought to be sound American doctrine. It is not the negro alone who is disfranchised, but every citizen. A wrong to any is a wrong to all. When any body of men, white or black, rich or poor, East or West, North or South, are kept by force or strategem from the free exercise of any of the privileges of citizenship, the liberties of all are imperiled.

The contest before us assumes all its difficulties from the fact that we enter the Presidential race handicapped by the certainty that in an electoral college of 444 members, 156 votes are now already absolutely secured in advance to the Democratic nominee, and that because of the solid South, kept permanently solid by a perpetual breach of the guaranties of the Constitution of the United States. They tell us the Republican party has met and fulfilled its destiny, and that our mission is ended. The mission of no progressive party is ever finished in a free, growing and expanding country, so long as there is a wrong to be redressed, so long as there is a right to be enforced; so long as all the privileges of citizenship are not freely enjoyed, and until equal and exact justice is obtained for every State as well as for every individual. So long will there be work for our party, and each Republican may exclaim—

> "I live to greet that season,
>   By gifted men foretold,
> When men shall live by reason
>   And not alone by gold.
> When man to man united,
>   And every wrong thing righted,
> This whole world shall be lighted,
>   As Eden was of old.

[Applause.]

"I live * * * *
    * * * for every cause that lacks assistance;
For every wrong that needs resistance;
For the future in the distance,
    And the good that I can do."

[Long continued applause.]

There were calls for "Reed."

The CHAIRMAN. The Honorable Thomas B. Reed is always in order in a Republican Convention. [Applause.]

Mr. Reed came to the platform.

The CHAIRMAN. *Gentlemen of the Convention :* The Honorable Thomas B. Reed, of Maine.

Mr. REED. *Mr. President and Fellow Citizens :* I want to add in the presence of this vast audience my hearty expression of faith in the future of the Republican party. [Applause.] Its past needs the endorsement of no man. That has the endorsement of history, for the deeds of the Republican party are history itself. [Applause.] And while we are prevented from pointing with pride to the achievements of our party on account of our tenderness for the Democracy [laughter and applause], nevertheless we sit here to-day rejoicing that our past history shows that from our birth until now our character has been such that it is a guaranty of the magnificent future which we are sure to have. [Applause.] It is true that we have done great things, but it is equally true that we have no right to rest upon them. Our past is glorious, but our future ought to be more so. [Applause.] It it true that we have given to this great country a wonderful physical prosperity. It is true that wealth has been poured into the laps of all our people by the great system which we believe in, and which we have carried out, and I say to you to-day that there is a nobler future, even than having given prosperity to a country, before the Republican party. [Applause.] And that nobler future is to give to every citizen of the United States the liberty of speech and action. [Cheers and applause.] Wealth and prosperity are noble, but human liberty is magnificent. [Great applause.]

There were continued calls for "McKinley," to which that gentleman arose and bowed his acknowledgments. There were also calls for "Ingalls" and "Foraker," but no responses.

The CHAIRMAN. There is no coercion in a Republican Convention. Gentlemen, General Clarkson is recognized.

General CLARKSON. *Mr. Chairman :* The National Committee has instructed me to recommend, further, to this Convention, the following officers for its temporary organization:

—2

Secretaries—Charles W. Johnson, Minneapolis; Carson Lake, New York; F. N. Arthurholt, Ohio; George Lee, San Francisco; Joseph O. Brown, Pennsylvania; W. P. Brownlow, Tennessee; Arthur S. Clark, Massachusetts.

Assistant Secretaries—Theodore F. Simmons, California; Philip Q. Churchman, Delaware; Aaron Bradshaw, D. C.; A. W. Monroe, Maryland; Charles S. Morriss, Kentucky; Charles Hopkins, Ohio; J. W. Dimmick, Alabama; James Blaine Walker, Montana; T. V. McAllister, Mississippi; Otto Gramme, Wyoming.

Reading Clerks—Charles F. Haney, Minnesota; James H. Stone, Michigan; John S. Kenyon, New York; H. S. Olliver, North Dakota; Charles Curtiss, Kansas; Charles Partridge, Illinois; Thomas B. Mills, Wisconin; W. E. Riley, Kentucky.

Official Stenographers—Theodore C. Rose, New York; James F. Burke, Pennsylvania.

The CHAIRMAN. *Gentlemen of the Convention:* You have heard the names recommended as temporary officers of this Convention; those of you who favor that recommendation please signify by saying "aye." Opposed, "no." (Carried unanimously.) The vote seems to be unanimous, and the Chair so declares.

Mr. WILLIAM J. SEWELL, of New Jersey. *Mr. Chairman:* I wish to offer a resolution.

The CHAIRMAN. Before presenting that resolution the Chair will announce that unless there is objection, until the permanent organization is effected this Convention will be governed by the rules of the last Republican National Convention. General Sewell offers the following resolution, which the Reading Clerk will read for the information of the Convention :

Resolved, That the roll of States and Territories be now called and that the Chairman of each delegation announce the names of the persons selected to serve on the several Committees as follows:

> Permanent Organization.
> Rules and Order of Business.
> Credentials, and
> Resolutions.

The resolution was adopted by the Convention.

The CHAIRMAN. The Reading Clerk will now call the roll of States and Territories, and the Chairman of each delegation as his State is called will please give the Secretary the information desired.

Chief Reading Clerk Charles F. Haney called the roll, and the several States and Territories reported the following, as members of the committees:

COMMITTEE ON PERMANENT ORGANIZATION.

Alabama	Iverson Dawson	New Hampshire	Dana W. King
Arkansas	Harmon L. Remmel	New Jersey	Wm. Barbour
California	E. P. Johnson	New York	Samuel Thomas
Colorado	Thomas C. Graden	North Carolina	Huge Cale
Connecticut	Timothy E. Hopkins	North Dakota	Thomas F. Marshall
Delaware	Geo. Fisher Pierce	Ohio	Geo. K. Nash
Florida	John F. Horr	Oregon	C. E. Wolverton
Georgia	J. Q. Gassett	Pennsylvania	Lyman D. Gilbert
Idaho	D. C. Lockwood	Rhode Island	Wm. Gregory
Illinois	Thomas S. Ridgway	South Carolina	Geo. I. Cunningham
Indiana	N. T. Depauw	South Dakota	Dr. Clark B. Alford
Iowa	G. M. Curtis	Tennessee	W. F. Poston
Kansas	A. H. Ellis	Texas	Locke McDaniel
Kentucky	D. J. Burchett	Vermont	Geo. T. Childs
Louisiana	J. Madison Vance	Virginia	Henry Bowen
Maine	John L. Cutler	Washington	John H. McGraw
Maryland	Allen Rutherford	West Virginia	Thomas E. Davis
Massachusetts	John W. Chandler	Wisconsin	W. E. Conger
Michigan	James H. Wilkinson	Wyoming	C. L. Vagner
Minnesota	Frank A. Day		
Mississippi	Wesley Crayton	Arizona	M. W. Stewart
Missouri	John B. Hale	Dist. of Columbia	John W. Freeman
Montana	A. B. Hammond	New Mexico	Tranquilino Luna
Nebraska	Geo. W. Holland	Oklahoma	D. W. Marquardt
Nevada	D. W. Bender	Utah	F. J. Cannon

COMMITTEE ON RULES AND ORDER OF BUSINESS.

Alabama	Wm. H. Harney	New Hampshire	Chas. T. Means
Arkansas	S. F. Stahl	New Jersey	Francis J. Swayze
California	R. D. Robbins	New York	J. W. Husted
Colorado	Hosea Townsend	North Carolina	E. A. Johnson
Connecticut	Allen W. Paige	North Dakota	W. H. Robinson
Delaware	G. W. Marshall	Ohio	J. A. Ambler
Florida	Joseph E. Lee	Oregon	O. C. Applegate
Georgia	E. S. Richardson	Pennsylvania	H. H. Bingham
Idaho	Willis Sweet	Rhode Island	Isaac L. Goff
Illinois	Joseph P. Roberts	South Carolina	W. D. Crum
Indiana	W. R. McKee	South Dakota	James Halley
Iowa	D. L. Heinsheimer	Tennessee	C. W. Garrett
Kansas	Eugene F. Ware	Texas	F. K. Chase
Kentucky	W. H. Milby	Vermont	E. P. George
Louisiana	Louis J. Souer	Virginia	John M. Langston
Maine	S. W. Bird	Washington	Nelson Bennett
Maryland	Martin M. Higgins	West Virginia	J. D. Hewett
Massachusetts	Geo. E. Freeman	Wisconsin	C. A. Booth
Michigan	W. H. Withington	Wyoming	E. R. Dinwiddie
Minnesota	S. G. Comstock		
Mississippi		Arizona	M. W. Stewart
Missouri	J. H. Rainey	Dist. of Columbia	George Holmes
Montana	S. S. Hobson	New Mexico	Nicholas Gallis
Nebraska	E. B. Warner	Oklahoma	D. W. Marquardt
Nevada	A. J. McDonell	Utah	O. J. Salisbury

COMMITTEE ON CREDENTIALS.

Alabama	Daniel N. Cooper	Illinois	S. H. Bethea
Arkansas	Thomas H. Barnes	Indiana	Hiram Brownlee
California	O. A. Hale	Iowa	F. W. Simmons
Colorado	B. Clark Wheeler	Kansas	S. I. Hale
Connecticut	F. B. Brandegee	Kentucky	John Feland
Delaware	George V. Massey	Louisiana	Thomas A. Cage
Florida	Henry S. Chubb	Maine	C. M. Moses
Georgia	R. D. Locke	Maryland	Alfred G. Sturgiss
Idaho	James M. Shoup	Massachusetts	William Cogswell

Michigan ....A. T. Bliss
Minnesota.......................R. C. Dunn
Mississippi............. John S. Burton
Missouri ....Henry Lamm
Montana......... ....P. McCormick
Nebraska........... ......C. A. McCloud
Nevada ....A. C. Cleveland
New Hampshire....Henry B. Quinby
New Jersey...........Wm. T. Hoffman
New York ....W. C. Wallace
North Carolina.......Dr. J. O. Willcox
North Dakota.............E. J. Gleason
Ohio ....:...............W. E. Crum
Oregon ....R. R. Hayes
Pennsylvania..........David H. Lane
Rhode Island..........Edward Thayer

South Carolina....John H. Ostendorff
South Dakota ....Jos. M. Greene
Tennessee.............. ....J. T. Settle
Texas.......... .... Henry Terrell
Vermont ....Fred E. Smith
Virginia ....M. F. Chamblin
Washington.............Wm. Kirkman
West Virginia...........Chas. B. Hart
Wisconsin............. ....A. E. Smith
Wyoming ....F. W. Mondell

Arizona............ ....M. W. Stewart
Dist. of Columbia....Andrew Gleason
New Mexico...........Thos. B. Catron
Oklahoma. ....A. J. Seay
Utah.....................O.. J. Salisbury

COMMITTEE ON RESOLUTIONS.

Alabama...... ....William Vaughan
Arkansas....................A. S. Fowler
California...............Geo. A. Knight
Colorado...............Henry M. Teller
Connecticut............James P. Platt
Delaware............. Jas. H. Wilson
Florida. ....Edward R. Gunby
Georgia .... R. R. Wright
Idaho ....W. B. Heyburn
Illinois.............. Joseph G. Cannon
Indiana.................. .....C. F. Griffin
Iowa..................... .....J. H. Gear
Kansas...................O. E. Learnard
Kentucky..........George Drury, Jr
Louisiana.... .....Robert F. Guichard
Maine.......... ....C. F. Libby
Maryland.......... Thomas S. Hodson
Massachusetts ...John Q. A. Brackett
Michigan .... Charles Austin
Minnesota..........George Thompson
Mississippi...... ....
Missouri.... ... .O. L. Houts
Montana .... Thomas Couch
Nebraska.............Charles H. Gere
Nevada..................John P. Jones

New Hampshire.......David R. Pierce
New Jersey... . ...Gilbert Collins
New York ....Edmund O'Connor
North Carolina. ....J. C. Pritchard
North Dakota ....John A. Percival
Ohio ....Joseph B. Foraker
Oregon ....J. Brown, Jr
Pennsylvania.......... .. H. W. Oliver
Rhode Island.........Frank G. Harris
South Carolina........ ... S. E. Smith
South Dakota....Edward C. Erickson
Tennessee...............Newton Hacker
Texas....................A. S. Rosenthal
Vermont...............Adna Brown
Virginia...............Edmund Waddill
Washington ....Edward Eldridge
West Virginia....John A. Hutchinson
Wisconsin............Lucius Fairchild
Wyoming,............. ......S. W. Downey

Arizona............ N. O. Murphy
Dist. of Columbia ....Perry H. Carson
New Mexico............J. A. Whitmore
Oklahoma................ . A. J. Seay
Utah...................F. J. Cannon

Mr. J. S. HAMMER, of Indian Territory. *Mr. Chairman:* The delegation from the Indian Territory represents 150,000 Republicans, and the National Committee has seen proper to give us seats on this floor, but has declined to give us representation, and we now appeal to the Convention for that right also.

The CHAIRMAN. The National Committee recommended that the representatives from the Indian Territory be admitted to seats without votes. Until that recommendation is changed, the Chair will have to declare the gentleman not in order.

The Chair desires to announce to the Convention and to the gentlemen who have been appointed members of the various Committees, that immediately upon the adjournment of this session they are requested to meet in committee rooms which have been prepared in the rear of the platform. Each room has been appropriately marked, and if you will meet promptly upon the adjournment of this meeting for the purpose of organization, you will greatly facilitate the work of the Convention.

The Chair wishes further to say that he has been asked to present to the Convention a memorial from the Federal Suffrage Association. I beg leave to suggest to this Association that they introduce their memorial after a permanent organization has been effected, when it will be referred to the Committee on Resolutions.

Gentlemen, what is your further pleasure?

Mr. WILLIAM MURRELL, of New Jersey. *Mr. Chairman*—

The CHAIRMAN. The Chair desires to request that each delegate, as he asks recognition of the Chair, state his name and delegation.

Mr. MURRELL. *Mr. Chairman:* I am an alternate-at-large from New Jersey. I desire, in order to prevent confusion hereafter, to get a ruling of the Chair. I was elected as alternate for the Hon. John I. Blair. That patriotic, distinguished and venerable Republican is not here, and there is another Republican from New Jersey who is now sitting in the seat of Mr. Blair, and attempting to represent—

The CHAIRMAN. The Chair must rule that this discussion is not now in order. It is a matter to be brought before the Committee on Credentials.

Mr. MURRELL. *Mr. Chairman:* According to the rules, as the roll is now made up, I am an alternate, and I ask the Chairman if I am entitled to the floor. If not, I will withdraw.

The CHAIRMAN. The gentleman is out of order at present.

Mr. SPOONER, of Wisconsin. *Mr. Chairman:* I move that the Convention do now adjourn until to-morrow morning at 11 o'clock.

The CHAIRMAN. The Chair refers the gentleman from New Jersey to the Committee on Credentials. He can have no standing in the permanent organization until that Committee reports in his favor.

Senator Spooner moves that the Convention do now adjourn until 11 o'clock to-morrow morning. Are you ready for the question?

The question was put and carried in the affirmative, and at 1:55 P. M. the Convention adjourned to 11 o'clock to-morrow.

SECOND DAY.

WEDNESDAY, June 8th, 1892.

The Convention was called to order at 11:47 A. M. by Chairman Fassett, who said:

Gentlemen, the Convention will kindly come to order. The proceedings of this day will be opened with prayer by the Right Reverend H. B. Whipple, D. D., LL. D., Bishop of Minnesota.

Bishop WHIPPLE. Almighty God, our Heavenly Father, who hath promised to give wisdom to those who reverently seek Thee, and who alone pourest into the hearts of men that most excellent gift of charity, send Thy blessing upon this Convention. Help them to realize that government is a sacred trust from God, who alone has the right to govern, and that in His love He hath permitted every nation to say in what form that trust shall be clothed. And grant, O Heavenly Father, that the one whom they shall select may be a man after Thine own heart, a lover of righteousness, the defender of the helpless and the guardian of the honor of our country. And give to this whole nation an understanding heart to obey Thee, that so truth and justice, religion and piety, peace and happiness may be insured unto us through all generations. And all this we humbly ask in the name of Thy Son, Jesus Christ, in whose words we sum up all our petitions. Our Father who art in heaven, hallowed be Thy name, Thy kingdom come, Thy will be done, on earth as it is in heaven. Give us this day our daily bread, and forgive us our trespasses as we forgive those who trespass against us. And lead us not into temptation, but deliver us from evil, for Thine is the kingdom, and the power and the glory, forever and ever. Amen.

PRESENTATION OF GAVEL.

Mr. JOHN L. WEBSTER, of Nebraska. *Mr. Chairman—*

The CHAIRMAN. The gentleman from Nebraska.

Mr. WEBSTER. I want to call attention to the fact that there is on the platform a gentleman from Nebraska, Mr. L. E. Walker, who desires to present a gavel to this Convention.

The CHAIRMAN. If there is no objection Mr. Walker will be recognized for that purpose.

Mr. WALKER. *Mr. Chairman and Gentlemen of the Convention:* Among the many masterpieces of Republican legislation, as numerous as the stars in our flag, the Homestead act of 1862, which for ten years was before Congress, and was finally vetoed in 1859 by Buchanan, and the Nebraska enabling act of 1867, are particularly cherished by the people of our state. Taking advantage of the beneficent provisions of the Homestead act thousands of returning soldiers acquired homes in Nebraska in 1865, thus becoming our prosperous and thrifty citizens, thereby enabling us to pass the act admitting Nebraska from ten to fifteen years sooner than otherwise; and, as a token of our appreciation, we desire to present this gavel. It is simple, but useful, historical and Republican. The wood from which it was made was grown upon what is known as the first or original homestead, located near Beatrice, Neb., entered January 1, 1863, by Daniel Freeman, who still owns and occupies his farm. The ends of the gavel are inlaid with silver coins, the one bearing the date of 1867 and the other 1892, which is significant that this year Nebraska celebrates her twenty-fifth or silver anniversary. With the hope that in 1917, when Nebraska celebrates her golden anniversary, that this great country may be governed by Republicans, we have the honor, on the part of the young and the old Republicans of Nebraska, to present the temporary Chairman of this Convention with this gavel.

The CHAIRMAN. On behalf of the Convention and on behalf of the temporary chairman, the Chair returns its very best thanks to Nevada.

(Cries of, "Nebraska," "Nebraska.")

The CHAIRMAN. There was so much silver about it, the mistake is excusable. The next business in order is the report of the Committee on Credentials. General William Cogswell, of Massachusetts, is recognized.

Mr. COGSWELL. *Mr. Chairman:* I am instructed by the Chairman of the Committee on Credentials to ask for further time in which to report, and that the committee may be given leave to sit continuously until it completes its labors.

Mr. J. C. SPOONER, of Wisconsin. *Mr. Chairman:* I rise for the purpose of asking the Chairman of the Committee on Credentials, if the Committee has made such progress as to enable him to inform the Convention when we may reasonably expect a report?

Mr. COGSWELL. *Mr. Chairman:* The answer is simply an individual opinion; and it is, that if the labors of the committee are attended with reasonable success it cannot hope to report before tomorrow.

The CHAIRMAN. In the absence of a motion all debate or remarks must be with unanimous consent.

Mr. SPOONER. I desire the privilege of interrogating the gentleman further. I desire to ask whether the business of the Committee is so far advanced that it is ready now, or will soon be ready to report to the Convention a list of uncontested delegates and alternates ?

Mr. COGSWELL. The question would seem almost to answer itself. It cannot require much time to report a list of uncontested delegates.

The CHAIRMAN. Gentlemen, are you ready for the question? There being no objection the Committee is extended permission to sit until they have completed their report. The next order of business is the report of the Committee on Permanent Organization. Mr. D. C. Lockwood, of Idaho, Chairman of the Committee, is recognized.

Mr. LOCKWOOD. *Mr. Chairman and Gentlemen of the Convention:* Your Committee on Permanent Organization have instructed me to make the following report:

We recommend for permanent Chairman of this Convention, Hon. William McKinley, of Ohio. (Cheers).

Your Committee further recommends for permanent Secretary of this Convention, Col. Charles W. Johnson, of Minnesota ; for Chief Reading Clerk, Charles F. Haney, of Minnesota. And the recommendation of the Committee further is that the present temporary working force of secretaries, assistant secretaries, reading clerks and stenographers be the permanent officers of this Convention.

Your Committee further recommends an honorary Vice-President and an honorary Secretary from each of the states.

I move the adoption of the report on Permanent Organization.

The report was adopted unanimously.

The following is the full list of the permanent officers of the Convention :

PRESIDENT.

HON. WM. MCKINLEY, JR..................................OF OHIO.

HONORARY VICE PRESIDENTS.

Alabama........ ....I. Green	New Jersey................G. A. Holsey
Arkansas......... ....Ferd. Havis	New York................Philip Brewer
California............. N. D. Rideout	North Carolina......: Charles A. Cook
Colorado.............Edw. V. Wolcott	North Dakota.........W. R. Robinson
Connecticut..................L. K. Cook	Ohio.... ....Gen. Asa Bushnell
Delaware........... J. Francis Bacon	Oregon......................T. H. Tongue
Florida.................S. H. Coleman	Pennsylvania................J. J. Custer
Georgia...............W. A. Pledger	Rhode Island........Charles Fletcher
Idaho......................J. M. Shoup	South Carolina. ...Paris Simkins
Illinois......Hon. Richard G. Oglesby	South Dakota ....N. E. Phillips
Indiana...................Lew Wallace	Tennessee...................T. L. Cate
Iowa.....................Eli Manning	Texas.......... ....R. B. Hawley
Kansas .... Calvin Hood	Vermont......... ...Hon. L. D. Hazen
Kentucky...............Leslie Combs	Virginia....................H. C. Wood
Louisiana............. Hon. D. Young	Washington.............J. A. Perkins
Maine......... Hon. Thomas H. Phair	West Virginia.............W. A. Miller
Maryland............Thorndyke Chase	Wisconsin..........Isaac Stephenson
Massachusetts......... R. S. Frost	Wyoming. ....C. N. Potter
Michigan................D. A. Blodgett	
Minnesota................M. H. Dunnell	Alaska..............Thomas S. Nowell
Mississippi.......: ...W. D. Frazie	Arizona................W. M. Stewart
Missouri.....Hon. F. G. Niedringhaus'	Dist. of Columbia.......J. F. Freeman
Montana ....A. J. Brelenburg	Ind. Territory...........Ridge Paschal
Nebraska....................Amos Cobb	New Mexico.. ....J. D. Ball
Nevada....................D. L. Bliss	Oklahoma................ ...M. J. Dean
New Hampshire.....Benj. A. Kimball	Utah...............................

HONORARY SECRETARIES.

Alabama...............A. H. Hendricks	New Hampshire..........Ira. N. Blake
Arkansas.. .... Henry M. Cooper	New Jersey................G. W. Jenkins
California..........Joseph S. Spear, Jr	New York............... Carson Lake
Colorado............. R. M. Donovan	North Carolina........ John C. Dancy
Connecticut..........Thomas Wallace	North Dakota.............E. J. Gleason
Delaware.............G. W. Marshall	Ohio.....................Amos Denison
Florida..................W. R. Long	Oregon................O. C. Applegate
Georgia............. ... ...J. T. Shepard	Pennsylvania............C. McConnell
Idaho ....M. B. Guinn	Rhode Island.........Henry A. Stearns
Illinois..................J. W. Ketchell	South Carolina... .....J. H. Fordham
Indiana...................W. J. Henley	South Dakota.........A. C. Johnston
Iowa.... ....J. E. Blythe	Tennessee................J. C. Napier
Kansas ....E. C. Little	Texas.................Walter T. Burns
Kentucky........... ......A. R. Dycke	Vermont........ ....N. W. Fisk
Louisiana...................J. L. Jones	Virginia....................P. H. McCall
Maine...............Hon. S. J. Walton	Washington.............John Clunen
Maryland................Samuel Root	West Virginia.... ....C. M. Hart
Massachusetts.......... E. U. Curtis	Wisconsin................A. J. Turner
Michigan....................J. H. Kidd	Wyoming...................F. N. Foot
Minnesota................C. E. Jackson	Alaska...................E. T. Hatch
Mississippi...............T. McAllister	Arizona ....
Missouri................Thomas J. Chew	Dist. of Columbia....Andrew Gleason
Montana ....Paul McConnell	New Mexico................M. A. Otero
Nebraska............C. P. R. Williams	Oklahoma ....D. W. Marquardt
Nevada......	Ind. Territory........Frank S. Genung

General Secretary—CHARLES W. JOHNSON, of Minnesota, Chief Clerk of the United States Senate.

Sergeant-at-Arms—CHANNING F. MEEK, of Colorado.

Chief Reading Clerk—CHARLES F. HANEY, of Minnesota.

Assistant Sergeants-at-Arms—Isaac M. Stevens, Colorado; Chas. L. Travis, W. M. Brackett, of Minnesota.

Additional Secretaries—Carson Lake, New York; F. N. Arthurholt, Ohio; George Lee, San Francisco; Joseph O. Brown, Pennsylvania; W. P. Brownlow, Tennessee; Arthur S. Clark, Massachusetts.

Assistant Secretaries — Theodore F. Simmons, California; Philip Q. Churchman, Delaware; Aaron Bradshaw, Washington, D. C.; A. Warfield Monroe, Maryland; Charles S. Morriss, Kentucky; Charles Hopkins, Ohio; J. W. Dimmick, Alabama; James Blaine Walker, Montana; T. V. McAllister, Mississippi; Otto Gramm, Wyoming.

Additional Reading Clerks—James H. Stone, Michigan; John S. Kenyon, New York; H. S. Olliver, North Dakota; Charles Curtiss, Kansas; Charles Partridge, Illinois; Thomas B. Mills, Wisconsin; W. E. Riley, Kentucky.

Official Stenographers—Theodore C. Rose, New York; James F. Burke, Pennsylvania.

The CHAIRMAN. The Chair will appoint as a Committee to escort the permanent Chairman to the platform Hon. Samuel Fessenden, of Connecticut, Senator Spooner, of Wisconsin, and Gen. Mahone, of Virginia.

Messrs. Fessenden, Spooner and Mahone escorted Governor McKinley to the platform.

The CHAIRMAN. *Gentlemen of the Convention:* Before presenting to you your permanent Chairman, the Chair desires to thank you most heartily for the kind forbearance which you have exercised toward him.

I now have the honor and the distinguished pleasure of introducing the Honorable William McKinley, Jr., of Ohio.

Temporary Chairman Fassett retired, and there were prolonged cheers for Governor McKinley.

Governor MCKINLEY. *Gentlemen of the Convention :* I thank you for the honor of presiding over the Tenth National Convention of the Republican party. Republican Conventions mean something. They have always meant something. Republican Conventions say what they mean and mean what they say. They declare principles, and policies, and purposes, and when entrusted with power, execute and enforce them. The first National Convention of the Republican party, thirty-six years ago, was held in the city of Philadelphia. The platform of that great Convention reads to-day more like inspiration than the affirmation of a political party. Every provision of that great instrument made by the fathers of our party are on the public statutes of our country to-day. Every one of them has been embodied into public law, and that cannot be said of the platform of any other political organization in this or any other country of the world. Whenever there is anything to be done in this country, and by this country, and for this country, the Republican party is called upon to do it. There is one thing that can be said about our organization that cannot be said about any other; it can look backward without shame or humiliation, and it can look forward with cheer and exultation. That cannot be said of any political organization other than ours in the United States. Gentlemen of the Convention, we are here to-day to make a platform and a ticket that will commend themselves to the conscience and the intelligence and the judgment of the American people. [Prolonged applause.] And we will do it. Whatever is done in this Convention either as to platform or as to ticket, will receive the approval of the American people in November of this year. [Great applause.] We have already heard some of the notes of victory, for this is a Republican year.

Rhode Island has spoken. Only yesterday Oregon spoke, electing three representatives—three Republican Representatives to the Congress of the United States; and when we get through with this Convention its conclusions will be the law of Republican action, as they will be the assurance of Republican victory. We are for a protective tariff and reciprocity. We propose to take no backward step upon either one of these great Republican principles. We stand for a protective tariff because it represents the American home, the American fireside, the American family, the American girl and the American boy, and the highest possibilities of American citizenship. We propose to raise our money to pay public expenses by taxing the products of other nations, rather than by taxing the products of our own. The Democratic party believe in direct taxation, that is, in taxing ourselves; but we don't believe in that principle so long as we can find anybody else to tax.

Our protective tariff not only does everything which a revenue tariff can do in raising all needed revenues, but a protective tariff does more than that. A protective tariff encourages and stimulates American industries and gives the widest possibilities to American genius and American effort. Does anybody know what tariff reform is? And that is to be the platform of our political opponents this year. What does it mean? You can study President Cleveland's utterances from the first one he made in New York, when he said he did not know anything about the tariff [laughter], until his last in Rhode Island, and you come away ignorant and uninformed as to what tariff reform means. Since the war there have been three great tariff reform bills proposed by the Democratic leaders, none of them alike, neither of them with the same free list, neither of them with the same tariff list, neither of them with the same rates of duty, but all made by the Democratic party upon the same principle to symbolize and represent tariff reform.

You may go to Mr. Mills, you may go to Mr. Springer, and you will find they differ totally; you may go to the House of Representatives at Washington, which was elected distinctively upon what they call a tariff reform issue, with two-thirds majority in the House, and what do you find? They passed three bills. Let me name them. First, free tin plate, leaving sheet steel, from which it is made, tariffed; that is, the finished product free and the raw material bearing a duty. Second, free wool to the manufacturer, and tariffed cloth to the consumer. Third, free cotton ties to the cotton states, and tariffed hoop iron to all the rest of the states. That is their idea of tariff reform. Gentlemen of the Convention, how do you like it? This contest that we enter upon is for the maintenance of protection and reciprocity; and I want to say here that there is not a line in that tariff bill that is not American; there is not a paragraph that is not patriotic; there is not a page that does not represent true Americanism, and the highest possibilities of American citizenship.

We are to declare ourselves upon other questions here to-day. We are to declare ourselves upon the question of a free ballot and a fair count. No platform should ever be made that does not reiterate that great constitutional guaranty, no Republican speech should ever be made that does not insist firmly and resolutely that the great constitutional guaranty shall be a living birthright, not a cold formality of constitutional enactment, but a living thing, which the poorest and humblest may confidently enjoy and which the richest and most powerful dare not deny. We can well leave to the Committee on Resolutions the duty of making a platform that shall represent the best thoughts, the best ideas and the best wisdom of the Republican party. When we go out of this Convention upon a true Republican platform we will go out marching to victory, no matter who may carry the banner.

There were loud cries for "Fred. Douglas," and Mr. Douglas stepped to the front of the platform and bowed his acknowledgments.

The CHAIRMAN. The next order of business is the report of the Committee on Rules and Order of Business. Gen. Henry H. Bingham, of Pennsylvania, is recognized.

Mr. BINGHAM. *Mr. Chairman and Gentlemen of the Convention:* I am directed by your Committee on Rules and Order of Business, to submit the following Rules for the government of the Convention:

RULE 1. The Convention shall consist of a number of delegates from each state equal to double the number of its Senators and Represtatives in Congress, six delegates from the Territory of New Mexico, two from each of the remaining territories, and two from the District of Columbia.

RULE 2. The rules of the House of Representatives of the Fifty-first Congress shall be the rules of the Convention so far as they are applicable and not inconsistent with the following rules:

RULE 3. When the previous question shall be demanded by a majority of the delegates from any State, and the demand seconded by two or more States, and the call sustained by a majority of the Convention, the question shall then be proceeded with and disposed of according to the rules of the House of Representatives in similar cases.

RULE 4. *It shall be in order to lay on the table a proposed amendment to a pending measure, and such motion, if adopted, shall not carry with it or prejudice such measure.*

RULE 5. Upon all subjects before the Convention, the States shall be called in alphabetical orders and next the Territories and District of Columbia.

RULE 6. The report of the Committee on Credentials shall be disposed of before the report of the Committee on Resolutions is acted upon, and the report of the Committee on Resolutions shall be disposed of before the Convention proceeds to the nomination of candidates for President and Vice-President.

RULE 7. When a majority of the delegates of any two States shall demand that a vote be recorded, the same shall be taken by States, Territories and the District of Columbia, the Secretary calling the roll of the States and Territories and the District of Columbia in the order heretofore stated.

RULE 8. In making the nominations for President and Vice-President, in no case shall the calling of the roll be dispensed with. When it appears at the close of any roll-call that any candidate has received a majority of all the votes to which the Convention is entitled, the President of the Convention shall announce the question to be: "Shall the nomination of the candidate be made unanimous?" But if no candidate shall have received such majority, the Chair shall direct the vote to be taken again, which shall be repeated until some candidate shall have received a majority of the votes; and when any State has announced its vote it shall so stand unless in case of numerical error.

RULE 9. In the record of the votes by States, the vote of each State, Territory and District of Columbia shall be announced by the Chairman; and in case the vote of any State, Territory or District of Columbia shall be divided, the Chairman shall announce the number of votes cast for any candidate, or for or against any proposition; but, if exception is taken by any delegate to the correctness of such announcement by the Chairman of his delegation, the President of the Convention shall direct the roll of members of such delegation to be called, and the result shall be recorded in accordance with the votes individually given.

RULE 10. No member shall speak more than once upon the same question, nor longer than five minutes, unless by leave of the Convention, except in the presentation of the names of candidates.

RULE 11. A Republican National Committee shall be appointed, to consist of one member from each State, Territory and the District of Columbia. The roll shall be called, and the delegation from each State and Territory and the District of Columbia shall name, through its chairman, a person who shall act as a member of such Committee. Such Committee shall issue the call for the meeting of the National Convention six months, at least, before the time fixed for said meeting; and each Congressional district in the United States shall elect its delegates to the National Convention in the same way as the nomination for a member of Congress is made in said district, and in territories the delegates to the Convention shall be elected in the same way as a nomination of a delegate to Congress is made, and said National Committee shall prescribe the mode for selecting the delegates for the District of Columbia. An alternate delegate for each delegate to the National Convention, to act in case of the absence of the delegate, shall be elected in the same manner and at the same time as the delegate is elected. Delegates at large for each State, and their alternates, shall be elected by State Conventions in their respective states.

RULE 12. The Republican National Committee is authorized and empowered to select an Executive Committee, to consist of nine members, who may or may not be members of the National Committee.

RULE 13. All resolutions relating to the platform shall be referred to the Committee on Resolutions without debate.

RULE 14. No persons, except members of the several delegations and officers of the Convention, shall be admitted to that section of the hall apportioned to delegates.

RULE 15. The Convention shall proceed in the following order of business.

First. Report of the Committee on Credentials.

Second. Report of the Committee on Permanent Organization.

Third. Report of the Committee on Resolutions.

Fourth. Naming members of National Committee.

Fifth. Presentation of Candidates for President.

Sixth. Balloting.

Seventh. Presentation of Candidates for Vice-President.

Eighth. Balloting.

Gen. BINGHAM. Your Committee would report that the rules submitted are, with two exceptions, those of the last National Convention, which were substantially those of the Conventions of 1880 and 1884. These rules were found to work smoothly, and, with an amendment to former rule three, adopting the rules of the House of Representatives of the Fifty-first Congress, and a new rule inserted proposing that a motion to table an amendment shall not carry with it or prejudice the pending measure, it is believed they will be satisfactory to the Convention. Your Committee deemed it proper to recognize specifically the rules of the last Republican House of Representatives, under which action, progress and results were made possible as against the rules of the present House, which permit indefinite filibustering, obstruction and non-action except when a report from the Committee on Rules is presented, a tyranny hitherto unknown in American history.

As illustrative of what is accomplished by the code of rules of the House of Representatives of the Fifty-first Congress, let me give you a brief catalogue, prepared by a neutral hand, and published in a neutral paper, of what was done by the Fifty-first Congress:

The McKinley tariff act, revising the entire series of schedules.

The administrative customs act.

The act to establish the World's Fair at Chicago.

The postal subsidy act, to open direct marine communication with Central and South American ports.

The opening and creation of the Territory of Oklahoma.

The act creating a commission for the proposed continental railroad through Mexico, Central and South America.

The act admitting Idaho and Wyoming as States.

The pension act, extending pensions to dependent soldiers and soldiers' widows.

The act to reduce pension fees from $10 to $2.

The French spoliation act.

The act to establish the regulations for vessels at sea adopted by the International Maritime Conference.

The act to refund the direct taxes collected from loyal States during the war.

The act making a general revision of the land laws.

The general land forfeiture act, securing the return of lands granted to railroads to the public domain open for settlement.

The completion of legislation dividing the Sioux Reservation and opening a part of it to settlement.

The act to reapportion Congressional representation according to the Eleventh Census.

The act to increase the endowment and equipment of State agricultural colleges.

The meat and cattle inspection acts in the interest of interstate and foreign commerce.

The act against gambling on race courses in the District of Columbia.

Various acts designed to improve the administration of the Post Office Department, and extend postal facilities.

The act increasing the monthly purchase of silver.

The original package act, allowing States having prohibitory laws to enforce them against shipments of liquor from other States.

The international copyright act.

These are the principal or important acts or laws of the Fifty-first Congress, and do not embrace or comprise many important bills passed by the House of Representatives, such as the bankruptcy bill, the bill to amend the election laws of the United States and to provide for their efficient enforcement, and others of lesser note.

The enactment of these laws, and the passage of these bills, were made possible by the code of rules adopted by the House of Representatives of the Fifty-first Congress.

With the new rule proposed, by which an amendment may be separated from the pending measure and tabled, if such be the wish of the Convention, without carrying with it or prejudicing such measure, it may be said that such is the present rule of the United States Senate, and is in harmony with advanced parliamentary practice. Since the Forty-eighth Congress this has been a rule of the Senate, and as we have present with us to-day a large number of Senators in delegate representative capacity, should discussion be determined upon that proposition which is wholly in the expedition of business and the saving of the delay of roll calls, I am very sure they will endorse, as your Committee has deemed wise to report, that rule which means acceleration and quickness in the discharge of the duties of this Convention.

It is suggested that perhaps, in reading Rule 1, I may have made an error in the use of the words. The rule there reads: "The Convention shall consist of a number of delegates from each State equal to double the number of its Senators and Representatives in Congress, six delegates from the Territory of New Mexico, two from each of the remaining Territories, and two from the District of Columbia."

Mr. S. M. CULLOM, of Illinois. *Mr. Chairman:* I desire to inquire whether the printed slip which has been handed to the delegates of the Convention is the exact report which the Chairman of the Committee has just read.

Mr. BINGHAM. With the exception which I have just stated.

Mr. CULLOM. That rule is right in the printed slip.

Mr. BINGHAM. What rule does the Senator from Illinois refer to?

Mr. CULLOM. I am not referring to any rule.

Mr. BINGHAM. There was an omission of the "Report of the Committee on Permanent Organization" in the Order of Business, which I have added.

Mr. CULLOM. I simply desire to know whether the delegates having these slips are to understand that these are the rules that have been reported by your Committee?

Mr. BINGHAM. With that one change which has been stated.

The CHAIRMAN. The question is upon agreeing to the report.

Mr. CULLOM. In the Order of Business as read it seemed to me in following the Chairman of the Committee as he read, that the announcements were different from what appear on this paper. I will ask to have re-read the Order of Business.

Mr. BINGHAM. "Rule 15. The Convention shall proceed in the following order of business:

"(1) Report of the Committee on Credentials."

"(2) Report of the Committee on Permanent Organization."

The printed slip requires the insertion of that report to correct the error of the printer.

Mr. CULLOM. And that has been done?

Mr. BINGHAM. The next is the "(3) Report of the Committee on Resolutions" and so on.

Mr. CULLOM. Read it all through.

Mr. BINGHAM. The next is the "(4) Naming of Members of the National Committee." The next is the "(5) Presentation of Candidates for President." The next is "(6) Balloting." The next is the "(7) Presentation of the Candidates for Vice-President," and the next "(8) Balloting."

Mr. CULLOM. That is understood.

T. B. KEOUGH, of North Carolina. *Mr. President:* I would like to call the attention of the Convention to one rule. In 1880 at Chi-

—3

cago, the Convention adopted the Congressional District as the unit of representation in the Convention. That entitled a member of the delegation to call the roll and poll his delegation if the vote is not correctly reported. Under Rule 7 there will be no opportunity to do that.

The CHAIRMAN. What rule does the gentleman refer to?

Mr. KEOUGH. To Rule 7.

The CHAIRMAN. Now, what is your inquiry?

Mr. KEOUGH. My inquiry is this: Does this preclude a member of a delegation from polling his own delegation, if he thinks the vote is not correctly reported?

The CHAIRMAN. Rule 9 says: "If exception is taken by any delegate to the correctness of such announcement by the Chairman of his delegation, the President of the Convention shall direct the roll of members of such delegation to be called, and the result shall be recorded in accordance with the vote individually given." Does that cover the gentleman's proposition?

Mr. KEOUGH. That is all right.

Mr. LOUIS E. McCOMAS, of Maryland. *Mr. Chairman :*

The CHAIRMAN. Mr. McComas, of Maryland, is recognized.

Mr. McCOMAS. I desire to ask the Chairman of the Committee to explain what change has been made in Rule 3 and the effect of it.

The CHAIRMAN. There has been no change in Rule 3. Rule 4 is a new Rule inserted in accordance with the practice of the Senate of the United States since the Forty-eighth Congress.

Mr. McCOMAS. Then I understand the Chairman to say that Rule 3 is precisely the same as it has been in former Conventions.

The CHAIRMAN. Yes, sir, precisely the same.

The motion to adopt the report of the Committee was agreed to.

The CHAIRMAN. The next order of business is the Report of the Committee on Resolutions. Is the Chairman ready to report?

Mr. J. B. FORAKER, of Ohio. *Mr. Chairman :* The Committee is not ready to report. We ask further time.

The CHAIRMAN. The Committee on Resolutions, through its Chairman, asks further time. Is there objection?

The Chair hears none, and further time will be granted.

The next order of business is the Naming of Members of the National Committee. The Secretary will call the roll of States.

Chief Reading Clerk Haney called the roll, and a portion of the names of the Committee were announced.

(A list of the National Committee as finally agreed upon will be found on a subsequent page.)

The CHAIRMAN. There are several resolutions which the Secretary desires to announce, which will be referred to the Committee on Resolutions.

Secretary JOHNSON. An address to the Republican National Convention, signed by the North Star Labor Club of Minneapolis.

A memorial from the Federal Suffrage Association of the United States, signed by Hon. M. D. Castle, of Sandwich, Illinois.

Another memorial on the same subject signed by Olympia Brown.

One from the United States Honest Money League, signed by its President.

The CHAIRMAN. These resolutions will be referred to the Committee on Resolutions.

Mr. J. S. PILLSBURY, of Minnesota. *Mr. Chairman :*

The CHAIRMAN. Governor Pillsbury, of Minnesota, is recognized.

Mr. PILLSBURY. I offer a resolution which I desire to have read and referred to the Committee on Resolutions.

The CHAIRMAN. Is there objection? (Cries of "Yes," "Yes.") There being objection, the resolution will go to the Committee on Resolutions without reading, under the rule.*

The next order of business is the "Presentation of Candidates for President."

Mr. M. H. DEYOUNG, of California. *Mr. Chairman :* I move that this Convention adjourn to 7 o'clock to-night. (Cries of "No," "No.")

Mr. J. J. INGALLS, of Kansas. I refer the Chairman to Rule 6.

The CHAIRMAN. The Rule referred to will be read.

Secretary JOHNSON read Rule 6 as follows:

"The report of the Committee on Credentials shall be disposed of before the report of the Committee on Resolutions is acted upon, and the report of the Committee on Resolutions shall be

---
*See Appendix.

disposed of before the Convention proceeds to the nomination of candidates for President and Vice President."

Mr. DeYOUNG. I move this Convention adjourn until to-morrow morning at 11 o'clock.

The CHAIRMAN. The gentleman from California moves that we adjourn to to-morrow morning at 11 o'clock. All in favor of the motion say "aye." All opposed "no."

The ayes have it.

Then at 12:50, p. m., the Convention adjourned until to-morrow at 11 o'clock a. m.

THIRD DAY.

MORNING SESSION.

THURSDAY, June 9th, 1892.

Chairman McKinley called the Convention to order at 11:25 A. M.

The CHAIRMAN. Prayer will be offered by Rev. William Brush, D. D., Chancellor of the Dakota University.

Dr. BRUSH. Let us pray:

We look to Thee, O Lord, for Thy gracious presence to encompass us as we now present ourselves at the very beginning of this session. We are unworthy to present ourselves before Thee, but we ask Thee to condescend to have mercy upon us and bridge the chasm occasioned by wickedness between Thee and our souls by the atonement of the Lord Jesus Christ. We thank Thee that, though we are unworthy, that Thou art infinitely exalted above all principalities and powers, and whilst Thou canst not look upon sin with any degree of allowance. Thou art full of compassion, Thou art replete in tenderness, Thou dost vouchsafe Thy gracious presence and impartest the influences of the Holy Spirit to enlighten the heart and to illuminate the understanding and to supply our every need through the riches of grace in Christ Jesus. O Lord, accept the gratitude of our hearts for all the multiplied blessings of Thy providence and grace in the past. As we refer to our individual history we are profoundly impressed ; as we refer to our National history we are reminded of Thy distinguished regard and supervision. Thou wast in the planting of the institutions of this great Republic, and Thou hast been

with it all through its history thus far and crowned it with success; and when darkness gathered over our Nation the bow of
promise overreached it. Oh, God, we thank Thee that Thou didst
go with us through the dark period of our National history, and
hast presided in the adoption of measures tending to conserve
the highest interests of the Nation in solving the problem of
reconstruction. O Lord, abide with our Nation still.

And now we ask Thee to command Thy blessing to rest upon
this representative body. O, may they be regardful of the constituents they represent, and may all things be subordinated to
the greatest aggregate good of the Nation. O Lord, may mere
partisanship stand back, and do Thou come Thyself to the front
and mold a platform of principles and policies that shall insure
the greatest measure of success for our common Nationality. As
Thou wast with Thine ancient people by a pillar of cloud by day
and a pillar of fire by night, so do Thou go before this Nation,
and lead it on to grander victories than it ever achieved in all its
past history. Command Thy blessing to rest upon the President
of this Nation and both branches of our National Legislature.
May they rise above the plane of mere partisanship to a compre-
hension of the higher interests of destiny and Nationality. Now
we commend ourselves to Thee, our homes and the citizens that
we represent. We ask Thee to be present in all these deliberations, and may the best possible results accrue from these proceedings. O Lord, bless us and guide us, and we would render
to Thee everlasting ascriptions and praises at last, through
Christ our Redeemer. Amen.

The CHAIRMAN. The regular order this morning is the report
of the Committee on Credentials, and I recognize Gen. Cogswell,
of Massachusetts, Chairman of that Committee.

Mr. COGSWELL. *Mr. President:* The Committee on Credentials is still in session. It has performed diligent work and
achieved reasonable progress. It hopes to be able to report in
full to-night at 8 o'clock. It asks further time.

Mr. SEWELL, of New Jersey. As it is impossible to go on with
any work in the Convention until the report of the Committee on
Credentials is made, I move that a recess be taken until 8 o'clock
this evening.

Mr. CULLOM, of Illinois. I ask that the gentleman will with-
hold his motion until I introduce a resolution for reference.

The CHAIRMAN. The gentleman from New Jersey moves that
this Convention take a recess until 8 o'clock this evening, and

pending that the gentleman from Illinois, Senator Cullom, desires to offer a resolution.

Mr. CULLOM. I ask that the following resolution be read and referred to the Committee on Resolutions.

The CHAIRMAN. The gentleman asks that the resolution be read in open Convention. Is there objection? [Cries of "read."]

ᵗChief Reading Clerk Haney read the resolution as follows:

"*Resolved,* That the 'World's Columbian Exposition' to be inaugurated in the City of Chicago in 1893 is rightfully considered by all our citizens, regardless of their political affiliation as a 'great national undertaking' and that, in recognition of its character and importance, Congress ought promptly to provide by appropriate-legislation such reasonable appropriation in and thereof as will enable the Government fully to discharge its express and implied obligations incident thereto; and as will insure the attainment of such results therefrom as will be commensurate with the dignity, progress, culture and development of a free and enlightened people." [Applause.]

Mr. CULLOM. I move that it be referred to the Committee on Resolutions.

The CHAIRMAN. The resolution under the rule will go to the Committee on Resolutions without debate.

Mr. ROBARTS, of Illinois. *Mr. Chairman:* I desire to offer a resolution and I would like to have it read and acted on this morning at this session.

The CHAIRMAN. The gentleman from Illinois asks unanimous consent for the reading of a resolution. Is there objection? There appears to be none.

Reading Clerk Stone, read the resolution as follows:

"*Resolved,* That every comrade of the Grand Army of the Republic not holding ticket of admission be admitted to standing room in this hall, and if any seats are vacant thirty minutes after the Convention shall have been called to order, such comrades shall be entitled to such vacant seats." [Applause.]

Mr. MASE, of New York. *Mr. Chairman:* I move that it be referred to the Committee on Resolutions.

The CHAIRMAN. It would properly go to the Committee on Rules and Order of Business.

Mr. ROBARTS. As a member of that Committee, I cannot object to that.

The CHAIRMAN. Then it will go to the Committe on Rules and Order of Business.

The gentleman from New Jersey, Mr. Sewell, moves that this Convention take a recess until 8 o'clock this evening. All favoring that say "aye." Those opposed "no."

·(Cries of "no," "no.")

The CHAIRMAN. As there is no demand for a division—

Mr. J. D. DAWSON, of New York. *Mr. Chairman:* I move for a division upon that vote.

The CHAIRMAN. The gentleman from New York demands a division.

The division was taken on a rising vote, and the Chair announced the result as follows:

Ayes, 407. Noes, 260.

The Convention, accordingly at 11:44 A. M., took a recess until 8 o'clock P. M.

THIRD DAY.

EVENING SESSION.

THURSDAY EVENING, June 9th, 1892.

Chairman KcKINLEY called the Convention to order at 8:52.

Mr. CHAUNCEY M. DEPEW, of New York. *Mr. Chairman—*

The CHAIRMAN. The gentleman from New York.

Mr. DEPEW. *Mr. Chairman:* I arise to a question of privilege; not high privilege, but pleasant privilege. We have present among our number a delegate, who has been a delegate to every National Convention of the Republican party since its organization; who has voted for every President of the United States for the last sixty years; who has served with distinction in Congress and in the Cabinet of the President of the United States; who is to-day eighty-three years of age, in full activity, and in the full possession of his faculties; and while England claims so much for Mr. Gladstone because at eighty-two he is so strong and so vigorous, America claims more for Colonel Dick Thompson, of Indiana, who is eighty-three years of age to-day. [Cheers.] I move you, sir, that the congratulations of this Convention be extended to him. [Applause and calls for "Thompson."]

Mr. C. F. GRIFFIN, of Indiana. *Mr. Chairman—*

The CHAIRMAN. The gentleman from Indiana.

Mr. GRIFFIN. In behalf of the delegation from Indiana, I desire to second the motion of the gentleman from New York.

The motion was unanimously adopted.

Mr. THOMPSON was conducted to the platform.

The CHAIRMAN. I have the pleasure of presenting to the Convention the Hon. Richard W. Thompson, of Indiana.   [Applause and cheers.]

Mr. THOMPSON. *Mr. Chairman and Gentlemen of the Convention:* Your action has awakened in my heart feelings which I have not words to express. I return to you my most sincere thanks and deepest gratitude. When I remember the events with which I have been associated in the political world, and find around me such an assemblage of those engaged in the common cause of preserving the welfare and the honor of this land, I feel as if I were young again. [Applause]. True, by the march which the dial has made, I am eighty-three years of age to-day. [Applause]. But I am not half that in reality because I am stimulated and emboldened by an undaunted Republican spirit, which animates me and which causes me to believe with an honest conviction that the destinies of this country are to be controlled by that great party for years and years to come. [Applause.]

Born as I was when the constitution of the United States was but 20 years old, I was reared and educated under revolutionary influences, and from my revolutionary ancestor I learned my Republicanism. [Cries of "good," "good," and applause.] They taught me to believe that the first and primary duty of the government of the United States was to take care of the interests of the people and to preserve all those great guaranties of the Constitution which are intended to secure to us, and to our children, the inalienable right of popular self-government. [Applause.] One of the instrumentalities by which that great right is to be preserved is the institution, under God, of the Republican party; [Applause] and we are to-day in the execution of the great trust which has been confided to us, to lay the foundation of another triumph upon the coming of November, which shall assure to us, and for years to come to our posterity, that this is the happiest, the most prosperous, the freest, and the grandest government upon the earth. [Applause.]

I cannot trespass upon your patience by entering upon the discussion of political questions now. I simply rose to return to you my sincere and heartfelt thanks for your congratulations, and to promise you in return that I will meet you here or some-where else in this broad land again, four years hence, [Applause and cries of "good", "good"] and I will do as I have done many a time before—aid you in selecting another Republican candidate for the Presidency. [Applause.] I have passed through, actively, fifteen Presidential campaigns. The first vote I ever cast for President of the United States was for Henry Clay [Cheers], the great champion of protection. [Applause.] The proudest vote I ever cast in my life, in a legislative body, was in 1842 for the tariff of that year [Applause], and I hope to see the time come when the public sentiment of this country shall so far vindicate that great bill which bears your honored name, sir, [the speaker turned to Chairman McKinley, and the Convention applauded vociferously], that neither faction nor party shall ever be able successfully to attack it.

Now, then, I promise you again that I will meet you four years hence. [Cheers.]

[During the cheers which followed these remarks, the electric lights flickered, and the Convention was enveloped in almost to-tal darkness for a few seconds.]

Your Chairman has instructed me to talk until the light comes back. [Light returned.] Am I not now, sir, released from the obligation imposed upon me? Gentlemen, in return for your congratulations I again repeat, I will meet you four years hence, and I hope to meet our honored Chairman also, that we may hail him as the author of a bill which has stood the test of four or five years of attack by its adversaries, and yet remains undis-turbed. [Applause.] The Democratic party proposes to destroy this bill by piecemeal, like rats gnawing at the ropes of a ship and seeking to sink it, while the great craft moves onward and bids defiance to the storm. [Applause.] I return you again my heartfelt thanks for your sympathy, your congratulation and your kindness. [Applause.]

ADMISSION OF VETERANS.

The CHAIRMAN. If there is no objection, I will recognize the Chairman of the Committee on Rules and Order of Business, General Bingham of Pennsylvania.

Mr. BINGHAM. *Mr. Chairman:* The Committee submit the following, as a substitute for the resolution referred to it.

Resolved: That as many of the Comrades of the Grand Army of the Republic as can be accommodated, and not holding tick-ets, shall be admitted to the Convention and seats unoccupied.

The motion was unanimously carried.

THE DISASTER AT TITUSVILLE.

Mr. J. J. CARTER of Pennsylvania. *Mr. Chairman—*

The CHAIRMAN. The gentleman from Pennsylvania.

Mr. CARTER. I have a communication which I desire to send to the platform, and have read for the information of this Convention.

The CHAIRMAN. The gentleman from Pennsylvania sends to the chair a communication which he desires read to the Convention, if there is no objection. The Chair hears none.

Reading Clerk PARTRIDGE read the following :

TITUSVILLE, PA., June 8, 1892.

Col. JNO. J. CARTER, T. B. SIMPSON, Delegates, Pennsylvania Delegation.

Our citizens earnestly request to have you notify the people of the country, through public announcement before the Convention, of the terrible loss of life and property and consequent suffering among poor people, from the recent flood and fire here and at Oil City. The proceedings of the Convention have absorbed the attention of the country and filled the newspapers to the exclusion of full accounts of our disaster, which will not be realized unless more directly brought to the notice of the public in this way ; thus preventing subscription to the relief fund now absolutely necessary to prevent additional suffering and death.

Make known the extent of our loss and assure the Convention that every dollar of relief furnished will be honestly and faithfully distributed, by competent and faithful citizens, among the sufferers.

(Signed)   E. O. EMERSON,
                         Mayor of Titusville.
                  W. G. HUNT,
                         Mayor of Oil City. ·

THE REPORTS OF THE COMMITTEE ON CREDENTIALS.

The CHAIRMAN. The regular order of business is the report of the Committee on Credentials, and the Chair recognizes the Chairman of that Committee, Gen. Cogswell of Massachusetts.

Mr. COGSWELL. *Mr. Chairman:* The Committee on Credentials closed its hearing at eight o'clock to-night. There has been no time to make a written report. Notice has been given to the majority that a minority report might be expected in regard to some of the contested cases. There has been no time for the minority to submit its views in writing. The majority, if the Convention is so minded, is prepared to report verbally, the action of the majority, and awaits the direction, Mr. President, of the Convention.

Mr. WILLIAM C. WALLACE of New York. *Mr. Chairman—*

The CHAIRMAN. The gentleman from New York.

Mr. WALLACE. On behalf of the minority I desire to present a partial report. As the gentleman from Massachusetts has already said, we have so recently adjourned that it has been impossible to obtain the minutes from which to complete this report for the information of this Convention; as a partial report from the minority of the Committee, I desire to submit the following.

The CHAIRMAN. The report of the minority will be received and submitted to the Convention after the report of the majority shall have been made. The gentleman from Massachusetts, Chairman of the Committee on Credentials, states to the Convention that he is not prepared with a written report at this time, but will proceed with a verbal report. If there be no objection he will proceed. The Chair does not hear any objection.

Mr. D. C. LOCKWOOD, of Idaho. *Mr. Chairman—*

The CHAIRMAN. Mr. Lockwood, of Idaho, is recognized.

Mr. LOCKWOOD. Do I understand that the Chairman of the Committee on Credentials has intimated to this Convention that there are to be two reports?

The CHAIRMAN. Yes, sir.

Mr. LOCKWOOD. A majority and a minority report?

The CHAIRMAN. Yes, sir.

Mr. LOCKWOOD. And that the majority are now ready to report, but that the minority have had no opportunity at this time to report?

The CHAIRMAN. No, the gentleman has misunderstood the statement made by the Chairman.

Mr. LOCKWOOD. That is the inquiry I wish to make.

The CHAIRMAN. The Chairman of the Committee on Credentials states that he is ready to make a report in behalf of the majority, but has had no time to put that report in writing. Mr. WALLACE, of New York, the representative of the minority, states that he has a partial report which he has sent to the Clerk's desk to be submitted after the Chairman shall have made his report.

Mr. LOCKWOOD. On behalf of the minority?

The CHAIRMAN. On behalf of the minority. Does the Chair hear any objections? The Chair hears none, and General COGS-WELL, Chairman of the Committee on Credentials, will proceed.

Mr. COGSWELL. *Mr. President:* The Committee on Credentials has considered the list of the uncontested delegates and has heard parties in twenty-four different contested cases. It recommends that the list submitted by the National Committee to the temporary organization be accepted as the list of duly accredited delegates and alternates, except in the cases to be hereafter mentioned.

Second. In the matter of contest in the eighth Alabama district, your committee finds for the sitting members and recommends that they retain their seats.

The same report is made as to the contest in the third Alabama district.

The same report is submitted in regard to the fourth Alabama district.

As to the contest for delegates at large from Alabama, your committee recommend that the contestants, Messrs. Noble, Smith, Dorsette and McEwen, be given seats.

In the fifth Alabama contest your committee find in favor of the sitting members, and recommend that they retain their seats.

In the contest of the ninth Alabama district, the committee recommend that the contestants, Messrs. Huston and Matthews, be seated.

As to the contest in the State of Kentucky your committee recommend that the contestants, Messrs. Mathews and Winstell be given seats.

As to the contest in Louisiana, as to the delegates at large, your committee finds in favor of the sitting members.

As to the contest in the first Louisiana district, the committee find for the contestants, Messrs. Booth and Lewis, and recommend that they be seated.

As to the contest in the second Louisiana district, your committee find for the sitting members.

The same finding in the fourth Louisiana district.

In the sixth Louisiana district your committee finds for Messrs. Donato and Breaux, the contestants, and recommend that they be given seats.

In the fourth district of Maryland the committee recommend that the contestants, Messrs. Supplee and Cummings, be seated.

In the contest in Mississippi of the delegates at large, the committee recommend, as does the National Committee, that the regular delegates and contestants both be seated, with the rights of a half a vote each.

As to the seventh Mississippi district the committee finds for the sitting members.

As to the contest in South Carolina on delegates at large, the committee find in favor of the sitting members.

In the contest in the fourth North Carolina district the committee recommend that Mr. Nichols, the contestant, be seated in place of Mr. Williamson, the sitting member.

In the sixth North Carolina district the committee find in favor of the sitting member.

In the seventh North Carolina district the committee recommend that Messrs. Walser, Bailey and Mott be seated, with the right to two-thirds of a vote each.

In the State of Texas, in the sixth district, and in all the contests, the committee find in favor of the sitting members.

In the District of Columbia, the committee find in favor of the sitting members.

In the Territory of Utah the committee recommend that the sitting members and the contestants, Messrs. Goodwin and Walling, be seated, with the right of one-half a vote each.

The member of the committee, Mr. Salisbury, of Utah, desires that I should note his dissent from the action of the committee in this last case.

I am authorized to report for the committee, that if the convention shall decide that the Indian Territory or Alaska is entitled to seats in this convention that it will be able at any time to report upon those who purport to be delegates from those respective Territories.

All of which is respectfully submitted for a majority of the committee, by its Chairman.

Mr. WALLACE, of New York. *Mr. Chairman—*

The CHAIRMAN. Does the gentleman from New York, Mr. Wallace, desire to present a verbal statement or does he desire that his report shall be read by the Secretary from the desk.

Mr. WALLACE. That is all the report which I am able to make, and I desire to have the Secretary read it from the desk.

The Secretary read the minority report as follows:

"In the disputed Alabama cases the delegates at large and the Ninth District considered by your Committee on Credentials, upon which they could not agree, the minority report as follows: That in their opinion the question as to the delegates at large is one largely, if not wholly, of regularity and organization. The State Convention was duly called for April 28th, 1892. The State Committee was duly called and it met the day prior thereto at Montgomery, at the office of the Collector of Internal Revenue at twelve o'clock, noon, of the 27th day of April, 1892, that being the time and place announced by said Moseley to members as the time and place of said committee meeting. The majority of the committee, a quorum being present, according to affidavits of members of said committee, the committee consisted of twenty members, after waiting a reasonable time, from an hour and fifteen to an hour and a half, a request was made of the Chairman, who was in another room on the same floor of the United States Government Building, to call the committee to order. This request was made several times. Finally, at about half past one o'clock, Chairman Moseley was again called in and requested to call the committee to order, a majority being present, when he said that he would adjourn the committee to meet at five o'clock P. M. Objection being made as to his right to adjourn the committee, a roll call being demanded by Richard W. Austin, who held his brother's, C. C. Austin's proxy, as a member of said committee, the Chairman replied that it was his private room, and he wanted it, and that the committee would adjourn until five P. M. as above stated by him. Thereupon, on motion the committee was called to order by the Secretary, a quorum and a majority bring present, according to the affidavits of members of said committee, the statement was made that the committee was ready and competent for business and proceeded to find a place of meeting for which a motion was made, put and carried, without a dissenting vote, to meet immediately at the Merchants Hotel. There at that time the committee met pursuant to adjournment, a quorum being present in person and by proxy, as shown by the original minutes of said meeting and by affidavits. The Secretary was directed to procure and prepare a hall in which to hold the convention and also named D. M. Long for temporary Chairman, John C. Binford for Secretary, and John M. Gee for Assistant Secretary. The Secretary, H. A. Wilson, whose duty it was and had been at previous state conventions to secure and prepare the hall, upon going to the Capitol found it in possession of guards and refused possession. These guards were two United States marshals, and two deputy internal revenue collectors, who refused admission or possession to him as such Secretary. These guards were placed there by Chairman Moseley. Then the Secretary, Mr. Wilson, secured the county court house, at which place, according to the sworn statements, 230 out of 332 legally elected delegates met on the succeeding day, April 28th, at 12 o'clock, noon. The State committee call had not stated the place of meeting in the city of Montgomery. At this convention and under the temporary organization thereof, as provided by the State committee the previous day at the Merchants Hotel, the following delegates at large, B. M. Long, William Vaughan, Iverson Dawson, and H. V. Cashin, and alternates, Thomason, Boyd, Binford and Braxdall, were duly elected and certified, and at such convention a new State committee was elected, and of which Hon. W. T. Stevens is Chairman and H. A. Wilson, Secretary. Then after performing all its business said convention adjourned *sine die.* Therefore we hereby recommend the placing upon the permanent roll the names of the above delegates and alternates. [Applause].

In the disputed Alabama case from the Ninth District, considered by your Committee on Credentials, upon which they could not agree, the minority thereof beg leave briefly to report that J. W. Hughes and W. H. Harney were elected delegates, and Henry Hall and J. O. Diffey, alternates to the National Convention; that the convention was held at Greensborough in said District on April 25, 1892, and all the delegates, thirty-four in number, participated in such convention as shown by the sworn statements of many delegates and others who participated therein. This convention was held with open doors at the Opera House in said city. Of the delegates who participated in said convention four were from the county of Blount (and there were no contests) who participated; fourteen from Jefferson, four from Bibbs, six from Hale and six from Perry county. According to sworn statements these delegates were elected at the regular call county conventions that comprise said District.

Another meeting which was claimed to be a District convention was also held in said city, on the same day, in the basement of the Colored Methodist church; at this latter meeting R. L. Huston and W. S. Matthews were elected delegates. According to a large number of affidavits, all who participated in that church house meeting merely claimed to be delegates but were not properly elected to said convention, but were men who were elected at bolting and pretended conventions. County meetings are conventions. The church meeting was held with closed doors guarded by door-keepers with instructions from the presiding officer to admit no one except upon his orders. Sworn statements show that such presiding officer was not a delegate to the District Convention and not a resident of the Congressional District, and was not the Chairman nor Secretary of the District Committee.

We therefore beg to recommend that the names of James W. Hughes and W. H. Harney as delegates, and Henry Hall and J.

O. Diffey as alternates be placed upon the permanent roll of the Convention.

David H. Lane,	A. T. Bliss,
J. M. Green,	W. E. Cramer,
J. F. Settle,	J. M. Shoup,
M. W. Stewart,	B. Clark Wheeler,
A. Gleason,	R. C. Dunn,
F. B. Brandagee,	A. E. Smith,
Paul McCormick,	F. A. Cage,
William C. Wallace,	Daniel N. Cooper.

Mr. COGSWELL. *Mr. Chairmen—*

The CHAIRMAN. The gentleman from Massachusetts, Gen. Gogswell.

Mr. COGSWELL. I move you, Mr. Chairman, that the report of the Committee be adopted as a whole.

Mr. CHAUNCEY I. FILLEY, of Missouri. *Mr. Chairman—*

The CHAIRMAN. The gentleman from Missouri.

Mr. FILLEY. I am delegated, Mr. Chairman, by the delegates, on behalf of the Republican organization and the Republican party of the State of Alabama, to ask this convention to substitute for the majority report, the report of the minority, and that the delegates therein recommended be seated. [Applause.] I do not propose to enter into the controversies of the Alabama Republicans. I do propose, however, on the part of the majority of Republican party in the State of Alabama to protest against the disorganization of the State and Congressional Committees, in the State of Alabama. [Applause.] Mr. Chairman, the State Convention was duly called on the 19th day of March, by the State Committee, to convene in the city of Montgomery on the 28th day of April. There was an omission, unintentional, however, as stated by the Chairman, and others of the Committee, and no place of meeting in the city of Montgomery was designated in the call. At that 19th day of March meeting also the State Committee was ordered to convene on a day prior to the meeting of the Convention, the 27th day of April, at the office of the Collector of Internal Revenue, the Chairman of the Committee, R. A. Moseley, Jr., and did meet at that office at 12 M., on the 27th day of April. That is, the majority of the Committee met there, as sworn to, and as represented by a copy of the State Committee, twelve or

thirteen members meeting there. They waited paitently for half
an hour and sent word in to the Chairman of the Committee, who
was in another office in the Government building in consultation
with leading Republicans and others, to have him come in and
convene the Committee—call it to order—and let it proceed to the
business for which it was convened. He however came into the
room and looking about said that there would be no meeting of
the Committee in his office. At about 1:15 a request was again
sent that he come in and call the Committee to order, and he
replied that that was his private office and he would adjourn the
Committee to meet at the grand jury room at 5 P. M. And again
at half past one o'clock a request was made, and he came in again
and said that no meeting could be held in that office. Then Mr.
Austin, who held a proxy of his brother, demanded that he call
the Committee to order and have the roll called, which he declined to do and left the room. Thereupon the Secretary of the
Committee, Mr. H. A. Wilson, did call the Committee to order
and proceeded with the roll call, twelve or thirteen of the twenty
members of the Committee answering thereto. Not only a
quorum but a majority.

The CHAIRMAN. The gentleman's time has expired.

Mr. FILLEY. Was there a limit to the time? I heard no limit
announced.

The CHAIRMAN. Under Rule 10 the time is limited, unless
unanimous consent is obtained.

Mr. FILLEY. I ask the consent of the Convention to proceed;
it will not take me five minutes longer.

The CHAIRMAN. The gentleman from Missouri asks unanimous consent to proceed. As the Chair hears no objection, Mr.
Filley may continue.

[Cries of "go on" and applause.]

Mr. FILLEY. A statement was made that the meeting should
not be held there. A motion was made to adjourn to the
Merchants Hotel, to meet at 3 P. M., which motion was carried
without a dissenting vote. At 3 P. M. the Committee assembled
at the Merchants Hotel and proceeded to name the temporary
officers for the next day for the Convention, and also to name a
Committee, Mr. Wilson, the Secretary of the Committee, and one

—4

other, to proceed to the State Capitol and arrange the seats in the hall for the delegates for the next day's Convention; and they proceeded to the hall and were denied admission, as stated in the report; finding the hall in the possession of two Deputy United States Marshals and two Deputy Collectors of Internal Revenue, and they were denied admission and possession of the hall. Then they went back to the Committee and proceeded to secure the Court House, at which, on the succeeding day, the majority of the delegates elected to the State Convention, met and elected delegates at large, which I, on behalf of the minority of the Committee, move you, sir, be substituted and given seats in this Convention.

Mr. GEORGE V. MASSEY, of Delaware. *Mr. Chairman:—*

Mr. G. A. KNIGHT, of California. *Mr. Chairman:—*

The CHAIRMAN. Recognitions will be alternated. I recognize the gentleman from Delaware, Mr. Massey, a member of the Committee, to speak in opposition.

Mr. MASSEY. *Mr. President:* For more than two days, as diligently and carefully as the Committee on Credentials was able to perform its duty, it has done it. I have listened, sir, with much interest and close attention to the honorable gentleman who spoke for Missouri, and as I listened and followed him I recognized exactly one side of this question, as we heard it before the Committee. It is proper to say, sir, and I say with great frankness, that in almost all these cases, and none more markedly than in this, was there a confusion of matters and conflicting testimony, from which your Committee to the best of its ability has evolved a conclusion satisfactory to a majority, and one entirely fair, as it believes, to this Convention and to the party. [Applause.] Every single proposition embodied in the narrative of the gentleman from Missouri presented in his speech just concluded, was before your Committee, and every single proposition as submitted by him, was the subject of contest and controverting proof. So that, without taking up the time of the Convention, and without trespassing upon their patience, it is sufficient to say in so far as this case is concerned that there was opposing testimony, and that in the conflict of testimony your Committee has evolved, to the best of their ability, by its majority vote, that

conclusion which it believes to be honest, just, conscientious
and equitable, in the light of all the facts, and it asks this Convention to sustain its report.

The CHAIRMAN. Mr. Knight, of California, is recognized.

Mr. KNIGHT. *Mr. Chairman and Gentlemen of this Convention:* I am in favor of the minority report in this Alabama
case, and I will tell you my reasons. It is an admitted fact that
we go before the people of this great Commowealth combatting
the Democracy of this Nation, and say that we have to face one
hundred and fifty-six solid votes from the solid South. Do you
recognize that we have nearly one hundred thousand officers
under our Government standing on guard in the Republican
party? If that great power; if that great machinery is to be put
in operation to advocate the will or the wish of any one man, let
me tell you the Republican party is in danger. [Cheers.] It
stands here admitted, fellow Republicans, that a Collector of Internal Revenue and two United States Marshals and two Deputy
Marshals stood guard and thwarted the will and the wish of the
people of Alabama. [Cheers.] Let this great body representing
the whole country tell them to keep their hands off and let Republicanism have its rights. [Cheers.] Republicans have a
right to talk; Republicans have rights to be exercised. Office-
holders have no right, when Republicans meet, to stand between them and the exercise of the rights of American citizenship and throw the weight of their votes, their force, and
their power for or against any one candidate. It is admitted,
fellow Republicans, that this United States Collector stood there
to thwart the will and the wish of the people of Alabama. I am
from a State where the Federal brigade take no part in politics,
and stand aloof. [Applause.] And if it be the fact that we not
only have to face one hundred and fifty-six electoral votes in the
Democratic party, but a hundred thousand office-holders to
thwart the will of Republicans, then, I say, I protest, [applause]
and I hope that the minority report in this particular case will
be sustained, and this Convention do that which is in harmony
with justice and in accord with right and stand by the truly
loyal Republicans of Alabama. Gentlemen, I thank you. [Long
continued applause.]

Mr. S. H. BETHEA, of Illinois. *Mr. Chairman:*—

The CHAIRMAN. The gentleman from Illinois.

Mr. BETHEA. I desire to say but a few words in behalf of this majority report. I join with the gentleman from California in saying that if it is right that this minority report should stand, then let it stand; but do not let it stand and overrule this majority report, unless you are sure it is right. Do not ask this Convention here to overthrow the results of the labors of these people upon a mere unfounded charge against an office-holder [Applause.] Every American citizen has his rights. If on the record and undisputed facts of this case, as agreed upon by the majority of this Committee, an office-holder happens to be sustained then it is right, and no mere charge should influence us· It is not a question, Mr. Chairman, of office-holder or no office-holder. I stand here representing the people of the Rock River Valley with whom there are no office-holders who have control in politics. I stand here representing nine-tenths of the Republicans there. I would not raise my voice in behalf of anything simply because there was an office-holder in it. I speak to you then upon the merits of this case, and what are they? I ask you gentlemen to consider them. What are they? Will you take the mere unfounded charge and statement of the gentleman from California, who was not upon the Committee, or the gentleman from Missouri, who was not upon the Committee, against the report of a majority of that Committee who sat patiently and listened to the evidence? [Applause.]

Mr. FILLEY, of Missouri. Will the gentleman allow me a word?

The CHAIRMAN. Does the gentleman from Illinois yield the floor to the gentleman from Missouri?

Mr. BETHEA. Yes, sir.

Mr. FILLEY. I will state to the gentleman that I gave three days and three nights until midnight, a much longer time than this committee has given, to this one contest. [Cheers.]

Mr. BETHEA. I will answer the gentleman. I submit that you started out in that committee prejudiced against us. [Applause.] I went into this committee and into this convention unpledged and unprejudiced, as did, I believe, many of the members of this committee. Now, then, the committee considered and listened to these people for hours in the Alabama case. They heard both sides; they heard the evidence as far as they could. Affidavits were submitted, in this as in all other cases, on both sides without number, and I found you could prove anything by almost anybody from that country. [There was hissing in the galleries.]

I perhaps stated that a little too strong, and I will withdraw that part of it. [Hisses and cries of "sit down."]

Mr. J. G. CANNON, of Illinois. *Mr. Chairman:* I rise to a question of order.

The CHAIRMAN. The gentleman will state his question.

Mr. CANNON. Would it be in order if the audience indulged in hissing, while any delegate is talking, to move to clear the galleries so we can proceed to business without interruption? [Applause.]

The CHAIRMAN. I think that would be in order under the rules of the 51st Congress, [applause and laughter,] which govern us.

Mr. CANNON. I give notice if hissing is repeated I will make that motion and insist upon a vote. [Cries "make it now."]

Mr. BETHEA. I will state to the Convention that I have no desire to cast any reflection upon any community, and did not intend to do so, but I will stick to my proposition that we found that the affidavits came in handy on both sides. Now as to the merits of the case. We believe from the evidence that this majority report finds in favor of that organization which is represented by the Chairman, and was represented by the majority of that Committee, which called the Convention. He issued the call; he got the Committee together. A majority was there, and as result of their action a Convention was called the next day, and the people representing the other side were the bolters of that Committee, and they called a bolters' Convention. Now, that is the result as we, the majority, have arrived at from the evidence, and I submit to this Convention that this Committee should be sustained.

Mr. E. O. WOLCOTT, of Colorado. *Mr. Chairman:*

The CHAIRMAN. Senator Wolcott, of Colorado, is recognized.

Mr. WOLCOTT. *Mr. Chairman, and Gentlemen of the Convention:* Inasmuch as the motion made by the gentleman from Massachusetts included all the contested cases, I venture at this time to say a word in behalf of the little sixth district of Kentucky; another case of a little too much internal revenue. [Applause.] The facts which I state are borne out by the testimony which I have seen, and the minority report upon them commends itself to every American who loves fair play, and I believe the delegates to this Convention want fair play wherever it hits. [Applause.] . There were in the Sixth District 123 delegates, of which 62 constituted a majority. There was a contest in one county comprising 40 delegates. The call was regularly made, unquestionably regular. At the appointed day 42 delegates, 41 from one county and 1 from another, constituting a majority of all, save the contested delegates, met. The friends of one set of the contesting delegates insisted that their delegates should be seated, and when this was refused, they took the 39 or 40 other men whose seats were not contested, and went to another hall, not included in the call, held a Convention of their own and now come up here with two delegates, which the majority of this Convention desire to seat, with a certificate of good character from Mr. Comingore, a Collector of Internal Revenue of the Sixth District. I hold in my hand, Mr. Chairman, a list of 130 odd office-holders, who are delegates to this Convention, nine-tenths of whom live in States where there is a hopeless Democratic majority. The trouble in this Committee as to these delegates comes not alone from these men, but it comes from a pressure of between two and three thousand government office-holders, who swarm the corridors of the hotels, and fill these galleries, and haunt the delegates, who ought to be in Washington and elsewhere attending to their business. [Cheers.]

[A cry of "sit down."]

Mr. WOLCOTT. I will not sit down. [Cheers.] We who are Republicans from Republican States, would like to have a little voice in naming a candidate for the Presidency. [Cheers.] Possibly the office-holders may name him, but I don't believe it. [Cheers.] But we from Republican States do ask the office-holding contingent, who are bringing a solid South against us, to at least conduct their side of the case in common decency, and common honor, so that we won't be ashamed to vote the ticket. [Prolonged applause and cheers.]

Mr. C. B. HART, of West Virginia. *Mr. Chairman:*—

The CHAIRMAN. The gentleman from West Virginia, Mr. Hart, is recognized.

Mr. HART. *Mr. Chairman:* In response to the terse, able and conclusive manner in which the distinguished Senator from Colorado has argued against the adoption of the report of the majority of the Committee on Credentials, I wish to say with equal conclusiveness that I come from a Southern State, and am not an office-holder. [Cheers.] I differ further from this distinguished gentleman. I come from a Southern State carried in 1888 by Mr. Cleveland, by the meagre majority of 500 votes, which State we expect as confidently as we expect to do anything, to turn over to the Republican party in next November, [Cheers], and we expect to do that, sir, with the nominee, barring no one, who may be the choice of this great Convention.

I do not come from a Republican State, unhappily; neither do I come from a State which threatens to go Democratic because a certain man may be nominated. [Cheers and applause.] When you get into my State, sir, there you find the power of the old Puritan type of Republican which knows nothing but the following of the flag and the Republican party. Now, I wish to say, sir, dropping this purely technical discussion of the subject introduced by my friend from Colorado, I wish to say in all soberness that your committee for three days has endeavored to do justice and to dispatch the business of the Committee, that it might contribute to the decent and orderly dispatch of the business of this Convention. It is true, in the nature of things it must be true, that in some cases, desiring to be fair, with such a mass of testimony from both sides, and with expert arguments brought forward on both sides, it may be, in view of all this, that the Committee may not have done exact justice in every particular case. The gentleman will understand that these decisions are frequently a matter of compromise, and I am able to say this for the Committee that, until the last moment, after three days of patient labor we did expect, by a policy of conciliation, by the fairly ascertained majority of that Committee, using its powers temperately, and I may say judicially, we did expect, and we were led to expect that we might come into this Convention with a unanimous vote which might receive the unanimous endorsement of this Convention. In conclusion I call attention to one fact, and it is an important fact, and in my mind a conclusive one, and it is this: it is not reasonable to believe, I submit, that the five gentlemen who have signed this minority report shall have more wisdom, more keenness of perception, more common honesty than the forty-four who approved the majority report. [Applause.]

Mr. DUFFIELD, of Michigan. *Mr. Chairman*—

The CHAIRMAN. Does the gentleman rise to oppose the report of the majority?

Mr. DUFFIELD. I rise to speak in behalf of the minority in the 9th District of Alabama.

The CHAIRMAN. Mr. Duffield, of Michigan, is recognized.

Mr. DUFFIELD. *Gentlemen of the Convention :* This Convention, if it does its duty, will nominate the next President of the United States. [Applause.] It will not do it, gentlemen, if we differ so much among ourselves, against our own people. I rise, Mr. Chairman, to call attention to this one consideration in the case of the delegates at large and of the Ninth District from Alabama. It is to be regretted, sir, that the majority report is verbal and states no facts, but simply conclusions. The record of the minority report states facts. The records of this Convention will then go out with nothing to sustain the majority report but the speeches of its advocates. But with the minority report stating such facts, about this man who invited that Convention into a grand jury room, and if any one believes that they will believe that he ought to be invited into a grand jury room with twelve men to indict him. [Applause.]

Therefore, Mr. Chairman, in view of the fact that the majority report contains no statement of fact, I say to this Convention, don't vote down the minority report, which will be a part of that record. [Applause.]

Mr. POWELL CLAYTON, of Arkansas. *Mr. Chairman :*—

The CHAIRMAN. Does the gentleman from Arkansas rise to sustain the report?

Mr. CLAYTON. For a few moments.

The CHAIRMAN. The Chair recognizes the gentleman from Arkansas.

Mr. CLAYTON. *Mr. Chairman:* Some allusion has been made here to officeholders. I have never filled a Federal office in my life, and none that did not come from my own State; therefore, I think I can speak dispassionately on this subject. The gentleman from Colorado has intimated that officeholders should return to Washington and attend to their business. There are various kinds of officeholders, among which are Senators of the United States. [Cheers.] I respectfully submit that if the officeholders leave this hall and go to their duties in Washington, my distinguished friend must go with them. [Applause.]

Mr. WOLCOTT (Colorado). *Mr. Chairman:* I desire to remind the distinguished gentleman from Arkansas—

The CHAIRMAN. Does the gentleman from Arkansas yield to the gentleman from Colorado?

Mr. CLAYTON. Yes, sir, for a moment.

Mr. WOLCOTT. I desire to remind the distinguished gentleman from Arkansas that if he does not hold office, he drags a beautiful lot of them always in his train, and while I hold office, it is not by appointment from the President of the United States, and I am there as I am here, to represent a Republican constituency. [Applause.]

Mr. POWELL CLAYTON. *Mr. Chairman:* If every delegate in this hall who does not represent a Republican constituency were to leave this hall, we would have a very great scattering indeed, and some of the largest and greatest States of them all would have to go out with us from the South. Now, I respectfully submit that all these outside matters ought not to be dragged in here. [Applause.] I have not dragged them in, nor has the majority. They have submitted this case upon the testimony, and I submit that this Convention should not be prejudiced in its mature judgment by this dragging in of officeholders, or by the slur that men who come here from the Southern States, men who have faced the horrors of Southern Democracy [applause] are to be pointed out and have it said that they cannot cast electoral votes. We have suffered enough from the enemy, without suffering from our friends. [Applause.] I beg of you to drop that slur. We are invited here by the National Committee, and if we do not stand upon an equality, then I say let us leave this hall and go home. [Cheers.]

Mr. CANNON, of Utah. *Mr. Chairman :—*

Mr. DEPEW, of New York. *Mr. Chairman :—*

The CHAIRMAN. Does the gentleman from New York rise to oppose the report?

Mr. DEPEW. The gentleman from New York rises to sustain the report, because the gentleman from New York understands that the speech of the gentleman from Arkansas (Mr. Clayton) was on neither side. [Laughter.]

The CHAIRMAN. The Chair would have to differ with the gentleman from New York, and recognize some one who desires to speak in opposition to the majority report. The Chair recognizes the gentleman from Utah, (Mr. Cannon), for that purpose.

Mr. CANNON. *Mr. Chairman:* I desire in behalf of the minority of the Committee on Credentials, to present a report which I hold in my hand, and have it read. I shall then ask recognition from the Chair in order to speak in opposition to the majority report.

Chief Reading Clerk Haney read the report as follows:

"*To the Republican National Committee:* The undersigned, a minority of your Committee on Credentials, respectfully report in favor of seating O. J. Salisbury and Frank J. Cannon as delegates, and George Sutherland and James Sharp as alternates, said delegates and alternates having been duly elected at a convention duly held on the 1st day of April, 1892, at Provo City, Utah Territory, by the Republican Party of said Territory, as recognized by the Republican National Committee, on the 24th day of November, 1891, and on the 6th of June, 1892, after due and full hearing. And the minority whose names are hereto undersigned further respectfully report that C. C. Goodwin and C. E. Allen, with their alternates contesting, are not entitled to seats in your Convention, for the reason that they do not represent said Republican Party in Utah, and were not elected by said party nor by any conventions held in said Territory by said party.

O. J. SALISBURY,
FRANK W. MUNDELL."

The CHAIRMAN. The gentleman from Utah, Mr. Cannon, is recognized.

Mr. CANNON. *Mr. Chairman and Gentlemen of the Conven-*

tion: I desire to speak in opposition to so much of the majority
report as is covered in the minority report by a contrary finding.

There are three parties in Utah, the Republican Party, the Democratic Party and the Liberal Party. The sitting delegates O. J.
Salisbury and Frank J. Cannon represent the Republican Party
of that Territory, consisting of nine thousand men, who vote the
Republican Ticket every time it is put in the field. [Applause.]
The two gentlemen whom it is proposed to seat with us, that we
may be compelled to share our votes with, by the majority report,
represent the Liberal Party, and a constituency which never
voted the Republican Ticket in Utah, from the day it was founded
to the present time. I assert that we might as well have a Democratic contingent coming in here to share our seats, as to have
these gentlemen come in to vote with us upon our two votes. The
mere fact, which will be asserted to you no doubt, if any one
shall speak in opposition to the minority report, that our Republicanism there is of recent growth and development, must not
stop us, it seems to me, if justice be done, because the question
is not how long a man has been a Republican but how good a
Republican he is. [Applause.] The objection which is raised to
us and to our having sole possession of these seats is that one of
us is a Mormon. I am he, and I will bear the burden. When the
Republican party declared in its platform that it would extermi-
nate the twin relics of barbarism, it fought one with the sword
and it fought one with intelligence, thank God. It conquered
with the sword and when it had finished its work in the South it
wrote with the hand of peace "fiat finis." Now it has accomplished just so much in Utah by school houses, by newspapers,
by law, and by the growth of intelligence, in the younger people
of that Territory. [Applause.] I say that now has come the time
to let the angel of peace write with the hand pointed to Utah
again. that it may no longer curse the Nation with the annoyance
which has always been springing up in demands for legislation
and platform planks. We in Utah want freedom. Where shall
we appeal for it except to the Republican Party, which is the
only guardian of freedom. [Applause.] I say if you seat these
men you seat them on the old issue. They do not know that
Brigham Young is dead. [Laughter.] He died when I was in

knickerbockers and I decline to be held responsible for old ser-
mons which he uttered in the early days of Utah. I appeal to
the Republican Party, which has been the liberty-giver ever
since the day that God Almighty called it into being. [Applause.]
I ask that this Convention will recognize Republicans in Utah
and not Liberals. If you shall decide in favor of the majority
report you make the Republican party in that Territory a shut-
tle-cock to be knocked back and forth by the two battledores of
Democracy and Liberalism, and I say this, that if you will give to
us our seats and the encouragement, thereby afforded, to go out
and work for Republicanism with heart and hope and strength,
we will give you a State of Utah that shall be Republican, some-
time, when you get ready for it. Not for years to come, but when
it does come it will be Republican. We will come not as Mor-
mons, but as intelligent American citizens, friends of the Republican Party. This is the first time that an appeal has ever been
made in a Republican Convention, to do something upon the
other side, for Utah. You have had planks in your platforms
time after time with regard to polygamy, with regard to domin-
ation of the Church over the State, now finish those by recogniz-
ing that the end of those questions has come, because it has
come. [Applause.]

Mr. DEPEW, of New York. *Mr. Chairman:—*

The CHAIRMAN. The gentleman from New York, Mr. Depew.

Mr. DEPEW. *Mr. Chairman:* I know nothing whatever about
the merits of this question, and after listening to the speeches
which have been made on both sides, I know less than I did
before. [Laughter.] We appointed a Committee here two days
ago of fifty members, upon Credentials, for the purpose of making up the lists of this Convention and ascertaining who were
entitled to vote. That Committee has sat for two days, has listened to the testimony, has given conscientious labor to the
questions, and has made its report. Of the fifty sixteen have
made a minority report. The gentleman from Missouri has
passed upon the question as a committee of one appointed by
himself, has made his report. [Applause and laughter.] The
gentleman from Colorado has appeared as the attorney of one
part of the report and has made his speech, incidental to the

expression of the terror with which he moves about this town for fear of the Internal Revenue Collector [applause]. As the United States Senate is a co-ordinate body in the confirmation of Federal officeholders, he is part of the creatures of his own creation. [Applause and laughter.] Now, we might sit here and listen to this debate for two weeks, and at the end of that time we would be no nearer the close than we are this minute. We have had this Committee. We can move through no other lines than by a Committee like this. Nearly two-thirds have joined in a report, and I suggest that we accept that report and end this discussion. [Applause and cries of "Question."]

Mr. WARNER MILLER. of New York. *Mr. Chairman—*

The CHAIRMAN. Mr. Miller, of New York.

Mr. MILLER. *Mr. Chairman and Gentlemen of this Convention:* We are not all know-nothings here, if my colleague is. [Applause and laughter.] I have attended several National Conventions and have listened to several reports from Committees upon Credentials, but, gentlemen, this is the first time, and I believe it is the first in the history of the Republican party, when the majority of the Committee have come before nine hundred delegates and simply given their conclusions, without giving us one single reason for them. [Applause.] If my colleague had listened to the reading of the minority report made by Mr. Wallace, of New York State, he would have known something about the facts of this case. The minority have presented a clear report here, which is unimpeached. No member of the majority of this Committee has, up to this moment, given this body one single reason why their report should be accepted, save simply that it is the majority report of the Committee. [Applause.] How large a majority report is it? Twenty-four to twenty-three. [Applause.] Does that weigh and outweigh everything else in this case? I have listened with patience to the speeches of the majority members of theCommittee and to the Chairman, and I repeat that not one single reason has been given for the majority report. We are told, however, that we are to accept that blindly because it is the majority report. Mr. President and gentlemen of this Convention, a National Committee composed of one from every State and Territory gave a number of days to the consideration of making up the roll of this Convention. The National Committee, which so gallantly and so successfully carried on the last campaign [applause] decided by a majority, by a vote of 28 to 21, they were Committee considered this carefully for days, when that National not beset by a great National Convention, and with the great interests which come into the Convention—when the question of the position of these different men as to the probable candidates before this Convention, was not considered—that Committee, I repeat, by a vote of 28 to 21, gave the seats to the four delegates at large in Alabama. And when this Credential Committee comes here with barely one majority and insists that their report must be taken because it is the report of the majority, without a single reason given, I put over against that claim the proposition that the National Committee by a majority of seven gave these men their seats. [Applause.]

Mr. President, I have little more to say upon this question. The reading of that minority report must carry conviction to every man who hears it unless it is impeached. It states the facts concisely. I will not repeat them. You have heard it read. It states them concisely and up to this minute no man has arisen here to deny it. The gentleman from Illinois did undertake to make a different statement, but he did not do it, Mr. President; and I submit, sir, that the minority report given here, until it is met and impeached by a carefully prepared document which will give us a different state of facts,—and I submit that they cannot be given,—that this Convention will be perpetrating a great outrage if it overturns the judgment of the National Committee.

I wish to raise a parliamentary question. I intended to have raised it before. As I understand it, the Chairman of the Committee on Credentials moved to adopt the entire report as it was. Upon that I demand a division, sir. Upon that demand we come first to the Alabama case, and upon that Mr. Filley has moved a substitute. That I hold to be the parliamentary position.

The CHAIRMAN. The gentleman from New York asks a division upon the report of the Committee, and asks for a vote first upon the Alabama case and upon the substitute submitted by the gentleman from Missouri, Mr. Filley.

Mr. COGSWELL. *Mr. President:* When representing a majority of this Committee I came to this hall and reported that less than 30 minutes before, the Committee had finished its last hearing of 24 cases, and that no time had been allowed for a written and elaborate report, and then awaited the pleasure of the Conven. tion, whether the Committee by its Chairman should submit a verbal statement of the doings of the Committee, and when the President of this Convention asked if there was objection to my stating verbally what we had done, and the gentleman from New York sat dumb in his seat, I say he should be dumb now, and not arraign the Committee for not making an elaborate report. [Cheers.] I ask for but fair play.

Mr. MILLER. Will the gentleman permit me a question?

The CHAIRMAN. Does the gentleman yield?

Mr. COGSWELL. I do not. Now, gentlemen of the Convention, the report I stated to you to-night was recapitulated before the full Committee a few minutes before its adjournment, and that report was agreed to, excepting that notice was given that there might be a minority report, and that has appeared signed by 16 out of 50; and this majority report is the report of 50 save 16 dissenting. Nothing but commendation has been made upon the work of the National Committee. I indorse that commendation; and your Committee out of 24 cases have come to a different conclusion in only seven, less than one-third. [Applause.] And in its deliberations it tried to discover the merits of each case. Each side was represented, and in every one the Committee believe they have reported to you, as nearly as they could, who were fairly, honestly and properly chosen to represent the Republican Party in this Convention. I therefore now move you, Mr. President, the previous question.

Mr. CRAPO, of Massachusetts. I desire to second that motion. [Cries for the question.]

Mr. YOUNG, of North Carolina. *Mr. Chairman:* I ask the floor for one minute again. The Chair stated he would recognize me after the gentleman from Massachusetts had spoken. I ask the gentleman to withdraw his motion for a moment.

The CHAIRMAN. I would be glad to do it if the gentleman from Massachusetts would withdraw his demand for the previous question. In that event the Chair would recognize the gentleman from North Carolina. [Cries of "question."]

Mr. OGLESBY, of Illinois. The gentleman is not of the majority and is not entitled to it.

Mr. COGSWELL. If the gentleman was on the opposite side I would withdraw the motion, but being on the same side I decline to do it because of the demand for the "question."

Mr. YOUNG. *Mr. Chairman:* I call for a division of the question. I wish the gentleman would withdraw the previous question for a minute, because the Chair announced that if I would yield to the gentleman from Massachusetts he would recognize me next. No Republican Convention can afford to do injustice. [Cries for the "question."]

The CHAIRMAN. The Chair desires to say that he has no control over this matter. The gentleman insists upon his demand for the previous question, and under the rule adopted by this Convention, it requires that a majority of the delegates from some State, shall demand the previous question, and that the demand be seconded by two or more States.

Mr. CRAPO, of Massachusetts. *Mr. Chairman:* The Massachusetts delegation demands the previous question.

The CHAIRMAN. The gentleman from Maryland seconds the motion.

The CHAIRMAN. West Virginia and New Jersey second the demand for the previous question.

Mr. QUAY, of Pennsylvania. *Mr. Chairman—*

The CHAIRMAN. The Chair will recognize the gentleman from Pennsylvania, Senator Quay.

Mr. QUAY. I desire the Chair to state the effect of the operation of the previous question.

The CHAIRMAN. The inquiry propounded by the gentleman from Pennsylvania, Mr. Quay, is as to the effect of this demand for the previous question. If the previous question should be sustained, the Chair would hold that it would be applicable not only to the majority, but to the two minority reports.

Mr. QUAY. Then Mr. Chairman, I beg to inquire if the minority report is sustained, what is the effect upon that portion of the report upon which we are not voting; the effect of the previous question upon it.

The CHAIRMAN. The minority report only applies to certain portions.

Mr. QUAY. We intend to move to strike out other portions of the report.

The CHAIRMAN. I understand that a demand was made by the gentleman from New York for a division upon all the contested cases raised by the minority report. So that if the previous question should be ordered, a vote would have to be taken upon these several divisions without debate.

Mr. QUAY. *Mr. Chairman:* The point is this: There are portions of the report of the Committee on Credentials which we propose to contest, upon which we have filed no written report. We intend to move to strike out and to amend the report so far as that is concerned.

Mr. MILLER, of New York. *Mr. Chairman:* We demand a division of the question. And that as already stated would call for a separate vote upon every portion of the report, upon each particular case. Of course, when a particular case comes up, the minority will be entitled to move to substitute another report for the majority report on that particular case.

The CHAIRMAN. In answer to the inquiry of the gentleman from Pennsylvania probably I had better state the proposition again. The Chair thought he had stated it so that it was heard by the entire Convention. The gentleman inquires as to the operation of the previous question if it be sustained. The Chair thinks it would apply to the majority and to the minority reports. It would operate upon all of them. But the Chair desires to state that he understands from the motion made by the gentleman from New York (Mr. Miller) that a separate vote can be demanded upon every finding of the majority report.

Mr. GOODWIN, of Michigan. *Mr. Chairman—*

The CHAIRMAN. For what purpose does the gentleman rise?

Mr. GOODWIN. I ask to have one thing explained before this Convention acts upon this question. I ask unanimous consent to make a statement.

—5

The CHAIRMAN. The gentleman from Michigan asks unanimous consent to make a statement. Is there objection?

A member of the New York delegation objected.

The CHAIRMAN. Objection is heard, and the question now is upon sustaining the demand for the previous question. Those favoring that—

A Delegate from South Carolina. *Mr. Chairman:* I rise on a question of information.

The CHAIRMAN. The gentleman will state his question.

The Delegate. I desire to inquire as to the majority report, seating the South Carolina delegation, as to what manner it was done. I desire to know the result of that matter.

The CHAIRMAN. The gentleman's inquiry is not one proper to be addressed to the Chair. The question is upon sustaining the the demand for the previous question.

A Delegate from Tennessee. *Mr. Chairman:* I rise for the purpose of appealing to this Convention. I ask that the gentleman from Michigan be heard in his request to make a statement.

The CHAIRMAN. The gentleman from Tennessee asks unanimous consent to be heard. Is there objection?

Several objections were heard.

The CHAIRMAN. There is objection.

A Delegate. I ask that the gentleman from Michigan be heard.

The CHAIRMAN. The question is upon sustaining the demand for the previous question.

A vote of the Convention was taken and the previous question was seconded.

Mr. MILLER, of New York. *Mr. Chairman:* I move to substitute the minority report in the Alabama case.

The CHAIRMAN. The first vote to be taken will be on the substitution of the minority report in the Alabama case for the majority report.

Mr. HISCOCK, of New York. *Mr. Chairman:* I rise for a parliamentary inquiry. I submit, sir, that the first question is upon seating in this Convention these gentlemen upon the regular roll whose seats are not contested. That is the first question.

WARNER MILLER, of New York. There can be no objection to that.

The CHAIRMAN. The Chair dislikes very much to do it, but is forced to overrule the point of order.

Mr. HISCOCK. Then I ask unanimous consent that the first vote be taken upon the seating in this Convention of those gentlemen whose seats are not contested.

The CHAIRMAN. The gentleman from New York, (Mr. Hiscock) asks unanimous consent that the first question shall be on the uncontested seats. Is there objection?

Mr. MASE, of New York, and others, "I object," "I object."

The CHAIRMAN. There is objection. All those in favor of substituting the minority report—

Mr. MASE, of New York. I withdraw the objection.

The CHAIRMAN. Does the Chair hear any further objection? There being no objection, the question is upon adopting the majority report as to the uncontested seats in this Convention.

The question was put and agreed to.

The CHAIRMAN. The question is now upon substituting the minority report in the Alabama case.

The Chair put the question.

The CHAIRMAN. The Chair is in doubt as to the vote.

Mr. MILLER, ot New York. Let us have a roll call on the question.

[Cries of "roll call," "roll call," and confusion.]

The CHAIRMAN. We must have order so that business may be done.

Mr. INGALLS, of Kansas. I desire the question stated by the Chair.

The CHAIRMAN. The question before the Convention is the substitution of the minority report in the Alabama case for the majority report.

Mr. MILLER, of New York. We demand a roll call.

There was much confusion in the hall.

The CHAIRMAN. There is a demand for a recorded vote.

Mr. QUAY, of Pennsylvania. Pennsylvania demands a call of the States.

Mr. MILLER, of New York. New York seconds that demand.

The CHAIRMAN. Pennsylvania demands a recorded vote upon this question, and New York seconds that motion. The Secretary will call the roll of States and Territories.

Mr. C. B. HART, of West Virginia. *Mr. Chairman:* I rise to a question of privilege.

The PRESIDENT. The gentleman from West Virginia rises to a question of privilege.

Mr. HART (from the platform). *Mr. Chairman:* My attention has been called by my colleague of the Committee, from Montana, to a misstatement which I made in the hearing of this Convention a few moments since. I desire to correct that misstatement. It is done at my colleague's request at this time and from this place, because in his opinion, the misstatement influenced unfairly some votes. Much as I desire the adoption of the majority report of the Committee, I much desire that justice may be done to the contestants—[Confusion and cries of "no," "no"] and contestees in this case—

A Delegate. *Mr. Chairman:* I call for the "question."

[Confusion and calls for the "question" among the delegates and cries of "regular order."]

The CHAIRMAN. I desire to say, gentlemen of the Convention, that Mr. Hart was recognized on this question to correct a statement made in his remarks, which he desired to do before the Convention.

A Delegate. Let him do it, and not make a speech.

Mr. HART. What I am saying is preliminary to the arithmetic of the case.

A Delegate. Drop the preliminaries.

A Delegate. I object to the gentleman making an argument.

Mr. HART. The gentleman does not object to my making a statement?

The Delegate. No, but I object to the gentleman making an argument.

Mr. HART. I stated that the minority report was signed by five members of the Committee. I so understood or I would not have so stated. I find by reference to that report which I have first heard read in this Convention and had no means of knowing otherwise, that it was signed by fifteen. [Cries for "roll call."]

The CHAIRMAN. The Secretary will proceed to call the roll of States.

A DELEGATE from Alabama. *Mr. Chairman:* I desire to make a motion.

A DELEGATE. *Mr. Chairman:* I make the point of order that when one motion was pending another is not in order.

The CHAIRMAN: The point of order is well taken.

READING CLERK CURTIS commenced calling the roll of States, and Alabama reported seventeen ayes and five noes, and the vote was announced.

Arkansas was then called and reported one aye and fifteen noes.

Mr. HISCOCK. *Mr. Chairman:* Are the contestants voting in their own cases?

The CHAIRMAN. The Chair has no information on that subject.

Mr. COGSWELL. Certainly, the report is against the sitting members.

Mr. HISCOCK. I suggest that fact should be ascertained.

The CHAIRMAN. From what State?

Mr. HISCOCK. From Alabama. Is the vote upon the Alabama case?

Mr. COGSWELL. *Mr. Chairman:* If the Convention will allow me—

Mr. HISCOCK. Has Alabama been called, and has she voted?

The CHAIRMAN. Alabama has been called and voted and her vote recorded, and we have gone to another State.

[Cries of "roll call," "roll call."]

Mr. DEPEW. I challenge the vote of Alabama.

Mr. FASSETT. A challenge is out of order at this time.

The CHAIRMAN. I do not understand whether the gentleman challenges the correctness of the vote or not.

Mr. DEPEW. I challenge the correctness of the vote of Alabama, and for this reason: There are nine delegates from that State who were placed on the roll by the National Committee. The majority report, upon which we are voting turns them out and puts nine more in their places, and they have no right to vote. [Applause.]

Mr. QUAY, of Pennsylvania. We are voting to retain in their places the men placed upon the temporary roll by the National Committee, and not to turn them out.

The CHAIRMAN. There should be no misunderstanding about this question, and no technical ruling upon a question so import-

ant and vital. As I understand it every delegate who was seated
in this Convention by the National Committee is entitled to enjoy
the privileges of this Convention [applause] until by a majority
vote they shall have been unseated; [applause] and these gentlemen have not yet been unseated. A question more serious, probably, than the one I have just stated, is the question whether a
delegate could vote in his own case, [cries of "that is the question
exactly,"] and upon that question the Chair is very much embar-
rassed. We are proceeding under the rules of the 51st Congress,
so far as they can be applicable to a National Convention. Rule 8
provides that every member shall be present within the hall, etc.,
and shall vote on each question put, unless on motion made
before division or the commencement of the roll call and decided
without debate, he shall be excused, or unless he has a direct
personal or pecuniary interest in the event of such a question.

Mr. HISCOCK. *Mr. Chairman:* I appeal to the President of the
Convention that under that rule in contested election cases the
sitting member has never been allowed to vote.

The CHAIRMAN. Does any gentleman desire to be heard upon
that point of order, and with respect to the right of these gentlemen to vote in their own cases? If so the Chair would be very
glad to hear from them.

Mr. MILLER, of West Virginia. I make this point of order:
That the question could only have been raised when the State of
Alabama was called; that other States have been called since that
time.

The CHAIRMAN. I do not think, with all deference to the gentleman's point, in a matter of this sort, so important to the integrity of our proceedings, that a technical point of that sort should
be raised. We want to decide precisely what is right, and make
a suitable precedent for future Conventions, and therefore I
should be very glad to hear from any gentleman who asserts the
right of a sitting member to vote in his own case.

Mr. RICHARDS, of Illinois. *Mr. Chairman:* I move you that
the vote of the State of Alabama be passed.

The CHAIRMAN. I fear that motion has come too late. [Cries
of "decision."]

Mr. SPOONER, of Wisconsin. *Mr. Chairman:*—

The CHAIRMAN. Senator Spooner, of Wisconsin.

Mr. SPOONER. It is a question of very little consequence, I think, what this vote may be. It is a matter of very great consequence that the National Republican Convention shall be right upon the question, and it is a universal law the world over—requiring no rule to affirm it—that no man shall be a judge in his own case. I would like to ask the Chair if in his experience as a member of Congress, he has ever known of a case where a man has been permitted to vote in his own case?

The CHAIRMAN. I do not recall any such case, yet I may not have observed all of the contested cases.

Mr. SPOONER. We are working under the rules of the 51st Congress, which state that no man can vote in a case in his own interest. Every delegate who is voting to determine the question whether he is a delegate or not, is certainly voting in his own interest.

Mr. FASSETT, of New York. *Mr. Chairman :—*

The CHAIRMAN. The gentleman from New York, Mr. Fassett.

Mr. FASSETT. *Mr. Chairman:* I take it there is no difference of opinion in this Convention as to the paramount importance of proceeding right. No man ever yet confessed himself willing to do wrong. It seems to me this question is not without embarrassments. If the position of Senator Spooner of Wisconsin is correct, then the proceedings of a Convention could be, at any time, brought to naught by any sufficient number of conspirators who chose to make a contest in each delegation. [Cheers.] And contestants could join together and paralyze the action of any Convention. It seems to me a ruling should be made that would make it possible for a preliminary organization, and for that purpose, Mr. Chairman, the National Committee has been recognized as the supreme tribunal for the making up of the roll, and the National Committee have made up the roll in order that we may do business; and until all contests are settled, and we have a permanent organization, the roll of the National Committee ought to be the roll to be called, and the names thereon ought to be permitted to be answered to, by their owners.

Mr. RICHARD W. AUSTIN, of Alabama. *Mr. Chairman—*

The CHAIRMAN.   The Chair recognizes the gentleman from Alabama.

Mr. AUSTIN.   *Mr. Chairman and Gentlemen of the Convention:* Representing the sitting members, upon the floor of this Convention, from the State of Alabama, permit me to say that all we want at the hands of this Convention, is justice.   I withdraw, in the interests of harmony, and in the interest of justice, the four votes from the State at large. [Applause.]

Now gentlemen, indulge me for but a moment.   I am a native of the South, the son of an old Whig, a Union man, and a lifetime Republican.   I was canditate for my party in the Congressional District of North Alabama two years ago, and we increased the Republican vote more than any Congressional District in the United States, Mr. McKinley's not excepted.   I ask you in behalf of the regular delegation, elected by four fifths of the Republicans of that State, to retain these men in their seats.

Mr. F. S. BAIRD, of Illinois.   I wish to call attention, Mr. Chairman, to the fact that but a few moments ago a motion was made and unanimously adopted that the delegates, whose names were reported upon as not being contested, were seated as the delegates of this Convention, and the gentlemen whose seats are being voted upon at this time, are not delegates, and have no right to vote.

I want to say right here that I have voted in favor of the minority report, for the very reason that it seemed to be fair upon its face; and for the further reason that there were no statements of facts made here by the majority report. [Cries of "out of order."]   Now Mr. Chairman, it is one of the oldest principles of law and of justice that no man should be a judge in his own case.

Mr. WOLCOTT, of Colorado.   *Mr. Chairman—*

The CHAIRMAN.   Senator Wolcott.

Mr. WOLCOTT.   The gentleman from Alabama arose and announced that he withdrew some votes, supposing he had the attention of the Chair.   He asked leave to withdraw their four votes.

The CHAIRMAN.   I understand that there are six votes involved in this controversy.   Will the gentleman from Alabama again state his purpose?

Mr. AUSTIN. We withdraw six votes, Mr. Chairman.

Mr. QUAY. Under the division of the question, the delegates from the districts certainly have the right to vote upon the question of the seating of the delegates at large.

The CHAIRMAN. I submit to the Convention that the delegates at large would be entitled to vote upon the contest between the district delegates, understanding as I do that there are different questions involved; and the district delegates would be entitled to vote for the delegates at large upon that question. [Applause and cries of "he is right."]

Now the State of Alabama will be called, and following the suggestion of the Chair the votes will be announced.

Reading Clerk Curtis resumed the calling of the roll, and Alabama reported, 13 ayes and 5 noes.

Mr. FORAKER. *Mr. Chairman:* I submit, under rule 7, that Alabama has two other votes.

The CHAIRMAN. Does the gentleman from Ohio make a further point of order?

Mr. FORAKER. I call the attention of the delegates from Alabama to the fact, for the purpose of ascertaining if they understood the matter, and voted in accordance with the ruling of the Chair.

The CHAIRMAN. Have they so voted?

Mr. AUSTIN. Yes, sir.

Reading Clerk Curtis resumed the call of the roll and Arkansas reported, 1 aye, 15 noes; California, 10 ayes, 8 noes; Colorado, 8 ayes; Connecticut, 9 ayes, 3 noes; Delaware, 2 ayes, 4 noes; Florida, 8 noes; Georgia, 1 aye, 25 noes; Idaho, 6 ayes; Illinois, 19 ayes, 28 noes.

Mr. CANNON, of Illinois. *Mr. Chairman:* I challenge the vote of Illinois, and demand a roll call of that State.

The CHAIRMAN. The gentleman from Illinois, Mr. Cannon demands a roll call of the delegates of his State. The Secretary will call the roll.

The Reading Clerk called the roll of the State of Illinois, and the following delegates voted aye:

J. H. Gilbert, George B. Swift, Samuel B. Raymond, W. R. Kerr, Earnest J. Magerstadt, William Lorrimer, Robert L. Martin, Frederick S. Baird, Henry Wolff, Arthur W. Pulver, Isaac L.

Ellwood, James B. Lane, W. S. Cowen, C. F. H. Carruthers, (Alternate for Dr. E. A. Wilcox, not present), Oscar G. Price, John A. Gray, Joseph F. Durant, Joseph D. Graff, Thomas J. Golden, James A. Gregory—twenty.

And the following delegates voted no: Shelby M. Cullom, Richard J. Oglesby, J. G. Cannon, Joseph Robbins, Miles Kehoe, Herman H. Kohlsaat, Jeremiah N. Sharp, S. H. Bethea, A. C. Stanly, William H. Stewart, W. H. Hannah, W. A. Rankin, Morris Rosenfeld, William A. Lorrimer, Edward A. Crandall, J. W. Kitchell, B. S. Shellabarger, John Kirby, Patrick Richards, Horace Dollarhide, Phillip W. Barnes, David H. Zepp, James P. McCashland, Louis Krughoff, T. S. Ridgeway, James M. Schumacher, J. P. Roberts and S. Lovejoy Taylor—twenty-eight.

Roll call continued:

Indiana, 30 noes; Iowa, 6 ayes, 20 noes; Kansas, 10 ayes, 10 noes; Kentucky, 6 ayes, 20 noes,

When Louisiana was called—

Mr. KELLOGG. *Mr. Chairman:* One of our delegates at large, Mr. Cage, who was a member of the Committee on Credentials, has been taken ill and has left the hall, requesting me to cast his vote in this case. Have I a right to do so? [Cries of "no," "no."]

The CHAIRMAN. If I understand the gentleman's inquiry, it is whether, there being an absent delegate, he is entitled to cast a vote for him, having been authorized to do so when the gentleman left the hall?

Mr. KELLOGG. Yes, sir.

The CHAIRMAN. The Chair would hold that the gentleman had no such right.

Mr. KELLOGG. If the Chair please, I desire to state that the alternate for the delegate was not able to procure a ticket and was unable to gain admission to the hall.

The Reading Clerk proceeded with the call, and Louisiana reported 11 ayes, 3 noes.

Mr. KELLOGG. *Mr. Chairman:* I desire that the vote be polled.

Mr. FILLEY, of Missouri. *Mr. Chairman:* I do not think the gentleman from Louisiana (Mr. Kellogg) was heard by the Chair.

The CHAIRMAN. Will the gentleman from Louisiana repeat the announcement.

Mr. KELLOGG. There is a request on the part of a delegate that the vote be polled, and I will therefore request that the vote be polled. [Cries of "no," "no."]

The CHAIRMAN. The Secretary will call the roll of delegates from Louisana.

Reading Clerk STONE called the roll of Louisiana delegates with the following result:

William Pitt Kellogg, aye; Robert F. Guichard, aye; Andrew Hero, Jr., aye; James Madison Vance, aye; Jacob Gray, aye; Paul Broyard, (no response); Joseph Wilkins, alternate, aye; Andrew W. Smyth, no; Richard Simms, aye; Thomas A. Cage, (no response).

The CHAIRMAN. Call the alternate.

Reading Clerk (continuing) Victor Rochou, (no response).

The CHAIRMAN. Proceed with the roll call.

READING CLERK. Jason L. Jones, aye; Albert H. Leonard, aye; William Harper, aye; John B. Donnally, no; David Young, aye; Louis J. Souer, (No response); Joseph Honore, Jr., alternate, (No response); William Duplessis, (No response); William Green, alternate, (No response).

Mr. KELLOGG, of Louisiana. *Mr. Chairman:* I desire to ask the name of the alternate of Robert S. Guichard from the State at large.

SECRETARY JOHNSON. Henry O. Maher.

Mr. KELLOGG. Mr. Guichard's vote is recorded, and Mr. Maher is in the State of Lousiana. I make the point that where there are four delegates and four alternates at large that in the absence of any delegate at large any alternate at large may act.

The CHAIRMAN. The Chair would hold that in the case of four delegates at large, and four alternates at large, in the absence of any delegate at large and of his alternate it would be the duty of the Secretary to call the next alternate.

Reading Clerk STONE. The vote stood: Louisiana, 11 ayes, 2 noes.

Reading Clerk (continuing). Maine, 12 ayes; Maryland, 16 noes; Massachusetts, 14 ayes, 16 noes; Michigan, 20 ayes, 8 noes.

When Minnesota was called.

A DELEGATE from Minnesota. *Mr. Chairman:* In the absence of a delegate, S. G. Comstock, we desire to have his alternate called.

The Reading Clerk called J. W. Reynolds, who voted aye, and and the vote stood: Minnesota, 11 ayes, 7 noes.

Reading Clerk (continuing): Mississippi, 6 ayes, 10½ noes; Missouri, 14 ayes, 19 noes; Montana, 5 ayes, 1 no; Nebraska, 6 ayes, 10 noes; Nevada, 6 ayes; New Hampshire, 2 ayes, 6 noes; New Jersey, 2 ayes, 18 noes.

Mr. MURRELL, of New Jersey. *Mr. Chairman:* I am the alternate of the Hon. John I. Blair, of New Jersey. He is not here, and I wish to vote in his place.

Mr. SEWELL, of New Jersey. *Mr. Chairman:* I make the point that this gentleman (Mr. Murrell), is not a member of this delegation.

Mr. MURRELL. *Mr. Chairman:* I demand a call of the roll.

Mr. SEWELL. The alternates from New Jersey are elected alternate without reference to any one particular member of the delegation, and it has been the practice for years to assign alternates when a vacancy occurs. The vacancy of John I. Blair has occurred, and Mr. Gaddis, in accordance with our custom, has been assigned, having received the largest number of votes at the State Convention.

Mr. MURRELL. I simply call for the roll furnished this Convention. The roll furnished by the Committee shows prima facie that I am the alternate.

The CHAIRMAN. Does the gentleman question the correctness of the announcement of the vote?

Mr. MURRELL. Yes, sir.

The CHAIRMAN. The Secretary will call the roll of New Jersey.

Mr. SEWELL. *Mr. Chairman:* I stand here to demand the right according to precedent. This is the fifth National Convention I have taken part in, and been chairman of a delegation from my State, and I know all about the precedents and we have been governed by this custom almost since the Republican party has had an existence. [Cries of "call the roll."] This gentleman has no business in the delegation until a vacancy occurs and it has been assigned to him by a majority of the delegates. [Cries of "call the roll."]

Mr. MURRELL. No delegation has power to deprive me of my rights.

The CHAIRMAN. The question raised by the gentleman is as to whether he is entitled to vote for his principal who is absent, he being the alternate— [A voice: "Who makes him so?"]

Mr. MURRELL. The people of the State Convention.

The CHAIRMAN. I desire to know how the delegates are chosen in the State Convention of New Jersey.

Mr. SEWELL. The delegates to this Convention were chosen by acclamation. The alternates were voted for, commencing with Mr. Gaddis who had 703 votes, running down to this man who had about 400. When a vacancy occured in the delegation, the delegation itself unanimously assigned the gentleman that had the 703 votes to fill the vacancy, and we will continue that down as vacancies occur.

Mr. DEYOUNG, of California. *Mr. Chairman:* The roll is the only thing we can be governed by. The roll shows this man an alternate of Mr. Blair, and he has a right to vote.

Mr. MURRELL. I demand the roll call.

The CHAIRMAN. The record of the National Committee, if the gentleman will permit me to state, reads as follows: "William J. Sewell, delegate, E. H. Kirkbride, alternate; John I. Blair and G. T. Cranmer, alternate.

Mr. MURRELL. The roll I am talking about is the roll I have been voting on all of the time from New Jersey. [Laughter.]

The CHAIRMAN. I am informed by the Secretary that this is the official roll given to us by the Committee, and we must be bound by that.

Mr. SEWELL. The roll referred to by the gentleman is an advertising sheet of one of these railroads. I have seen it myself. [Laughter.]

The CHAIRMAN, I know of no other rule of this Convention, and I shall hold that Mr. George Cranmer is the alternate of John I. Blair. Continue the calling of the roll.

New York was the next State called and the vote announced as follows: New York, 45 ayes, 27 noes.

Mr. J. A. SLEICHER, of New York. *Mr. Chairman:* I rise to a question of information. One of our delegates is ill and his alternate is not here and another alternate has been substituted. I want to know if we have a right to make such a substitution.

Mr. FASSETT. *Mr. Chairman:* On the naked question as put by the gentleman from New York I think the Chair would not be in possession of sufficient information to give the proper answer. In the Convention which delegated to two gentlemen the duty of representing one of the districts of New York, it was reserved to them to appoint a substitute in case of the sickness of the principal and the absence of the alternate; acting upon that Mr. Stearns in one of our districts asked permission that that direction and rule of the local district be recognized by the delegation from the State of New York. It was so recognized by the unanimous votes of 71 representatives from the State of New York and upon that showing his name was placed upon the roll by the National Committee. His name has been uncontested upon the roll and the uncontested roll has been adopted by this Convention.

Mr. SLEICHER. I desire to say that at the meeting of our delegation the name of Mr. Stearns was suggested in the absence of both delegate and alternate, and Mr. Fassett himself arose in his seat and declared it would be the understanding that this applied simply for the present. I want to know whether outsiders are entitled to vote here.

The CHAIRMAN. I would inquire of the gentleman from New York if the name of Mr. Stearns is on the roll of uncontested delegates that was passed upon by the Convention to-night.

Mr. SLEICHER. I think not.

The CHAIRMAN. I will inquire of the Secretary.

Secretary JOHNSON. The name of Mr. Stearns appears on the roll as a delegate from the Fourteenth District of New York.

The CHAIRMAN. The name of Mr. Stearns appears as a dele. gate from the Fourteenth District.

Mr. SLEICHER. And is to be counted?

The CHAIRMAN. The Chair would therefore hold that we are to be bound by the report of the Committee which the Convention has adopted.

Reading Clerk Curtis continued the call of the roll: North Carolina, 10 ayes, 14 noes, (one absent).

DELEGATE. I call for the poll of the North Carolina delega. tion.

The CHAIRMAN. Does the gentleman from North Carolina question the announcement?

DELEGATE. I do.

The CHAIRMAN. Call the roll.

Reading Clerk Curtis called the roll with the following result:

Peter C. Pritchard, no; Elihu A. White, no; Henry P. Cheatham, no; John C. Dancy, no; Clay M. Barnhard, aye; Hugh Cale, no; John H. Hannon, aye; Charles A. Cook, no; A. R. Middleton, (absent); J. E. O'Hara, alternate (absent); George C. Scurlock, no; J. H. Williamson, aye; Edward A. Johnson, no; T. B. Keough, no; J. A. Cheek, aye; Archibald Brady, no; James H. Young, no; J. J. Mott, one-half vote, aye, Zebulon V. Walser, one-half vote, no.

Mr. YOUNG, of North Carolina. *Mr. Chairman:* The Committee on Credentials decided that each of those gentlemen should have two-thirds of a vote.

The CHAIRMAN. I will say to the gentleman that the Convention has not yet passed upon the report of the Committee on Credentials.

The roll call then proceeded as follows:

William A. Bailey, one-half vote, aye; Joseph O. Wilcox, no; Reuben L. Jenkins, no; Charles J. Harris, aye; R. W. Logan, no.

The SECRETARY. North Carolina, 6½ ayes, 13½ noes.

Reading Clerk (continuing):

North Dakota, 4 ayes, 2 noes; Ohio, 27 ayes, 19 noes; Oregon, 6 ayes, 2 noes; Pennsylvania, 54 ayes, 9 noes; Rhode Island, 3 ayes, 5 noes; South Carolina, 6 ayes, 12 noes; South Dakota, 5 ayes, 3 noes; Tennessee, 12 ayes, 10 noes; Texas, 9 ayes, 20 noes (1 absent); Vermont, 5 ayes, 3 noes.

(At this point the electric lights flickered and went out, and a lamp was brought in but proved entirely insufficient for the purpose of enabling the transaction of business.)

(About twenty minutes after twelve Mr. Foraker, of Ohio, stepped up to the front of the platform and inquired of President McKinley, "Can't you go ahead?" to which the presiding officer replied, "Can we do it?" to which Mr. Foraker replied, "Of course we can.")

The CHAIRMAN. The Secretary will proceed with the call of the roll.

Mr. MCDANIEL, of Texas. *Mr. Chairman:* I question the vote of Texas as announced and wish to have the delegation polled. [Cries of "too late," "too late."]

The CHAIRMAN. What is the next State?

The SECRETARY. Vermont is next.

The CHAIRMAN. It must be manifest to everybody that it is impossible to go on in an orderly manner with business in such a light. I cannot see the gentleman who is questioning the correctness of the count.

Mr. C. L. McGEE, of Pennsylvania. *Mr. Chairman:* I rise to a point of order. The State of Texas was recorded; the State of Vermont has been called and it is not in order for any gentleman to challenge the correctness of the vote of the State of Texas.

A DELEGATE. There is nothing in order but the roll call. I call for the regular order.

Mr. FASSETT, of New York. *Mr. Chairman:* Owing to the darkness and the danger that may occur from the use of matches and the impossibility of doing business, I move that we adjourn till to-morrow morning at ten o'clock. [Cries of "no," "no."]

A DELEGATE. *Mr. Chairman:* I make it a point of order that no motion is in order during a roll call.

(After waiting several minutes further for light, Mr. Miller of New York addressed the Convention as follows :)

Mr. MILLER. *Mr. Chairman and Gentlemen of this Convention:* For one, I am not willing to sit here in the present condition of affairs. I think we owe it to ourselves, and to the people in the galleries, that this audience should now disperse as quietly as possible, and I ask unanimous consent—[Cries of "I object, I object."]

Mr. MILLER. I ask unanimous consent—[Repeated cries of "object," "object."]

Mr. MILLER. Very well, then I leave this hall.

(At this point, after a lapse of about fifteen minutes, the electric current was again turned on and after the applause had subsided, the Convention again proceeded with its business.)

The CHAIRMAN. The Convention will come to order. The gentleman from Texas challenges the correctness of the count announced. The gentleman from Pennsylvania raises the point of order, that the questioning came too late. The Chair sustains the point of order, because we had already passed to Vermont and called that State. The Secretary will proceed. [Applause.]

Reading Clerk (continuing):

Virginia, 15 ayes, 9 noes ; Washington, 8 ayes ; West Virginia, 2 ayes, 10 noes ; Wisconsin, 9 ayes, 15 noes ; Wyoming, 2 ayes, 4 noes ; Arizona, 1 aye, 1 no ; Dist. of Columbia, 2 ayes ; New Mexico, 6 noes ; Oklahoma, 2 noes ; Utah, 1 aye, 1 no.

Secretary JOHNSON. Total $423\frac{1}{2}$ ayes and 463 noes.

The CHAIRMAN. On this vote for the substitute of the minority report in Alabama the ayes are 423½ and the noes 463, and the motion is lost.

THE ALABAMA CASE.

The following is a statement of the vote on the motion to substitute the minority for the majority report in the Alabama case:

	AYES	NOES		AYES	NOES
Alabama	13	5	New York	45	27
Arkansas	1	15	North Carolina	6½	13½
California	10	8	North Dakota	4	2
Colorado	8		Ohio	29	19
Connecticut	9	3	Oregon	6	2
Delaware	2	4	Pennsylvania	54	9
Florida		8	Rhode Island	3	5
Georgia	1	25	South Carolina	6	12
Idaho	6		South Dakota	5	3
Illinois	20	28	Tennessee	12	10
Indiana		30	Texas	9	20
Iowa	6	20	Vermont	5	3
Kansas	10	10	Virginia	15	9
Kentucky	6	20	Washington	8	
Louisiana	11	2	West Virginia	2	10
Maine	12		Wisconsin	9	15
Maryland		16	Wyoming	2	4
Massachusetts	14	16	Arizona	1	1
Michigan	20	8	Dist. of Columbia	2	
Minnesota	11	7	New Mexico		6
Mississippi	6	10½	Oklahoma		2
Missouri	14	19	Utah	1	1
Montana	5	1			
Nebraska	6	10	Totals,	423½	463
Nevada	6		Total vote, 886½.		
New Hampshire	2	6	Necessary for choice. 444.		
New Jersey	2	18			

The CHAIRMAN. Is there a further division demanded?

Mr. QUAY. Yes, sir.

Mr. CHRISTOPHER L. MAGEE, of Pennsylvania. *Mr. Chairman:* Do I understand that that vote seats the delegates from Alabama who were reported in favor of by the majority of the Committee?

The CHAIRMAN. That will be so when the majority report is adopted.

Mr. MAGEE. I move the adoption of the majority report.

Mr. J. L. CARNEY, of Iowa. *Mr. Chairman:* I move now that we adjourn until 10 o'clock to-morrow morning.

The CHAIRMAN. The gentleman from Iowa moves that the Convention adjourn until ten o'clock to-morrow morning.

Mr. DEYOUNG, of California. I move that the hour be eleven o'clock.

—6

The CHAIRMAN. The motion is that we adjourn to meet to-morrow morning at ten o'clock. The affirmative vote is now being taken.

Upon the motion to adjourn a division was demanded, and a rising vote was taken.

The CHAIRMAN. On this vote the ayes are 271 and the noes, 372 ; so the motion to adjourn is lost. [Applause.]

Mr. DEPEW, of New York. I now call for the question on the adoption of the majority report.

Mr. TELLER, of Colorado. I move we now adjourn until 11 o'clock to-morrow morning.

Mr. CANNON, of Illinois. *Mr. Chairman:* Upon that motion I make the point of order that no business has intervened and it is evidently a dilatory motion.

The CHAIRMAN. The gentleman from New York demands a vote upon the motion for the adoption of the majority report upon the Alabama case.

Mr. QUAY, of Pennsylvania. The Alabama delegates at large.

Mr. DEPEW. *Mr. Chairman:* What I want to get at is simply this: The gentleman from Pennsylvania moved to substitute the minority for the majority report in the Alabama case. On a call of the roll the Convention has refused to substitute the minority for the majority report. Now, I desire to ask, what I think will be a pro forma vote, that we adopt the majority report so far as that extends in the matter.

The CHAIRMAN. The question raised by the gentleman from Pennsylvania is, that the vote was only had as to the delegates at large.

Mr. DEPEW. Then I ask for the adoption of the majority report on the question raised.

Mr. QUAY. I call for the roll call of States.

Mr. CHAIRMAN. All those in favor of the adoption of the majority report as to the delegates at large from Alabama, will say "aye."

The vote was taken.

The CHAIRMAN. The ayes seem to have it, but the Chair is reminded that there is a demand for a call of States by the gentleman from Pennsylvania, (Mr. Quay.) However the gentleman is not entitled to a roll call until one State is seconded by two others.

Mr. QUAY. The State of Pennsylvania calls for the calling of the roll by States, on the motion for the adoption of the majority report of the Committee on Credentials as to the four delegates at large from Alabama.

Seconded by New York and Colorado.

Mr. SPOONER. What is the question?

The CHAIRMAN. The question is upon the adoption of the majority report in the Alabama case.

Mr. QUAY. As to the delegates at large from that State?

The CHAIRMAN. As to the delegates at large from that State. The Secretary will now call the roll of States.

Reading Clerk Stone called the roll:

Alabama, 56 ayes, 13 noes.

Mr. HISCOCK. I wish to inquire in this case whether the contesting delegates have voted.

The CHAIRMAN. They have not voted.

The roll call proceeded:

Arkansas. 15 ayes, 1 no; California, 8 ayes, 10 noes; Colorado, 8 ayes, 8 noes.

Mr. DUFFIELD, of Michigan. *Mr. Chairman:* I rise for information. There is so much confusion that we do not know how the question is stated or what will be the result of a vote "aye" or "no." Will the Chair please explain?

The CHAIRMAN. The question is on the adoption of the majority report in the Alabama case, as to the delegates at large.

The roll call proceeded as follows:

Connecticut, 9 ayes, 3 noes; Delaware, 4 ayes, 2 noes; Florida, 8 ayes; Georgia, 26 ayes; Illinois, 26 ayes, 18 noes; Indiana, 30 ayes; Iowa, 20 ayes, 6 noes; Kansas, 10 ayes, 8 noes; Kentucky, 22 ayes, 4 noes; Louisiana, 3 ayes, 11 noes; Maine, 11 noes; Maryland, 16 ayes; Massachusetts, 13 ayes, 13 noes; Michigan, 11 ayes, 11 noes; Minnesota, 6 ayes, 8 noes; Mississippi, 11 ayes, 5½ noes; Missouri, 24 ayes, 8 noes; Montana, 1 aye, 4 noes; Nebraska, 10 ayes, 6 noes; Nevada, 6 noes; New Hampshire, 5 ayes, 1 no; New Jersey, 18 ayes, 2 noes; New York, 28 ayes, 44 noes; North Carolina, 15 ayes, 6 noes; North Dakota, 2 ayes, 4 noes; Ohio, 26 ayes, 15 noes; Oregon, 2 ayes, 6 noes; Pennsylvania, 9 ayes, 54 noes; Rhode Island, 3 ayes, 5 noes; South Carolina, 15 ayes, 3 noes; South Dakota, 3 ayes, 5 noes; Tennessee, 10 ayes, 6 noes; Texas, 19 ayes, 9 noes; Vermont, 2 ayes; Virginia, 8 ayes, 15 noes; Washington, 8 noes; West Virginia, 10 ayes, 2 noes; Wisconsin, 14 ayes, 9 noes; Wyoming, 4 ayes, 2 noes; Arizona, 1 aye, 1 no; District of Columbia, 2 noes; New Mexico, 6 ayes; Oklahoma, 2 ayes; Utah, 1 aye, 1 no.

Mr. BUCKLEY, of Connecticut. *Mr. Chairman:* There is an error in the record of the vote of Connecticut. It should be recorded 3 ayes and 9 noes.

Mr. HOPKINS, of Connecticut. *Mr. Chairman:* I challenge the vote of Connecticut.

The CHAIRMAN. The gentleman from Connecticut challenges the correctness of the announcement of the vote of Connecticut, and the Secretary will call the roll.

Chief Reading Clerk Haney called the roll as follows:

Morgan G. Bulkley, no; James P. Platt, no; Timothy E. Hopkins, aye; Lorrin A. Cooke, aye; Thomas Duncan, no; Thomas A. Lake, absent, (alternate also absent); Thomas M. Wallace, no; E. Irving Bell, absent; William I. Lewis, absent; Frank B. Brandegee, no; Edwin Milner, absent; John A. Porter, alternate, aye; Allan W. Page, no; Thomas G. Bradstreet, aye.

Reading Clerk. Connecticut, 4 ayes, 6 noes.

The CHAIRMAN. On the motion to adopt the majority report in the Alabama case the ayes are 476 and the noes 365½. [Cheers.] The motion is agreed to and the majority report of the Committee is adopted.

The following is a statement of the vote on the adoption of the majority report as to the delegates at large from Alabama:

	AYES	NOES		AYES	NOES
Alabama	5	13	New Jersey	18	2
Arkansas	15	1	New York	28	44
California	8	10	North Carolina	15	6
Colorado		8	North Dakota	2	4
Connecticut	4	6	Ohio	26	15
Delaware	4	2	Oregon	2	6
Florida	8		Pennsylvania	9	54
Georgia	26		Rhode Island	3	5
Idaho		6	South Carolina	15	3
Illinois	26	18	South Dakota	3	5
Indiana	30		Tennessee	10	6
Iowa	20	6	Texas	19	9
Kansas	10	8	Vermont	2	
Kentucky	22	4	Virginia	8	15
Louisiana	3	11	Washington		8
Maine		11	West Virginia	10	2
Maryland	16		Wisconsin	14	9
Massachusetts	13	13	Wyoming	4	2
Michigan	11	11	Arizona	1	1
Minnesota	6	8	Dist. of Columbia		2
Mississippi	11	5½	New Mexico	6	
Missouri	24	8	Oklahoma	2	
Montana	1	4	Utah	1	1
Nebraska	10	6			
Nevada		6	Totals,	476	365½
New Hampshire	5	1	Total vote, 841½.		

Mr. ELLIOTT F. SHEPARD, of New York. *Mr. Chairman:* I ask unanimous consent to present a resolution at this time.

The CHAIRMAN. The gentleman from New York, Mr. Shepard, asks unanimous consent to present a resolution at this time.

Mr. SHEPARD, of New York. *Mr. Chairman:* I have been asked to present this resolution. It is a matter of humanity, and is in relation to the application for relief in behalf of Titusville and Oil City, and it is simply this:

That the Secretary of this Convention, Mr. C. W. Johnson, is authorized to receive any contributions which any one chooses to give him, and that he will see that the contributions go to the proper authorities for the relief of the sufferers by those great fires and floods.

The resolution was put to a vote, and unanimously agreed to.

THE PLATFORM.

Mr. J. B. FORAKER. *Mr. Chairman:* I ask the unanimous consent of the Convention that we may read without debate the resolutions that I have been instructed by the Committee on Resolutions to report to the Convention for adoption. There is a reason why this should be done, and I trust no objection will be made. It will require only a very few moments.

The CHAIRMAN. Is there any objection? The Chair hears none.

The resolutions were read by Gov. Foraker as follows:

The representatives of the Republicans of the United States, assembled in general convention on the shores of the Mississippi river, the everlasting bond of an indestructible Republic, whose most glorious chapter of history is the record of the Republican party, congratulate their countrymen on the majestic march of the nation under the banners inscribed with the principles of our platform of 1888, vindicated by victory at the polls and prosperity in our fields, workshops and mines, and make the following declaration of principles:

We reaffirm the American doctrine of protection. We call attention to its growth abroad. We maintain that the prosperous condition of our country is largely due to the wise revenue legislation of the Republican congress.

We believe that all articles which cannot be produced in the United States, except luxuries, should be admitted free of duty, and that on all imports coming into competition with the products of American labor, there should be levied duties equal to the difference between wages abroad and at home. We assert that the prices of manufactured articles of general consumption have been reduced under the operations of the tariff act of 1890.

We denounce the efforts of the Democratic majority of the House of Representatives to destroy our tariff laws by piece meal, as manifested by their attacks upon wool, lead and lead ores, the chief products of a number of States, and we ask the people for their judgment thereon.

We point to the success of the Republican policy of reciprocity, under which our export trade has vastly increased, and new and enlarged markets have been opened for the products of our farms and workshops.

We remind the people of the bitter opposition of the Democratic party to this practical business measure, and claim that, executed by a Republican administration, our present laws will eventually give us control of the trade of the world.

The American people, from tradition and interest, favor bi-metallism, and the Republican party demands the use of both gold and silver as standard money, with such restrictions and under such provisions, to be determined by legislation, as will secure the maintenance of the parity of values of the two metals so that the purchasing and debt-paying power of the dollar, whether of silver, gold or paper, shall be at all times equal. The interests of the producers of the country, its farmers and its workingmen, demand that every dollar, paper or coin, issued by the government, shall be as good as any other.

We commend the wise and patriotic steps already taken by our government to secure an international conference, to adopt such measures as will insure a parity of value between gold and silver for use as money throughout the world.

We demand that every citizen of the United States shall be allowed to cast one free and unrestricted ballot in all public elections, and that such ballot shall be counted and returned as cast; that such laws shall be enacted and enforced as will secure to every citizen, be he rich or poor, native or foreign born, white or black, this sovereign right, guaranteed by the Constitution. The free and honest popular ballot, the just and equal representation of all the people, as well as their just and equal protection under the laws, are the foundation of our Republican institutions, and the party will never relax its efforts. until the integrity of the ballot and the purity of elections shall be fully guaranteed and protected in every State.

SOUTHERN OUTRAGES.

We denounce the continued inhuman outrages perpetrated upon American citizens for political reasons in certain Southern States of the Union.

FOREIGN RELATIONS.

We favor the extension of our foreign commerce, the restoration of our mercantile marine by home-built ships, and the creation of a navy for the protection of our National interests and the honor of our flag; the maintenance of the most friendly relations with all foreign powers; entangling alliances with none; and the protection of the rights of our fishermen.

We reaffirm our approval of the Monroe doctrine and believe in the achievement of the manifest destiny of the Republic in its broadest sense.

We favor the enactment of more stringent laws and regulations for the restriction of criminal, pauper and contract immigration.

MISCELLANEOUS.

We favor efficient legislation by Congress to protect the life and limb of employes of transportation companies engaged in carrying on interstate commerce, and recommend legislation by the respective States that will protect employes engaged in State commerce, in mining and manufacturing.

The Republican party has always been the champion of the oppressed and recognizes the dignity of manhood, irrespective of faith, color or nationality; it sympathizes with the cause of home rule in Ireland, and protests against the persecution of the Jews in Russia.

The ultimate reliance of free popular government is the intelligence of the people, and the maintenance of freedom among men. We therefore declare anew our devotion to liberty of thought and conscience, of speech and press, and approve all agencies and instrumentalities which contribute to the education of the children of the land, but while insisting upon the fullest measure of religious liberty, we are opposed to any union of Church and State.

We reaffirm our opposition, declared in the Republican platform of 1888, to all combinations of capital organized in trusts or otherwise, to control arbitrarily the condition of trade among our citizens.

We heartily indorse the action already taken upon this subject, and ask for such further legislation as may be required to remedy any defects in existing laws, and to render their enforcement more complete and effective.

We approve the policy of extending to towns, villages and rural communities the advantages of the free delivery service, now enjoyed by the larger cities of the country, and reaffirm the declaration contained in the Republican platform of 1888, pledging the reduction of letter postage to 1 cent at the earliest possible moment consistent with the maintenance of the Post Office Department and the highest class of postal service.

CIVIL SERVICE.

We commend the spirit and evidence of reform in the civil service, and the wise and consistent enforcement by the Republican party of the laws regulating the same.

NICARAGUA CANAL.

The construction of the Nicaragua canal is of the highest importance to the American people, both as a measure of national defense and to build up and maintain American commerce, and it should be controlled by the United States government.

TERRITORIES.

We favor the admission of the remaining Territories at the earliest practicable date, having due regard to the interests of the people of the Territories and of the United States. All the Federal officers appointed for the Territories should be selected from bona fide residents thereof, and the right of self-government should be accorded as far as practicable.

ARID LANDS.

We favor the cession, subject to the homestead laws, of the arid public lands, to the States and Territories in which they lie, under such Congressional restrictions as to disposition, reclamation and occupancy by settlers as will secure the maximum benefits to the people.

THE COLUMBIAN EXPOSITION.

The World's Columbian Exposition is a great national undertaking, and Congress should promptly enact such reasonable legislation in aid thereof as will insure a discharge of the expenses and obligations incident thereto, and the attainment of results commensurate with the dignity and progress of the Nation.

INTEMPERANCE.

We sympathise with all wise and legitimate efforts to lessen and prevent the evils of intemperance and promote morality.

PENSIONS.

Ever mindful of the services and sacrifices of the men who saved the life of the Nation, we pledge anew to the veteran soldiers of the Republic a watchful care and recognition of their just claims upon a grateful people.

HARRISON'S ADMINISTRATION.

We commend the able, patriotic and thoroughly American administration of President Harrison. Under it the country has enjoyed remarkable prosperity and the dignity and honor of the Nation, at home and abroad, have been faithfully maintained, faithful and we offer the record of pledges kept as a guarantee of performance in the future.

The CHAIRMAN. The question is upon—

Mr. HISCOCK. *Mr. Chairman:* It was understood that the resolutions were to be introduced only; it is not in order to move their adoption.

Mr. FORAKER. I move the adoption of the resolutions.

Mr. HISCOCK. I raise the point of order that it is not in order to ask their adoption until the roll of the Convention is completed.

The CHAIRMAN. When the gentleman from Ohio arose and asked unanimous consent, he asked for consent to present these resolutions for consideration.

Mr. HISCOCK. I did not so understand it.

Mr. DEPEW. I trust there will be no objection. I hope this will go through. It is one of the best platforms I ever heard in my life. [Applause.]

Mr. FORAKER. *Mr. Chairman:* I stated to Gen. Cogswell that I would ask for unanimous consent to read the resolutions, but that I would not ask that they be considered now.

Mr. HISCOCK. There is only one reason I have for asking a delay until morning. I know there are gentlemen in the Convention who have considered the resolution in respect to the ceding of the arid lands in the States and Territories, and I merely ask it, in order that they may consider that resolution and see whether they wish to antagonize it or not.

The CHAIRMAN. The question is upon agreeing to the resolutions reported from the Committtee.

The question being put the resolutions were unanimously adopted, amid great cheering.

Mr. DEPEW. I move that the Convention now adjourn until 11 o'clock to-morrow morning.

The motion was agreed to, and the Convention, at 1:27 A M., adjourned until 11 o'clock A. M. Friday, June 10th.

FOURTH DAY.

MORNING SESSION.

FRIDAY MORNING, June 10th, 1892.

The Convention was called to order by Chairman McKinley at 11:37 A. M.

The CHAIRMAN. The Convention will please be in order. Prayer will now be offered by the Rev. Wayland Hoyt, D. D., pastor of the First Baptist Church of Minneapolis.

Dr. HOYT. *Let us pray:* Oh Lord, our God, Thou art very great ; Thou art clothed with honor and majesty. Thou hast prepared Thy throne in the heavens and Thy kingdom ruleth over all. Thy mercy is from everlasting to everlasting upon them that fear Thee, and Thy righteousness to children's children, to such as remember Thy covenant and remember Thy commandments to keep them. We praise Thee, O God, we acknowledge Thee to be the Lord. Most humbly and heartily we beseech Thee for Thine especial blessing upon this National Convention. Oh, thou Father of Light, in Whom is no variableness, neither shadow of turning, Who giveth to all men liberally and upbraideth not, we beseech Thee send upon Thy servants charged here with such momentous trust even Thine own wisdom. May he whom they shall select to be their standard-bearer be one chosen even of Thyself, a man after Thine own heart. Bless Thou our country, our fair heritage, founded and preserved and consecrated as it has been by the toil and by the blood of patriots. May righteousness dwell within its borders. May intelligence and well ordered liberty ; may safe and happy homes, and the universal recognition of the rights of citizenship, which our Constitution has put into the hands of free men, be studiously maintained. For such great and holy ends we pray Thee bless especially the deliberations, utterances and choice of these Thy servants. All of which we ask in the name and for the sake of Him who has taught us to say :

Our Father who art in heaven, hallowed be Thy name. Thy kingdom come, Thy will be done on earth as it is in heaven. Give us this day our daily bread, and forgive us our debts as we forgive our debtors. And lead us not into temptation, but deliver us from evil, for Thine is the kingdom and the power and the glory forever. Amen.

THE ALABAMA CASE.

The CHAIRMAN. *Gentlemen of the Convention :* The regular order of business this morning is the futher consideration of the report of the majority of the Committee on Credentials; and the question before the Convention is the substitution of the minority report for the majority report in the contest in the Ninth District of Alabama.

Mr. MATTHEW S. QUAY, of Pennsylvania. *Mr. Chairman—*

·The CHAIRMAN. The gentleman from Pennsylvania is recognized.

Mr. QUAY. *Mr. Chairman :* I desire to say that so far as the friends of the minority report are concerned, that they will make no further opposition to the majority report. It may be adopted by a *viva voce* vote, and on one ballot.

The CHAIRMAN. The gentleman from Pennsylvania, Mr. Quay, announces on the part of those opposed to the majority report, that they will make no further opposition thereto. [Applause.]

The question, therefore, is upon the adoption of the majority report. Those favoring that report will say aye.

The motion prevailed unanimously. [Applause.]

THE UTAH CASE.

The CHAIRMAN. It is proper that I should say to the Convention that the gentleman from Utah, a member of the Credential Committee, filed a minority report in addition to the one filed by the gentleman from New York. Does the gentleman from Utah desire a vote upon his report?

Mr. CANNON. I do, sir.

The CHAIRMAN. Those favoring the report of the minority in regard to the Utah contest, will say "aye;" contrary, "no."

The motion was put and declared lost.

The CHAIRMAN. Those who favor the adoption of the majority report will say "aye;" contrary, "no."

The motion to adopt the majority report prevailed.

ALASKA AND THE INDIAN TERRITORY.

Mr. C. W. FULTON, of Oregon. *Mr. Chairman:* I understand from the report of the Committee on Credentials that the question of the admission of delegates from Alaska depends upon the further action of the Convention, and I therefore move you that the two delegates from Alaska be admitted to seats in this Convention.

The CHAIRMAN. The Chairman of the Committee on Credentials informs the Chair that they made no report as to Alaska.

A DELEGATE. I move that the resolution of the gentleman be referred to that Committee for consideration.

Mr. COGSWELL, of Massachusetts. *Mr. Chairman—*

The CHAIRMAN. The gentleman from Massachusetts.

Mr. COGSWELL. If the Convention will allow seats to the delegates from Alaska, the Committee on Credentials is already able to report who are the accredited delegates. That is in their report made last night.

Mr. FULTON. I move that the degates be allowed representation.

The CHAIRMAN. The gentleman from Oregon moves that the two delegates from Alaska be entitled to seats upon this floor. Is there any discussion desired? [No response.]

The question being put to a vote was unanimously agreed to.

Mr. POWELL CLAYTON, of Arkansas. *Mr. Chairman:* I now move that the two delegates from Indian Territory be allowed seats on this floor.

The CHAIRMAN. The gentleman from Arkansas now moves that the two delegates from the Indian Territory be entitled to seats on this floor.

The question being put to a vote was unanimously agreed to.

OKLAHOMA, SOUTH CAROLINA AND ALABAMA.

Mr. A. J. SEAY, of Oklahoma Territory. *Mr. Chairman:* We elected six delegates from Oklahoma at a meeting called for that purpose, and in behalf of twenty-five thousand Republicans of that Territory, we ask that they be placed upon the roll and entitled to vote six votes in this Convention. [Cries of "no," "no," "no."]

Mr. EMERY, of South Carolina. *Mr. Chairman:* I wish to state in behalf of a contesting delegation from South Carolina, that they have come two thousand miles for a hearing in this Convention, and that the Committee appointed by this Convention to pass upon their claim to contested seats, has refused to hear them, and we desire this Convention to say whether or not they endorse that action.

Mr. T. B. JOHNSON, of South Carolina. *Mr. Chairman:* I rise to a point of order. The gentleman now speaking is not a member of any delegation.

The CHAIRMAN. The point of order is well taken, and is sustained.

I desire to state that it is very important that each State that has not already done so, should report to the Secretary the name of their National Committeeman.

Mr. AUSTIN, of Alabama. *Mr. Chairman:* I desire to state for the information of this Convention that the Alabama delegation met this morning at 9:30 and that there were twelve members present, whose seats have been practically settled and agreed upon by both the majority and minority of the Committee on Credentials, and that Mr. William Youngblood received thirteen votes of the twenty-two delegates from Alabama. As to the thirteen votes there is no question as to the legality of twelve of them, which is one more than a majority of our entire delegation.

Mr. WALKER, of Alabama. *Mr. President:* There are twelve delegates regularly elected and seated by this Convention, whose names I have, and who ask that Allen E. Parsons be made a member of the National Committee for Alabama. If there is any objection I ask that the delegation be polled.

Mr. AUSTIN. *Mr. President:* I beg the pardon of this Convention on account of the conduct of Republicans from Alabama. [Cries of "regular order."]

The CHAIRMAN. Will the gentleman state the vote for the National Committeeman by the seated delegates?

Mr. AUSTIN. I will.

The CHAIRMAN. The regular order is being demanded, and unless that is done at once, that order must be proceeded with.

Mr. AUSTIN. *Mr. Chairman:* They have changed one member of the delegation, who kept the minutes and recorded his own vote for the election of William Youngblood.

The CHAIRMAN. If there is no objection, Alabama may have further time to correct its arithmetic. [Laughter.]

Will some member of the Committee on Credentials give the name of the National Committeeman from Alaska?

The gentleman from Massachusetts, Gen. Cogswell, has a partial report to make from his Committee.

Mr. COGSWELL. *Mr. Chairman:* I submit the following report and ask to have it read.

Chief Reading Clerk Haney read the report as follows:

Indian Territory—Delegates, Ridge Paschal, John S. Hammer; alternates, F. S. Dunning, J. W. Roberts.

The CHAIRMAN. Those favoring the adoption of the report will say "aye."

The report was adopted.

The Secretary announced the following additional report of the Committee on Credentials:

Alaska delegates—Thomas S, Nowell, E. F. Hatch.

The CHAIRMAN. Those favoring the adoption of the report will say "aye."

The report was adopted.

The following is the list of delegates and alternates, with their post office address, as contained in the majority report, corrected in accordance with the action of the Convention:

Delegates to the Republican National Convention held at Minneapolis, Minn., June 7th to 10th, 1892.

ALABAMA.

Delegates.   *Alternates.*

AT LARGE.

Stephen N. Noble..............Anniston	John V. McDuffie............Hayneville
Wm. H. Smith.. ....Birmingham	Ben De Lomos..... ....Hayneville
Cornelius N Dorsette. .... Montgomery	Jeremiah C. Blevins........... .....Selma
Anderson N. McEwen............Mobile	Peter J. McEntosh............Tuscaloosa

DISTRICTS.

1—Prelate D. Barker........ ...Mobile	John W. Taylor................Choctaw
William Mathews.............Dayton	Henry J. Europe.................Mobile
2—Charles O. Harris ......Montgomery	John G. Scott.................Brewton
James H. Perdue. ....Greenville	George H. Patrick.........Montgomery
3—Alfred H. Hendricks.........Opelika	Horace H Powell................Ozark
Ishmael N. Fitzpatrick.......Opelika	John C. Jemison.............Suspension
4—Harvey A. Wilson..........Lomax	Thomas W. Allen..............Talladega
Charles P. Bland.... ......Piedmont	Wiley A. Hudson.............Anniston
5—Julian H. Bingham...........Bingham	Charles M. Prescott... ....Roanoke
Benjamin W. Walker.........Cowles	Samuel Lee ....Burkeville
6—Daniel N Cooper........ Hamilton	Howell N. Goins.............Tuscaloosa
Ignatius Green...........Tuscaloosa	Leslie M. Crawford..... ... .Eutaw
7—Millard F. Parker............Cullman	Edward M. Dale........ ....Attalla
Owen T. Holmes,...... ...Albertville	Henry C Forbes.............Russellville
8—Richard W. Austin..........Decatur	Augustus W. McCullough...Huntsville
Frederick C. Ashford......Courtland	Charles D. Donegan.........Huntsville
9—Robert L. Houston......Birmingham	Albert T. Walker......... Birmingham
Alex. L. Mathews....Greensborough	Stephen Childs....................Marion

ARKANSAS.

AT LARGE.

Powell Clayton. ......Eureka Springs	Logan H. Roots..............Little Rock
Henry M. Cooper...........Little Rock	Jesse C. Duke....... ....Pine Bluff
Miffin W. Gibbs.............Little Rock	Lewis J. Best...................Bearden
Louis Altheimer.............Pine Bluff	Frank W. Tucker..........Clover Bend

DISTRICTS.

1—Harmon L. Remmel.........Newport	John S. Parker.............Paragould
Elias C. Morris ....Helena	Henry H Wilson...............Augusta
2—Ferd Havis ....Pine Bluff	Thomas H. Kersh............ . Varner
Thomas H Barnes........Fort Smith	Peter L. Youngue..... ......Monticello
3—Henry B. Holman........Washington	J. D. Walker.............Arkadelphia
Alfred A. Tufts.............Camden	A. C. Foster. ....Texarkana
4—Asberry S. Fowler.......Little Rock	William B. Haines.........Little Rock
John E. Bush... ....Little Rock	William La Porte...........Little Rock
5—Solomon F. Stahl.........Bentonville	W. B. Morton ....Harrison
Frank R. McKibben,..... Van Buren	Carlton C. Patton.........Fayetteville
6—Oscar M. Spellman....... Lake Farm	S. B. P. Weaver.................Brinkley
Harry H. Myers............Brinkley.	David D. Cole....................Beebe

CALIFORNIA.

Delegates. *Alternates.*

AT LARGE.

M. H. DeYoung............San Francisco	Isaac Trumbo.............San Francisco
Charles N. Felton...........Menlo Park	Philo J. Hersey.............Santa Clara
E. F. Spence.................Los Angeles	Harrison G. Otis ....Los Angeles
N. D. Rideout...............Marysville	J. R. Carrick ....San Francisco

DISTRICTS.

1—Daniel T. Cole.......Mountain House	S. J. Matthews.....................Ukiah
E V. Spencer.............Susanville	J. T. Matlock....................Red Bluff
2—John F. Kidder.........Grass Valley	N. Sposati.......................Stockton
A. J. Rhoades.............Sacramento	E. C Voorhies..............Cedar Creek
3—Eli S. Denison.............Oakland	R. F. Christ.....................Oakland
R. D. Robbins...........Suisin City	H A McCraney.............Lakeport
4—E. S. Pillsbury..........San Francisco	Reuben H. Lloyd........San Francisco
Joseph S. Spear, Jr....San Francisco.	D. S. Dorn.............San Francisco
5—O. A. Hale...................San Jose	Mitchell Phillips.................San Jose
George A. Knight......San Francisco	John T. Dare ....San Francisco
6—E. P. Johnson... ....Los Angeles	J Frankenfield...............Los Angeles
R. E. Jack........A....San Luis Obispo	John T. Porter......... .... Watsonville
7—P. Y. Baker...................Vesalia	W. H. Scribner.........Bakersfield
R. W. Button.................Colton	A. S. Emery.................Oakdale

COLORADO.

AT LARGE.

Henry M. Teller............Central City	Benjamin Guggenheim .... Pueblo
Edward O. Wolcott.......... ...Denver	Joseph Williams.................Denver
Hosea Townsend........... ... Silver Cliff	Charles M. Corlett..........Monte Vista
Jared L. Brush................. Greeley	Silas Hanchett............Idaho Springs

DISTRICTS.

1—J. F. Sanders...................Denver	Edward H. Hall.............Fort Collins
Francis M. Downer........Longmont	Philo B. Upson. .... Sedgwick
2—B. Clark Wheeler...............Aspen	William A. Smith............Canon City
Thomas C. Graden..........Durango	Dexter T. Sapp.................Gunnison

CONNECTICUT.

AT LARGE.

Morgan G. Bulkley.............Hartford	Linus B. Plimpton............ Hartford
James P. Platt........... .....Meriden	William C. Hough. ....Essex
Timothy E. Hopkins .....Danielsonville	Frederick C. Palmer......:New London
Lorrin A. Cooke.................Riverton	David Strong....................Winsted

DISTRICTS.

1—Thomas Duncan ....Poquonock	H. Lewis Peck............. .....Bristol
Thomas A. Lake ....Rockville	Ebenezer C. Dennis ..Stafford's Springs
2—Thomas Wallace..............Ansonia	John B. Doherty.............Waterbury
E. Irving Bell ....Portland	William I. Lewis..............Westbrook
3—Frank B. Brandegee.....New London	W. C. Mowrey..... ....Norwich
Edwin Milner............Moosup	John A. Porter.............Pomfret
4—Allan W. Paige.........Birmingham	John W. Strickland..............Bristol
Thomas D. Bradstreet....Thomaston	Granville M Breining......New Milford

DELAWARE.

AT LARGE.

Anthony Higgins............Wilmington	William M. Winston........Wilmington
James H. Wilson.............Wilmington	Hugh C. Browne ....Wilmington
George V. Massey........... ...Dover	J Colby Smith. ....Willow Grove
J. Francis Bacon............Georgetown	Daniel J. Layton...........Georgetown
George W. Marshall.............Milford	Paris T Carlisle, Jr... ..... Frederica
George F. Pierce.................Milford	Henry P. Cannon ....Bridgeville

FLORIDA.

Delegates.   *Alternates.*

AT LARGE.

Delegates	Alternates
Joseph E. Lee........ ....Jacksonville	John R. Scott................Jacksonville
John G. Long..............St. Augustine	Nelson C. Wamboldt........Jacksonville
James A Spann...............Pensacola	Morris M. Moore.................Orlando
Edward R. Gunby ....Tampa	Carl C. Crippen ....Eustis

DISTRICTS.

1—William R. Long...........Monticello	Wm. G. Stewart. Jr.........Tallahassee
John F. Horr.... ....Key West	Martin W. La Rue..... ....Bartow
2—Henry S. Chubb..........Winter Park	Charles B. Tompkins.... .. ..Jasper
S. H. Coleman..............Gainesville	Robert R. Robinson ....Ocala

GEORGIA.

AT LARGE.

Alfred E. Buck............ ......Atlanta	Lewis M. Pleasant.............Savannah
William A. Pledger..............Athens	Thomas J. Helm..(........ .... Rome
William W. Brown........... .....Macon	Noah Johnson...............Sandersville
Richard R. Wright... .. ..College	Frank J. Wimberly.........McDonough

DISTRICTS.

1—Michael J. Doyle..........Savannah	William H. Styles ....McIntosh
Samuel B. Morse ....Savannah	William E. Moore..............Gayton
2—Benjamin F. Brimberry .....Albany	Charles W. Arnold... ....Albany
Carey B. Barnes ... .Cuthbert	Julius Cæsar Few...........Thomasville
3—Charles E. Coleman...........Macon	Paul C. Coley............Hawkinsville
Edward S. Richardson..Marshalville	Robert W. Everett ....Hawkinsville
4—John T. Shepherd.........Columbus	John D. Lovejoy.............Greensville
Andrew J Laird ....La Grange	Richard I. O'Kelly............Grantville
5—Christopher C Wimbish.....Atlanta	Henry W. Walker...............Atlanta
Edgar A. Angler.............Atlanta	Jackson McHenry...............Atlanta
6—Richard D. Locke......... .....Macon	Robert M. Logan.......... . .....Macon
Frank Disroon....... ......Macon	Isaac W. Wood.................Forsythe
7—W. T. Blackford ....Graysville	James H. Rinard.............Tallapoosa
John Q. Gassett ....Cartersville	D. C. Warren................Acworth
8—Madison Davis ....Athens	George W. Gantt..............Eatonton
Joseph W. Jones.............Madison	Harrison Harris ....Madison
9—Sion A. Darnell..............Atlanta	Christopher C. Haley ....Jasper
Andrew J. Spence... ....Cornelia	M. C. Wilcox........ . ....Demorest
10—Judson W. Lyons.............Augusta	William Yancey ....Beasley
John M. Barnes............Thomson	Andrew M. Brown........Sandersville
11—John H. Deveaux........ ..Brunswick	Abraham L. Tucker..... ....Waycross
William H. Matthews....Brunswick	William Jones...................Valdosta

IDAHO.

AT LARGE.

Fred T. Dubois.... ....Blackfoot	James Gunn......................Hailey
Willis Sweet... ....Moscow	O. L. Heightman.... .....Rathdrum
James Shoup....................Challis	A. W. Hagar.............Mountain Home
W. B. Heyburn.................Wallace	I. C. Moore...............Pocatello
Montie B. Guinn................Caldwell	G. C. Patten...... ....Montpelier
D. C. Lockwood.......... ......Pocatello	J. M. Brunzell..........Reynolds Creek

ILLINOIS.

AT LARGE.

Shelby M. Cullom.............Springfield	Thomas Vennum................Watseka
Richard J. Oglesby......... ..Elkhart	Benjamin O. Jones...........Metropolis
Joseph G. Cannon.............Danville	Richard M. Skinner.........Princeton
Joseph Robbins..................Quincy	Frank S. Whitman. ....Belvidere
James H. Gilbert...............Chicago	William D. Preston.............Chicago
Miles Kehoe................... ....Chicago	William E. Kent.................Chicago
George B. Swift............. . Chicago	Niels Juul..........................Chicago
Samuel B. Raymond...........Chicago	Elwyn B. Gould.......... ....Chicago

ILLINOIS—Continued.

DISTRICTS.

Delegates.	Alternates.
1—W. R. Kerr..................Chicago	Edwin H. Morris..................Chicago
Herman H. Kohlsaat.......Chicago	David W. Wood................Chicago
2—Ernst J. Magerstadt........Chicago	Charles W. Woodman............Chicago
William Lorimer............Chicago	Michael T. Barrett.............Chicago
3—Robert L. Martin...........Chicago	Thomas W. Sennott.............Chicago
Frederick S. Baird...........Chicago	Meyer R. Mandelbaum..........Chicago.
4—Henry Wulff ....Chicago	John Worthy..................Chicago
Arthur W. Pulver............Chicago	John M. Roach...............Chicago
5 -Isaac L. Ellwood.............DeKalb	David D. Sabin ....Belvidere
James B. Lane.................Elgin	Flavel K. Granger.......West McHenry
6—Winfield S. Cowan.........Shannon	Edwin H. Keeler.................Rockford
Jeremiah N. Sharp........Stockton	George W. Perkins................Polo
7—Solomon H. Bethea............Dixon	W. S. Frost..................Lee Center
Alfred C. Stanley........Rock Falls	William H. Carson............Hennepin
8—M N. M. Stewart........Wilmington	James Stein......................Morris
W. N. Hanna.................Lisbon	Archibald Means................Peru
9—Edward A. Wilcox...........Minonk	C. F. H. Carrithers............Fairbury
William A. Rankin..........Onarga	James Wilson ....Watseka
10—Oscar F. Price............Galesburg	Newton J. Smith.............Toulon
John A. Gray...... ......Lewistown	E. E Harding................Peoria
11—Morris Rosenfeld............Moline	Harry F. McAllister..........Oquawka
William A. Lorimer...........Aledo	Reese H. Griffith..............Rushville
12—Edwin A. Crandall.... ....Barry	George B. Child................Hardin
Joseph F Durant.............Quincy	Charles A. Martin............Virginia
13—John W. Kitchell...............Pana	F. H. Blane..............Petersburg
Joseph P. Graff.............Pekin	Gilbert Drennan.............Pawnee
14—David S. Shellabarger.......Decatur	James E. Hill..................Lincoin
John Kirby...............Monticello	Charles M. Wing.............Bement
15—Patrick Richards............Urbana	Patrick Burke................Urbana
Horace Dollarhide............Paris	William Ellis.................Tuscola
16—Thomas J Golden........Marshall	James E. Wharf.................Olney
Philip W Barnes....Lawrenceville	F. M. Brock.................Fairfield
17—David H. Zepp............Nokomis	Charles M. Webster.........Shelbyville
James A. Gregory........Lovington	William P. Stewart...... Carlinville
18—James T. McCasland..East St. Louis	David R. Sparks.................Alton
Louis Krughoff...... ......Nashville	Hardy C. Voriss............ Waterloo
19—Thomas S. Ridgway..Shawneetown	Charles H. Sneed.................Benton
James M. Shoemaker..McLeansboro	Allen Bleakley................Carmi
20—Joseph P. Robarts.......Mound City	Thomas H. Sheridan..........Golconda
S. Lovejoy Taylor............Sparta	W. I. Smith...................Vienna

INDIANA.

AT LARGE.

Richard W. Thompson......Terre Haute	Calvin Cowgill.................Wabash
Stanton J. Peelle...... ....Indianapolis	George L. Knox............Indianapolis
Newland T. DePauw........New Albany	James H. McNeely...... ....Evansville
Charles F. Griffin............ Hammond	W. H. Elliott.:................New Castle

DISTRICTS.

1—George P. Heilman.......Evansville	James R. Adams. ....Petersburg
Frederick P. Leonard....Mt. Vernon	Clarence P. Laird.............Rockport
2—Edward F. Meredith....Washington	William R. McMahan ....Huntingburg
Howard R. Lowder......Bloomfield	Hillary Q. Houghton............Shoals
3—Jasper Packard........New Albany	John W. Martin............Scottsburg
James Graham............. Madison	Cadwallader Jones.........Charlestown
4—Claude Cambern....... Rushville	Erasmus S. Powell..........Shelbyville
George M. Roberts....Lawrenceville	William D Willson..............Osgood
5—Joseph B. Homan...........Danville	Silas A. Hays..........Greencastle
Nathaniel U. Hill......Bloomington	Henry S. Rominger...............Hope
6—Isaiah P. Watts........Winchester	Leander P. Mitchell........New Castle
Charles W. Stivers.........Liberty	Francis T. Roots..:........Connersville
7—Winfield T. Durbin...... Anderson	Thomas J. Cook............Indianapolis
Roger R. Shiel.........Indianapolis	W. R. King................Greenfield
8—William R. McKeen...Crawfordsville	William Leavitt..............Brazil
Lew Wallace.........Crawfordsville	Isaac H. Kalley..............Sullivan
9—James M. Reynolds........Lafayette	George E. Nolin.............Boswell
Americus C. Daily.........Lebanon	Dennis J. Mendenhall ......Westfield

—7

INDIANA—*Continued.*

Delegates.　　　　　　　　　　　*Alternates.*

DISTRICTS.

10—Alexander R. Shroyer...Logansport　　William Spangler.............Winamac
　　Mordecai F. Chilcote.....Rensselaer　　William C. Leatherman ....Valparaiso
11—Hiram Brownlee............Marion　　Hiram E Grove.................Bluffton
　　Silas A. Pulse.............. ...Warren　　Byron L. Myers ....Peru
12—William L. Penfield..........Auburn　　Augustus A. Chapin.......Fort Wayne
　　Robert P. Barr..........Kendallville　　Stephen A. Fuller..... ....Angola
13—Lemuel W. Royse...... .. ..Warsaw　　Harry B. Tuthill...........Michigan City
　　Charles W. Miller...... .....Goshen　　George A. Scott............. ....Knox

IOWA.

AT LARGE.

James S. Clarkson........... .....Des Moines　　Bruce C. Seaman.............Davenport
John H. Gear..... ....,..Burlington　　George E. Taylor. ....Oskaloosa
Edgar E. Mack..............Storm Lake　　Albert B. Cummins..........Des Moines
Daniel C. Chase............Webster City　　William Eaton....................Sidney

DISTRICTS.

1—Marcus Simpson........ Burlington　　Jackson Roberts.............Washington
　　W. S. Withrow........ ...Mt. Pleasant　　O. S Todd.........Columbus Junction
2—George M. Curtis.............Clinton　　John M. Buchanan.............Victor
　　John H. Munroe.. ....Muscatine　　J. C. Campbell...............Bellevue
3—Charles W. Mullan ....Waterloo　　J. A. Rogers.................Clarion
　　Charles H. Tidd.............,.Geneva　　Moulton Hartness.... ....Greene
4—Robert H. Fairbairn..New Hampton　　Andrew C. Walker...........Northwood
　　George E. Marsh...............Osage　　J. Cliff Crawford...............Waukon
5—James L. Carney..... Marshalltown　　Thomas E. Booth..............Anamosa
　　John T. Moffitt................Tipton　　B. Murphy...... ....Vinton
6—Francis W. Simmons.......Ottumwa　　John A. Riggen..............What Cheer
　　J. R. Gorrell..... ....Newton　　C. L. Robberts...................Grinnell
7—Homer C. Boardman........Nevada　　Robert A. Crawford............Altoona
　　W. H. Berry..............Indianola　　Isaac B. Hendershot..............Otley
8—N. P. Nelson.................Conway　　James C. Barrows...........Centerville
　　Eli Manning...............Charlton　　W. A. DeLashmutt..... ....Mt. Ayr
9—David L. Heinsheimer....Glenwood　　Mahlon J. Davis...................Lewis
　　Ernest E. Hart........Council Bluffs　　Charles P. Sheffer .... Red Oak
10—James P. Conner. .. ..Denison　　Torkild A. Rossing.................Bode
　　Eugene Secor. ....Forest City　　Robert Struthers.................Rolfe
11—James W. Reed........ .. Ida Grove　　William M. Smith... ....Sheldon
　　G. W. Pitts..............Orange City　　Alonzo C. Parker..... ....Spencer

KANSAS.

AT LARGE.

John J. Ingalls............ :....Atchison　　A. B. Keller...............Leavenworth
Calvin Hood............ .. ..Emporia　　Charles W. Hull ....c.Kerwin
A. H. Ellis .... Beloit　　George N. Mickel.............Stockton
C. C. James........ ....Lawrence　　Ira F. Collins ....Sabatha
L. A. Bigger.............. ..Hutchinson　　E. N. Emmons ....:..
E. C. Little....................Abilene　　H. F. Mason.............Garden City

DISTRICTS.

1—Cyrus Leland, Jr..................Troy　　L. F. Randolph..............Nortonville
　　S. H. Kelsay........ ....Atchison　　A. H. Knecht ....Louisville
2—O. G. Leonard.. .... .Lawrence　　E. C.Owens;.............. ....
　　Eugene Ward ....Fort Scott　　John McCasslin.................Kincaid
3—H. F. Hatch........ ..Arkansas City　　E. F. Adams. ....Sedan
　　A. D. Gibson.................:....Neosho　　A. C. Stich...............Independence
4—O. W. Little...... ....Alma　　W. E. Brown ....Augusta
　　I. N. Nye...............Eureka　　W. F. Waller..........Council Grove
5—John Davidson.........Junction City　　H. G. Higginbotham... .....Manhattan
　　Perry Hutchinson........Marysville　　A. Gilbert................Minneapolis
6—C. K. Curtis....... ....Topeka　　F. F. Burke ....Stockton
　　J. M. Miller............................　　M. K. Brown ....Goodland
7—Robert Page..... ....Ashland　　H. P. Myton...............Garden City
　　L. J. Hale.................LaCrosse　　W. C. Weeks....................Norwich

KENTUCKY.

Delegates.	*Alternates.*

AT LARGE.

William O. Bradley............Lancaster	John M. Logan.................Kilgore
George Denny................Lexington	W. H. Clark.........Middlesboro
Jordan Jackson.............Lexington	Thomas L. Walker...........Lexington
John Feland...... ....Owensboro	James M Beatty............Beattyville

DISTRICTS.

1—Alfred D. Crosby ....Mayfield	John F. Hall..................Paducah
O. Ross Baker. ....Princeton	Hugh F. McNary.............Princeton
2—A. H. Anderson... .....Hopkinsville	W. H. Hunter.....Owensboro
E. G. Sebill, Jr.............Henderson	Robert H C Mitchell.........Henderson
3—W. Godfrey Hunter.......Burksville	Thomas Sympson ....Franklin
William Turner......Bowling Green	William Lee Turner ....Russellville
4—Henry C. Martin.......Munfordville	William Forman.............Bardstown
W. H. Millby.............Greensburg	S. B. Smith...............Elizabethtown
5—Augustus E. Wilson.......Louisville	Julius A. Stege................Louisville
Horace Scott.............Louisville	Frank Kreiger................Louisville
6—T. B. Matthews.........Covington	Daniel C. Hemingway........Covington
M. Winstell.... ....Covington	John W. Smoot... .... .Covington
7—Llewellen P. Tarlton......Frankfort	Roger W. O'Conner. ... .Lexington
Leslie Combs.............Lexington	Richard P. Stoll.............Lexington
8—Curtis F. Burnam.... .....Richmond	Thomas Todd ....Shelbyville
Daniel R. Collier.........Louisville	Thomas M Cardwell......Harrodsburg
9—D. J. Burchett.............Louisa	Joseph A Sparks.............Vanceburg
W. H. Cox................Maysville	W. W Culverson................Ashland
10—Daniel Davis.............Paintsville	F. H. Hawkins..........Mount Sterling
J. B. Marcum................Jackson	George C. Perry ....Paintsville
11—Alfred R. Dyche... ...... .London	John M. Green.................Pineville
James Denton.............Somerset	William T. Dicken...............Albany

LOUISIANA.

AT LARGE.

William Pitt Kellogg......New Orleans	Alexander Boarman.........Shreveport
Robert F. Guichard......New Orleans	Henry O. Maher.........Donaldsonville
Andrew Hero, Jr ....New Orleans	Henry H. Blunt...........New Orleans
James Madison Vance ....New Orleans	John H. Lowery.............Plaquemine

DISTRICTS.

1—John W. Booth.....Pointe a la Hache	Joseph Fabacher, jr........New Orleans
James Lewis............New Orleans	W. J. Rodolph..............New Orleans
2—Andrew W. Smyth......New Orleans	Ernest Duconge...........New Orleans
Richard Simms...............Central	Monroe Williams. .,.......New Orleans
3—Thomas A. Cage............Houma	Victor Rochon..... .....St. Martinsville
Jason L. Jones...........Plaquemine	F. M. Tucker...............Morgan City
4—Albert H. Leonard.......Shreveport	A. J. Smith.................Bossier
William Harper... .....Shreveport	Moses Sterrett.. .. ..Shreveport
5—John B. Donnally...Lake Providence	Edward W. Wall ....Vidalia
David Young.................Vidalia	William W. Johnson.......... Tallulah
6—J. B. G. Donato..... .....Opelousas	Louis Creuzot ....Marksville
John E. Breaux.......Pointe Coupee	Alfred Washington.......Baton Rouge

MAINE.

AT LARGE.

Edmund B. Mallett, jr........Freeport	John F. Jamesen. ....Cornish
Charles E. Littlefield.........Rockland	Joseph C Holman...........Farmington
Edmund F. Webb...... .....Waterville	John A. Woodsum ....China
John L. Cutler.................Bangor	Wainright Cushing. ....Foxcroft

DISTRICTS.

1—Charles F. Libby............Portland	John E. Warren......Cumberland Mills
Charles M. Moses.........Biddeford	George Goodwin...........Wells Branch
2—Sidney M. Bird...... .....Rockland	Joel Wilbur.... ....Avon
Milton C. Wedgewood.......Lewiston	John M. Glidden. ....New Castle
3—Sylvester J. Walton.......Skowhegan	Edward F. Davies...............Castine
William M. Ayer... ....Oakland	David H. Smith..............Winterport
4—Charles A. McCullough ... ...Calais	Charles P. Allen.............Presque Isle
Thomas H. Pnair........Presque Isle	Nelson S. Allen ....Dennysville

MARYLAND.

Delegates.   *Alternates.*

AT LARGE.

James A. Gary ....Baltimore   James Wallace................Cambridge
Louis E. McComas...........Hagerstown   William E. Tilghman........Baltimore
Thomas S. Hodson............Baltimore   Joseph Parker.................Baltimore
Alexander Shaw.......... ....Baltimore   William H. Butler, jr........Annapolis

DISTRICTS.

1—Martin M. Higgins............Easton   Franklin H. Harper.. .. ....Still Pond
   Edward S. S. Turner......Nanticoke   B. Frank Lankford.......Princess Anne
2 -Samuel Roop... ....Westminster   Robert L. Christie........... ...Colora
   John T. Ensor...........Baltimore   Edmund M. Hoffman....... . Baltimore
3—Charles F. Riehl...........Baltimore   Jacob A. Seaton..............Baltimore
   Thorndike Chase.. ......Baltimore   Charles H. Ayers........Baltimore
4—J. Frank Supplee...........Baltimore   Frank G. Duhurst............Baltimore
   Harry S. Cummings ......Baltimore   Charles H. Gray........ ....Baltimore
5—Charles E. Coffin...........Muirkirk   Joseph F. Carter........... . Dorsey
   Richard Winter.............Chaptico   Franklin H. Covington.Broome's Island
6—A G. Sturgis......... ...Oakland   Robert R. Henderson .....Cumberland
   Allan Rutherford......Gaithersburg   John W. Cable...............Chewsville

MASSACHUSETTS.

AT LARGE.

William W. Crapo...... ...New Bedford   Michael J. Murray............Fitchburg
John Q. A. Brackett..........Arlington   Howes Norris. ....Cottage City
William Cogswell.............Salem   Butler R. Wilson.................Boston
W. Murray Crane................Dalton   Hiram T. Cady...........North Adams

DISTRICTS.

1—William B. Plunkett......... Adams   Charles S. Shattuck............Hatfield
   Robert B. Crane.........Westfield   Edwin Baker............Shelburne
2—Henry S. Dickinson.....Springfield   George W. Johnson..........Brookfield
   John L. Otis....................Leeds   Charles W. Hazelton.....Turners Falls
3—Samuel Winslow....... ...Worcester   Philip W. Moen............Worcester
   Charles N. Prouty......... ..Spencer   George L. Hyde....... ...West Boylston
4—George F. Fay...... ...... Fitchburg   Moses P. Palmer.................Groton
   Albert Clark..............Wellesley   Edward M. Rockwell........Leominster
5—Frederick Lawton...........Lowell   John Kilburn..... ......Lowell
   Francis H. Appleton.......Peabody   William N. Wood...............Andover
6—Elisha P. Dodge. .....Newburyport   Nathaniel C. Bartlett........ Haverhill
   William Reynolds......Marblehead   David I. Robinson...........Gloucester
7—Rufus S. Frost...............Chelsea   Frederic H. Odiorne.......... Malden
   Josiah C. Bennett............Lynn   Jeremiah J. McCarthy.....Charlestown
8—Charles Fairchild............Boston   Charles Franklin Sprague.......Boston
   Edward Glines ....Somerville   Samuel H. Pool.................Boston
9—Jesse M. Gove... ......East Boston   Everett Allen Davis ....Boston
   A. C. Ratshesky......... ....Boston   J. F. Malone..... ....Boston
10—Archibald T. Davidson.......Boston   John Shaw................Quincy
   Harrison H. Atwood. ....Dorchester   Benj. F. S. Bullard.............Boston
11—John W. Candler..........Brookline   Edward B. Wilson.....West Newton
   Edwin U. Curtis........ . Boston   Sidney Cushing.................Boston
12—George E. Freeman.......Brockton   Benjamin S. Lovell.......... ...Weymouth
   Willis K. Hodgman.........Taunton   Robert O. Harris.... East Bridgewater
13—Walter Clifford ....New Bedford   William A. Nye.... .....Bournedale
   John H. Abbott...........Fall River   Silas P. Richmond............Freetown

MICHIGAN.

AT LARGE.

Dexter M. Ferry................. Detroit   John J. Evans...............Battle Creek
Charles W. Wells................Saginaw   Fabian J. Trudell........Iron Mountain
Delos A. Blodgett.........Grand Rapids   Frank H. Ranney............Charlevoix
James M. Wilkinson..........Marquette   Rasmus Hanson.................Grayling

MICHIGAN—Continued.

| Delegates. | Alternates. |

DISTRICTS.

Delegates.	Alternates.
1—Henry M. Duffield............Detroit	T. H. Newberry..... ....Detroit
William H. Elliott.............Detroit	Joseph R. McLaughlin..........Detroit
2—William H. Withington......Jackson	Charles E. Hiscock...........Ann Arbor
William S. Wilcox.............Adrian	James T. Hurst...............Wyandotte
3—Charles Austin... ....Battle Creek	Corvis M. Barre...............Hillsdale
Charles L. Truesdell...... Quincy	Elbert S. Roos.............. Kalamazoo
4—Fred E. Lee ....Dowagiac	Frank B. Watkins......Hopkins Station
George W. Merriam.........Hartford	R. B. Messer. ....Hastings
5—James H. Kidd..... ....Ionia	John B. Perham.... ....Spring Lake
L. M. Sellers... ....Cedar Springs	Ernest B. Fisher...........Grand Rapids
6—Marshall E. Rumsey..........Leslie	Edward G. McPherson............Howell
Salmon S. Mathews..... ....Pontiac	James R. Hosie................Wayne
7—John W. Porter ....Port Huron	Silas B. Spier...............Mt. Clemens
George W. Jenks.........Sand Beach	Henry Howard. ....Port Huron
8—Aaron T. Bliss ... .Saginaw	James A. Trotter.. ....Vassar
William M. Kilpatrick ......Owosso	Otis Fuller.....................St. Johns
9—Charles M. Hackley.......Muskegon	J. R. Butler.... ....Frankfort
Fred A. Diggins......... .....Cadillac	Henry W. Newkirk... ....Luther
10—Selwyn Eddy...............Bay City	Theodore W. Crissey......... Midland
Robert J. Kelley.............Alpena	George E. Frost...... ....Cheboygan
11—George P. Stone.............Ithaca	Arthur A. Bleazby....... ......Calkaska
Thomas T. Bates .....Traverse City	Francis H. Dodds...... ....Mt. Pleasant
12—Orrin W. Robinson..........Chassell	John P. Christopher......... Bessemer
John Q. Adams............Negaunee	George Kemp........ ...Sault Ste Marie

MINNESOTA.

AT LARGE.

J. S. Pillsbury...............Minneapolis	Kee Wakefield....................Glencoe
F A. Day.......................Fairmont	J. N. Stacy.................Monticello
Stanford Newell.. ... .St. Paul	E. R. Cornwell..............Plainview
F. B. Daugherty....... ....Duluth	E. E. Corliss...............Fergus Falls

DISTRICTS.

1—W. H. Yale....... ....Winona	A. T. Stebbins ....Rochester
M. H. Dunnell..... ....Owatonna	J. P. Horland................Albert Lea
2—Daniel Shell............Worthington	D. C. Hopkins............... ..Madelia
A. F. Jacobson..........Lac qui Parle	D. A. McClarty............ Granite Falls
3—D. S. Hall....................Stewart	L. P. Dodge...... ....Farmington
F. C. Jackson.......... ....Northfield	E. C. Campbell.............. Henderson
4—George Thompson............St. Paul	H. F. Barker................Cambridge
Albert Berg............Centre City	T. C. Clark.................Stillwater
5—W. H. Eustis.............Minneapolis	C. A. Smith.................Minneapolis
S. P. Snider..............Minneapolis	S. E. Olson........ ....Minneapolis
6—R. C. Dunn................Princeton	J. M. Markham... .. ..Aitken
F. H. Hilliard ....Verndale	D. C. Dunham............. ......Anoka
7—S. G. Comstock.. ....Moorhead	J. W. Reynolds..............Elbow Lake
M. A. Wallan...............Glenwood	A. Greenlund.................. ....Warren

MISSISSIPPI.

AT LARGE.

John R Lynch ....:.............Natchez*	Henry Kernaghan...............Jackson
George M. Buchanan ....Holly Springs*	M. A. Montgomery................Oxford
George W. Gayles...........Gaylesville*	A. B. Poston............... Kosciusko
William H. Gibbs. ....Jackson*	David Knox.......... ......Greenville
James Hill ....Vicksburg*	....
A. T. Wimberley.......New Orleans, La*	....
W. E. Mollison.............Mayersville*	....
John McGill......................Jackson*	....

* ½ vote each.

MISSISSIPPI—Continued.

| Delegates. | Alternates. |

DISTRICTS.

Delegates.	Alternates.
1—H. C. Powers... ....Starkville	A. M. McMaster ....Burnsville
A. S. Shannon..............Shannon	J. H. Nichols..............Starkville
2—John S. Burton........Holly Springs	John A. Mahon............Holly Springs
Frank P. Hill...............Sardis	Austin Bell. ....Hernando
3—A. G. Pearce.. ....Greenville	J. E Ousley.... ....Rosedale
Wesley Crayton........... Vicksburg	G. W. Gilliam................ .....Lula
4—S. S. Matthews...... ......Winona	B. W. Foree........ ....West Point
W. D. Frazee...........Okolona	R. Collins.................Granada
5—J. I. Garrett.............Yazoo City	S. L. Jones.................Meridian
W. H. Mounger......... .....Paulding	A. Frazier ....Kosciusko
6—Fred W. Collins......... .. Summit	H. C. Griffin ....Natchez
George F. Bowles. ....Natchez	W. P. Locker ....Bay St. Louis
7—J. Meredith Matthews........Winona	A. C. Wanzer. ....Jackson
L. K. Atwood.................Bolton	F. B. Pratt........................Canton

MISSOURI.

AT LARGE.

William Warner ....Kansas City	Thomas B. Houghawout.. .... Carthage
Chauncey I. Filley.............St. Louis	Joseph H. Pelham.............Hannibal
Richard C. Kerens.............St. Louis	Leon H. Jordan........... ..Kansas City
A. C. Dawes ....St. Joseph	William A. Hobbs ....St. Louis

DISTRICTS.

1—James H. Kinnear. ....Kirksville	Alfred F. Poulton ....Canton
Ephraim Magoon...........Clarence	Evan Jones......................Hannibal
2—John B. Hale...........Carrollton	Louis Benecke ....: Brunswick
John F. Hawley .. ..Chillicothe	J. E. Swanger ....Milan
3—Joseph E. Black, Jr........Richmond	Elijah S. Gurney................Kidder
Henry C. Miller. ....Princeton	Charles W. Fry... . ...Grant City
4—Thomas J. Chew ....St. Joseph	Joseph Hansen............St. Joseph
William F. Rankin...........Tarkio	John Kennish............Mound City
5—William W. Morgan.....Kansas City	Joseph McCoy........ .....Independence
Erwin S. Jewett........Kansas City	John Wellborn...............Lexington
6—J. C. Lepscum ....Clinton	William H. H. Cundiff..... Pleasanthill
Oliver L. Houts........Warrensburg	B. L. Morrison.....................Jerico
7—Henry Lamm.................Sedalia	John R. Vance............. Marshall
George A. Ramsey.......Springfield	T. J. Aiken.................. Humansville
8—William P. Freeman.... Tuscumbia	Giles Bell ....Fulton
Charles C. Bell...........Booneville	Isaac Hoskinson........ ......Lebanon
9—J. C. Parish................Vandalia	George Kraettly.............Hermann
Thomas C. Wilson.......... ....Troy	Benjamin L. Emmons......St. Charles
10—Henry Beach...........St. Louis	Julius Wurtzberger............St. Louis
George Autenreith. ... ..Clayton	James W. Owens............Washington
11—Clark H. Sampson..... ..St. Louis	Julius Lehman.................St. Louis
Charles F. Wenneker..... St. Louis	William F. Schaeffer.............St. Louis
12—Frederick G. Niedringhaus.St.Louis	Michael Foerstel.. ....St. Louis
Nathan Cole................St. Louis	Charles Turner..............St. Louis
13—E. A. Rozier..........St. Genavieve	S. W. Crawford ....DeSoto
John H. Rainey......... ..Piedmont	Dr. Watts..................Marshfield
14—Madison B. Clark....... West Plains	Desevigne S. Crumb............Bloomfield
Wm. Regenhaudt...Cape Girardeau	Isaac M. Davidson ....Poplar Bluff
15—Franklin E. Williams..........Joplin	Joseph Thompson............Mt. Vernon
Joseph C. Seabourn..Southwest City	Washington A. Sanford...Minden Mines

MONTANA.

AT LARGE.

Thomas Couch............. ......Butte City	W. B. Hall....................Centreville
N. J. Biedenberg.......Deer Lodge City	Adolph Eliel..................... Dillon
A. J. Seligman.................Helena	George F. Cowan................ Boulder
A. B. Hammond................Missoula	A. J. Bennett.............Virginia City
Paul McCormick............ ... Billings	John R. King................Livingston
S. C. Hobson..................Lewiston	E. K. Abbott.....White Sulphur Springs

NEBRASKA.

AT LARGE.

John L. Webster. .... Omaha	Josiah L. Keck................Kearney
E. D. Webster............. .....Stratton	Whitfield H. Needham......Bloomfield
Lucius D. Richards............ Fremont	Matthew A. Dougherty........Ogalalla
Amasa Cobb ....Lincoln	Alonzo P. Tarbox............. ....Gandy

MONTANA—*Continued.*

Delegates.		Alternates.

DISTRICTS.

1—Charles H. Gere .... Lincoln
  George W. Holland......... Falls City
2—Cunningham R. Scott.......... Omaha
  J. C. Thompson........... ...... Omaha
3—Loren Clark............... ... Albion
  Atlee Hart...... ....Dakota City
4—Charles A McCloud........... ... York
  Lewis E Walker.............. Beatrice
5—Chas. P. R. Williams....Grand Island
  Walter E. Babcock...... Cambridge
6—Zachary T. Funk.......... Ainsworth
  Erwin B. Warner....... North Platte

Malcolm Stewart..................... Vesta
William H. Newell........ Plattsmouth
Millard F. Singleton............. Omaha
James Hassett....... ....Papillion
George W. Clark............. Humphrey
Herbert P. Shumway..........Wakefield
Edward E. Good.................. Wahoo
Henry C. Manary................Carlton
Charles W. Meeker............. Imperial
Albert W. Mock........... ......Nelson
E. S. Chadwick.... ....St. Paul
Asa B. Wood...................... Gering

NEVADA.

AT LARGE.

Duane L. Bliss .... Carson City
A. J. McDonnell.... .. ....Virginia City
Murray D. Foley............... ... Reno
A. C. Cleveland...............Cleveland
John A. Blossom,........Battle Mountain
W. T. Smith ... . Elko

William M. Stewart.........Carson City
John P. Jones.... ....Gold Hill
Horace F. Bartine...........Carson City
F. G. Newlands...................Reno
A. C. Hamilton ....Virginia City
David A. Bender ....Carson City

NEW HAMPSHIRE.

AT LARGE.

Frank C. Churchill. ....Lebanon
Benjamin A. Kimball. . .....Concord
Henry B. Quinby.... .. ..Lakeport
Charles T. Means............Manchester

Joseph Lewando................Wolfboro
Dexter Richards. ....Newport
Rosecrans W. Pillsbury ....Derry
George G. Davis...............Marlboro

DISTRICTS.

1—David R. Pierce..........Great Falls.
  Ira N. Blake..............Northwood
2—George F. Cruft........ .. Bethlehem
  Dana W. King........ ....Nashua

Charles Williams ....Manchester
Amos C. Chase...... ....Kingston
Thomas J. Walker.......... Plymouth
Charles A. Jones .Hillsborough Bridge

NEW JERSEY.

AT LARGE.

William J. Sewell.............. Camden
John I. Blair .... Blairstown
George A. Halsey.... ....Newark
Garret A. Hobart.............. Paterson

L. H. Kirkbride ....Mt. Holly
Elisha B. Gaddis................Newark
George T. Cranmer .... .Toms River
William Murrell ....Jersey City

DISTRICTS.

1—David Baird...... ....Camden
  Daniel Elmer ....Bridgeton
2—Washington A. Roebling.....Newton
  Henry Thorn ....Burlington
3—Benj. F. Howell .....New Brunswick
  William T. Hoffmann ....Freehold
4—Francis J. Swayze ....Newton
  George W. Jenkins........Morristown
5—John E. Miller.............Englewood
  William Barbour ....Paterson
6—Herman C. H. Herold ....Newark
  Frank M Parker........ ....Newark
7—Gilbert Collins ....Jersey City
  Thomas McEwan, Jr...Jersey City
8—Alexander Gilbert..........Plainfield
  Elias M. Condit..........West Orange

Charles W. Starr..............Woodbury
D. Harris Smith .... Salem
Albert M. Bradshaw.........Lakewood
Edward S. Lee............Atlantic City
A. B. Rohn, Jr..... . ...Raritan
George A. Hill...............Raritan
John H. Wilson.... ....,,Montclair
Allen Emory...................Frenchtown
Cornelius S. Bliss..............Paterson
Joseph H. Quackenbush.. ...Paterson
H. M. Baxter....................Newark
Peter Ulrich....................Newark
Zebina K. Pangborn.......Jersey City
John Reid ....Hoboken
Charles W. Fuller..............Bayonne
Foster M. Voorhees...........Elizabeth

NEW YORK.

Delegates.	Alternates.

AT LARGE.

Delegates.	Alternates.
Frank Hiscock..................Syracuse	Daniel H. McMillan............Buffalo
Thomas C. Platt................Oswego	George C. Buell ....Rochester
Chauncey M. Depew..........New York	John F. Parkhurst................Bath
Warner Miller.................Herkimer	William R. Weed...............Potsdam

DISTRICTS.

Delegates.	Alternates.
1—Carl S. Burr..............Commack	Frederick P. Morris...........Flushing
Benjamin H. Warford...Tottenville	William Richensteen..Long Island City
2—Robert A. Sharkey.........Brooklyn	Henry R. Williams......Gravesend. L. I
Charles A. Moore ....Brooklyn	Reuben Leland.......... ......Brooklyn
3—J. A. Fuller................Brooklyn	....
Wm. Wallace................Brooklyn	James M. Fuller ....Brooklyn
4—Theodore B. Willis.........Brooklyn	George B. Forrester...........Brooklyn
John J. Schlusser ....Brooklyn	R. Ross Appleton ....Brooklyn
5—Joseph Benjamin............Brooklyn	Samuel W. Murphy............Brooklyn
Charles T. Hepp ....Brooklyn	Benjamin Raphael ....Brooklyn
6—John E. Milholland ....New York	William H. Gedney........ ... New York
Herman O. Armour ......New York	John C. Dodd. ....New York
7—John D. Lawson..... ....New York	Denis Shea...............New York
Charles H. Murray.......New York	Patrick Elliff ....New York
8—Horace Porter.............New York	Gustav A. Schurmann........New York
Samuel Thomas ....New York	Patrick J. O'Brien ....New York
9—Jacob M. Patterson.......New York	Henry C. Botty ....New York
George Hilliard..... ....New York	John R. Nugent..............New York
10—S. Van Rensselaer Cruger, New York	Nathaniel A. Prentiss ......New York
William Henkel...........New York	Frank H. Daly...............New York
11—Frederick S. Gibbs........New York	Charles T. Pohlemus........New York
Sheridan Shook...........New York	Robert A. Greacen...........New York
12—William Brookfield ......New York	John Little..... . ...New York
Elliott F. Shepard ....New York	Michael Goode..... ....New York
13—David F. Porter............New York	David Freidsam...............New York
John Reisenweber... ...New York	Charles F. Bruder.... ....New York
14—William H. Robertson.....Katonah	Henry C. Henderson........Westchester
J. Thomas Stearns.................	C. Adelbert Becker. ....New York
15—Thomas W. Bradley........Walden	Joseph M. Dickey..............Newburgh
Clarence Lexow................Nyack	Louis F. Goodsell........Highland Falls
16—Louis F. Payn...... .....Chatham	Lewis H. Vail............. Poughkeepsie
Willard H. Mase.........Mattewan	Daniel Kent............... .....Patterson
17—George H. Sharp........Kingston	John E. Lasher........ ....Saugerties
J. Leroy Jacobs.............. Cairo	Alexander Cumming..........Coxsakie
18—John A. Quakenbush.....Stillwater	Zephania T. Magill..... ....Troy
Henry G. Burleigh........Whitehall	James H. Thompson........Greenwich
19—John A. Scheicher...........Albany	Henry A. Strong..............Cohoes
Thomas Austin..... .....Albany	John G. Ward......Coeymans Junction
20—John Sanford.. ....Amsterdam	James P. Argersinger...... Johnstown
Harvey J. Donaldson...Ballston Spa	Edward C. Whitmeyer.....Schenectady
21—Frank S. Witherbee....Port Henry	M Nelson Dickinson.....Warrensburgh
Edward C. O'Brien.....Plattsburgh	Isaiah Gibson..................Malone
22—Edmund S. Goodale......Watertown	Edward B. Bulkley. ....Antwerp
Carlton E. Sanford..........Potsdam	John A. Haig...............Madrid
23—James S. Sherman............Utica	Martin R. Lefevre ....Beaver Falls
V. Lansing Waters....... .Lowville	William E. Lewis..................Utica
24—Henry G. Munger..........Herkimer	Eugene A. Hinds......Richfield Springs
Hobart Krum.,.........Schoharie	Melvin W Harroway...Richmondsville.
25—William B. Cogswell.......Syracuse	Daniel Rosenbloom............Syracuse
Rufus T. Peck. .. ..Cortland	Charles A. Brooks..............Marathon
26—Edmund O'Connor.....Binghamton	James Forsyth................Oswego
Abram J. Decker...........Waverly	Clarence Carskadden........ Oneida
27—James W. Dunwell............Lyons	John T. Mott................Oswego
Gorton W. Allen. ....Auburn	Lamott M. Blakely...............Lyons
28—J Sloat Fassett............Elmira	Oliver P. Hurd................Watkins
John W. Dwight......... ...Dryden	William M. Sweet............Waterloo
29—Morris F. Sheppard.......Penn Yan	Charles S. Hoyt.................Dundee
Franklin D. Sherwood.Hornellsville	Benjamin F. Odell, jr............Phelps
30—Hulbert H. Warner.......Rochester	John A. Barhite.............Rochester
Frederick E. Gott......Spencerport	George A. Goss........ ..... Pittsford
31—William C. Watson..........Batavia	Frank H. Wyckoff...............Perry
Nathan S. Beardslee........Warsaw	Oscar Munn................Clarendon
32—John L. Williams.............Buffalo	Nicholas J. Mock. ....Buffalo
Philip Becker......... ......Buffalo	Daniel J. Kennedick.........Buffalo
33—Henry H. Persons......East Aurora	Christian Schwinger ....Tonawanda
Willis H. Howes.........Lockport	Charles B. Gaskill........Niagara Falls
34—Nicholas V. V. Franchot..... Olean	Hurlburt L. Phillips........Jamestown
John McEwen........ ....Wellsville	Watson W. Bush..............Rushford

NORTH CAROLINA.

Delegates.	Alternates.

AT LARGE.

Jeter C. Pritchard ....Marshall	John S. Fisher...... ....Tryon
Elihu A. White.................Raleigh	Edward S. Walton ....Morganton
Henry P. Cheatham.............Halifax	Harkless G. Gussom.............Edenton
John C. Dancy............. .Wilmington	Harrison B. Brown.............Asheville

DISTRICTS.

1—Claude M. Bernard........Greenville	J. P. Butler.. ....Williamston
Hugh Cale.............Elizabeth City	William L. Griffin.......... Edenton
2—John H. Hannon..... . ...Halifax	Daniel W. Patrick. ....Snow Hill
Charles A. Cook...... ......Warrenton	John W. Pope................ ..Raleigh
3—Abraham R. Middleton..Kenansville	James E. O'Hara...........Fayetteville
George C. Scurlock.......Fayetteville	Duncan J. McRae...............Carthage
4—John Nichols ....Raleigh	James H. McCain.................Raleigh
Edward A. Johnson..........Raleigh	William S. Mitchell.... ....Raleigh
5—Thomas B. Keogh.........Greensboro	Edward F. Parham ....Wentworth
James A. Cheek..........Hillsboro	William H. Crews, Jr............Oxford
6—Archibald Brady..........Charlotte	John L. Matheson.............Lilesville
James H, Young.. .....Wilmington	John S. Lewis ....Lumberton
7—Zebulon V. Walser......Lexington ⅔	Andrew C. Cowles...........Statesville
William A. Bailey.........Advance ⅔	William E. Henderson ....Concord
Dr. J. J. Mott..................... ⅔	....
8—Joseph O. Wilcox...........Dresden	A. L. Hendrix........... .....Ronda
Laban L. Jenkins............Gastonia	William S. Linville ....Winston
9—Charles J. Harris...........Dillsboro	William W. Rollins............Asheville
R. W. Logan.......... ..Rutherfordton	Henry C. Hunt.................Asheville

NORTH DAKOTA.

AT LARGE.

Thomas F. McHugh..............Grafton	Amun M. Tofthagen.. ....Lakota
John A. Percival...........Devil's Lake	Abner L. Hanscomb .. ..Towner
William H. Robinson ....Mayville	Oscar Barrett....................Steele
Gerald Pierce.................Bismarck	R. G. Mitchell........ ....Sheldon
Thomas Marshall............ Oakes	Olney G. Meacham. ... .Carrington
Edgar J. Gleason............Spiritwood	George H. Bingenheimer........Mandan

OHIO.

AT LARGE.

*William McKinley, jr...... .....Canton	*Melvin M. Boothman ....Bryan
*Joseph B. Foraker..........Cincinnati	*Robert M. Nevin................Dayton
*Asa S. Bushnell..............Springfield	*Ebenezer W. Poe................Columbus
*William M. Hahn... . ...Mansfield	*John S. Atwood...................Ripley

* NOTE.—A claim having been made that the official roll of the Convention as submitted by the National Committee, and the Committee on Credentials, and agreed to by the Convention, was incorrect respecting the alternate of Hon. Wm. McKinley, the following correspondence is submitted:

CHAS. W. JOHNSON, Secretary.

DAYTON, OHIO, June 22d, 1892.

DEAR SIR.—I was first alternate at large from Ohio, and as such, took Gov. McKinley's place in the delegation when he was chosen Permanent Chairman. It was I who called attention to the fact that at his request I had cast one of the original two votes, in the Ohio delegation, for Harrison for President. The stenographer has credited it to "Mr. Boothman." The Convention list of delegates and alternates and proceedings will show the accuracy of all above statements Please have correction made in published reports and oblige.

Yours Truly,

R. .M. NEVIN.

C. W. JOHNSON, Permanent Sec'y, etc., Minneapolis, Minn.

WASHINGTON, July 9, 1892.

MY DEAR SIR.—Your esteemed favor of the 22d of June was duly received. but I could not then reply to it, as I had not received the official report of the stenographer of the convention, and I had sent him my own official papers to be embodied in the official report, and could not refer to them. The stenographer has

OHIO—Continued.

Delegates.	Alternates.

DISTRICTS.

Delegates.	Alternates.
1 George B. Cox.............Cincinnati	Louis Kruckemeyer.........Cincinnati
Charles Fleischmann.....Cincinnati	Henry B. Morehead.........Cincinnati
2—Norman G. Kenan........Cincinnati	George H. Jackson.. ....Cincinnati
George B. Fox............Lockland	August H. Bode...............Cincinnati
3—W. E. Crume..... .... Dayton	Charles E. Pease......... ....Dayton
R C. McKinney... ....Hamilton	P. S. Elkenberry...............Eaton
4—Levi S. Jamison............ ..Celina	Benjamin M. Moulton.............Lima
James I. Allread.........Greenville	W. D. Davies.....................Sidney
5—Guilford L. Marble.........Van Wert	William H. Begg ......Columbus Grove
Oscar Eaton..................Bryan	Kidder V.Haymaker..... .. ....Defiance
6—Erskine Carson............Hillsboro	John Little .... Xenia
George W. Stanley...... Lebanon	Simeon G. Smith... ....Wilmington
7—Oliver S. Kelly........ Springfield	Morris H. Messe............Circleville
D. I. Worthington.Washington, C.H	Sherman Leach .. ..London
8 –C. C. Harris............. ....Findlay	R. G. Leibrand................Delaware
Isaac N. Zearing......Bellefontaine	H. H. Williams. ....Urbana
9—William H. Tucker...........Toledo	George B. Spencer..............Weston
John B. Wilson......Bowling Green	Alfred L. Sargent.............. ....Delta
10—Lucien J. Fenton........Winchester	Luther M. Beman............. Thurman
Samuel Llewellyn......... Coalton	Forrest E. Dougherty...... ...Waverly
11—John C. Entriken........Chillicothe	David L. Sleeper................. Athens
Charles E. Spencer...New Lexington	Robert S. Wilcox.....Hamden Junction
12—George K. Nash............Columbus	John B. McNeill...............Lancaster
Cyrus Huling..... ......Columbus	Daniel Crumley..... ....Lancaster
13—George C. Gormley.........Bucyrus	John C. Johnson...............Fremont
Wilbur C. Brown...........Fostoria	Samuel H. Hunt.......Upper Sandusky
14—W. C. Cooper... ....Mt Vernon	James R. Alsdorf............Mt. Vernon
Harry Griffith.... ....Mt. Gilead	D. C. Crockley..... ....Mansfield
15—John H. Riley............. Marietta	H. J. Cleveland..............Caldwell
Wm, A. Johnson,..........Zanesville	Cyril Hawkins.....McConnellsville
16—Isaac H. Taylor...........Carrollton	R. A. McDonald......... .... Carrollton
G. A. Keepers............Bealsville	A. C. Armstrong.............Woodsfield
17—M. Luther Smyser........... Wooster	A. R. Miller............ .. ....Newark
William C. Lyon...........'..Newark	W. A. Himebaugh............Coshocton
18—Jacob A. Ambler............Salem	John N. Taylor........East Liverpool
George E. Baldwin ....Canton	John A. Logan, jr........ Youngstown
19—Charles W. F. Dick............Akron	Sagito J. Smith... ....Conneaut
William Ritezel........ .....Warren	John Mehara.............. ....Ravenna
20—Isaac P. Lamson.........Cleveland	William M. Bayne............Cleveland
James A. Allen...........Painesville	Evelyn S. Pardee............Wadsworth
21 –Louis Black...............Cleveland	George A. Meyer......... ......Cleveland
Amos Denison ....Cleveland	Harry M. Fowler....... .....Cleveland

now sent me his report together with my official papers, and I am now able to answer you definitely. As a matter of fact, and of record (by the official roll of the convention furnished to me by the National Committee, and subsequently by the report of the Committee on Credentials), you were not the first alternate, and you were not Gov. McKinley's alternate. You were the alternate for Gov. Foraker. Gov. McKinley's alternate was Mr. Boothman.

What the Ohio delegation may have done towards placing men in different positions from that reported to me, I have no means of knowing.

The official report of the stenographer does not show who voted in Gov McKinley's place for Harrison. You may have done so on the first ballot taken. But when Gov. McKinley demanded that the delegation be polled, he voted in his own name, as you are doubtless aware. I am anxious to make any corrections of errors in the record, but in this matter I am sure the record is right.

Very Truly Yours,

CHAS. W. JOHNSON, Sec'y, etc.

HON. R. M. NEVIN, Dayton, Ohio.

DAYTON, OHIO, July 11th, 1892.

MY DEAR SIR.—I don't know who furnished you the list of delegates and alternates at large from Ohio, but whoever did was wrong. I was at our State Convention and know. Gov. McKinley was chairman of our State Convention. I enclose you my credentials, which please return. I *was* the first alternate, and Gov. McKinley's alternate, and on all questions until he challenged the vote of Ohio and voted himself for Harrison, I voted in his stead, not by action of the Ohio Delegation, but by action of the *State Convention* that elected me. E. W. Poe was Gov. Foraker's alternate, and Mr. Boothman was third on the list and alternate of Wm. M. Hahn. All I wanted corrected was that when I stated in open convention that I was one of the two who originally voted for President Harrison as Gov. McKin-

OREGON.

Delegates.		Alternates.	
AT LARGE.			
C. W. Fulton	Astoria	I N. Sanders	Union
Charles M. Donaldson	Baker City	Ezra L .Smith.	Hood River
C. E. Wolverton	Albany	McKinley Mitchell.	Gervais
Robert R. Hays.	Portland	Harrison R. Kincaid.	Eugene
DISTRICTS.			
1—Thomas Tongue	Hillsboro	Lewis C. Garrigus	Marshfield
Oliver C. Applegate	Olene	J. S. Cooper	Independence
2—Joseph Simon	Portland	Samuel Elmore	Astoria
Jonathan Bourne, Jr	Portland	J. M. Long	Portland

ley's alternate, that it should be credited to me and not to Mr. Boothman. If there is any doubt as to this, Gov. McKinley can easily settle it. Please advise me.

Truly Yours,

R. M. NEVIN.

C. W. JOHNSON, Sec'y, etc.

ENCLOSURE.

To the Committee on Credentials of the National Republican Convention:

GENTLEMEN:—Pursuant to call of the National Republican Committee, issued November 24, 1891, the Republicans of Ohio in State Convention assembled at the city of Cleveland, April 27 and 28, 1892, did by a unanimous vote, select to represent them at the National Convention to be held at Minneapolis, Minn . June 7, 1892, for the purpose of nominating candidates for President and Vice-President of the United States, to be voted for at the National election of 1892, and the transaction of such other business as may be brought before it, the following delegates at large:

WILLIAM McKINLEY, JR.
JOSEPH B. FORAKER.
WILLIAM M. HAHN.
ASA S. BUSHNELL.

At the same time and place four alternate delegates, to act in the absence of any or all of the above named delegates, were chosen as follows:

ROBERT M. NEVIN.
EBENEZER W. POE.
M. M. BOOTHMAN.
JOHN S. ATWOOD.

These are the credentials of the aforesaid delegates and alternates, severally and collectively.

In witness whereof, we have hereunto subscribed our names this fourth day of May, 1892.

WM. McKINLEY, JR.,

JOHN R. MALLOY, Secretary. Chairman of Convention.

WASHINGTON, July 14th, 1892.

MY DEAR SIR:—I received your esteemed favor of the 11th on yesterday, and should have replied at once but for the press of matters connected with my duties here.

From the papers sent by you I am fully satisfied that you are right respecting your claim to be Gov. McKinley's alternate, but I am powerless to change the roll or the report of the Committee on Credentials.

I have decided, however, so that your situation may be fully stated, to print in the official proceedings as a foot-note the correspondence we have had, together with your credentials. This involves the whole case.

I have not been able to find in the report of the stenographer any mention whatever of your explanation to the convention of your vote, nor is Boothman's name mentioned in that connection. I have a recollection, however, of some one rising in the Ohio delegation making such an explanation as you refer to, and this is also borne out by that of several newspaper correspondents now here, who were at the convention. I trust this may prove entirely satisfactory to you, as my desire is that you shall be fully set right.

Very truly your obedient servant,

CHAS. W. JOHNSON.

Secretary.

PENNSYLVANIA.

Delegates.   *Alternates.*

AT LARGE.

Hamilton Disston..........Philadelphia	William B. Ahern..........Philadelphia
William ᴊ. Elkins..........Philadelphia	Samuel L. Clements.......Philadelphia
William Flinn ....Pittsburg	James A. Dale................York
Henry W. Oliver..............Pittsburg	John W. Young.... ......Tunkhannock
Frank Reeder ....Easton	Joseph Bosler....................Ogontz
Samuel A. Davenport.... ... .Erie	Adam C. Hawkins.............Bradford
Henry C. McCormick.....Williamsport	Morgan B. Williams........Wilkesbarre
Lyman D. Gilbert.. ....Harrisburg	Lemuel Googins............ ..Pittsburg

DISTRICTS.

1—Henry H. Bingham.....Philadelphia	Amos M. Slack. ....Philadelphia
Oliver Wilson...........Philadelphia	Andrew F. Stevens........Philadelphia
2—David H. Lane.........Philadelphia	Courtland K. Bolles.......Philadelphia
Jacob Wildemore.......Philadelphia	Henry I. McIntyre..........Philadelphia
3—Theodore B. Stulb.... .Philadelphia	Joseph H. Clemmer.........Philadelphia
James B. Anderson.....Philadelphia	Harry Hunter ....Philadelphia
4—George S Graham.....Philadelphia	Robert Osborne.............Philadelphia
A. S. L. Shields.........Philadelphia	George J. Elliott............Philadelphia
5—David Martin...........Philadelphia	Robert B. Burns............Philadelphia
John S. McKinlay.....Philadelphia	Wilbur F. Short............Philadelphia
6—Enos Verlenden, Jr...........Darby	John A. Watts..............Thurlow
Thomas S. Butler.....West Chester	Merit M. Missimer.. ....Warwick
7—Jacob A Strassburger ...Norristown	Daniel A Shiffert............Pottstown
E. Wesley Keeler.... ...Doylestown	T Howard Atkinson.......Buckingham
8—Maurice C Lukenbach....Bethlehem	Thomas C. Walton.........Stroudsburg
William H. Stroh .....Mauch Chunk	James S. Drake ....Milford
9—Augustus M. High.........Reading	Webster B. Kupp ....Gibraltar
James Thomas............Catasauqua	Franklin H. Hersh............Allentown
10—Dr. John P. Miller..........Oak Hill	J. Harold Wickersham........Lancaster
George R Sensenig........Lancaster	Henry B. Keller ....Ephrata
11—Edward N. Willard.........Scranton	Conrad Schroeder..... .... Scranton
Benjamin Hughes..........Scranton	Edward Miles...............Dalton
12—Alex Farnham ....Wilkesbarre	Isaac P. Hand............Wilkesbarre
William J. Scott............Belbend	William F. Adams.............Hazelton
13—Alexander Scott...........Frackville	John I. Mathias...........Mahony City
Christian Lenker..Schuylkill Haven	John F. Gressang............Pottsville
14—John E. Fox..............Harrisburg	John Wister.................Duncannon
Jacob H. Grove............Lebanon	Eli Wallace.... ......Newmanstown
15—Galusha A. Grow.........Glenwood	Martin B. Allen..............Honesdale
Fred I. Wheelock.............Eaton	J. W. Hurst ....
16—Albert M. Bennett.......Covington	Elias Deemer..... ....Williamsport
William I. Lewis.......Coudersport	Samuel McClintock..............Salona
17—William C. McConnell.....Shamokin	Christian E. Geyer...........Catawissa
William L. Gouger........Danville	William C. Farnsworth.......Sunbury
18—Carl F. Espenschade....Mifflintown	Thomas B. Reed...........Lewistown
Jerry J. Cromer ......Fort Littleton	Benjamin F. Wagenseller...Selinsgrove
19—Charles H. Mullin..Mt. Holly Springs	Winfield S. Schroder.........Gettysburg
John C. Lower...........Gettysburg	George S. Krug................Hanover
20—Henry W. Storey.........Johnstown	John R. Scott... ....Somerset
John H. Jordan. ... .Bedford	Jasper Augustine...............Somerset
21—J. Owen Edelblute.......Brookville	William J. Mitchell...... ......Indiana
Norman K. Coller.........Leechburg	Hugh B. McIntire.......... ......Kent
22—Joseph O. Brown ....Pittsburg	John Gripp...............Pittsburg
Christopher L. Magee.....Pittsburg	Henry P. Ford................. Pittsburg
23—William Witherow.........Allegheny	Frank J. Torrence.......... .Allegheny
Josiah N. Davidson.......Allegheny	John C. Hetzel...............Allegheny
24—Frank M. Fuller..........Uniontown	Robert J. Black.............McKeesport
George M. VonBonnhorst..Pittsburg	James M Reed ....Connellsville
25—Matthew S. Quay.............Beaver	James J. Davidson...............Beaver
David W. Pearson....New Castle	Edward E. Abrams... ....Butler
26—Charles M. Reed. ....Erie	C. George Olmstead...............Corry
John J. Carter.....Titusville	Joshua Douglass...............Meadville
27—William W. Brown........Bradford	John C. Russell........North Clarendon
Thomas B. Simpson.....Oil City	John S. Wiley. ....Emporium
28—Daniel C. Oyster..... ......Ridgway	Frank L. Shallenberger.....Callensburg
A. Wayne Cook............Tionesta	James A. Fieder..... ....Bellefonte

RHODE ISLAND.

Delegates.   Alternates.

AT LARGE.

William G. Roelker......... Providence.
Samuel P. Colt.............. Providence
Willam Gregory............. Wickford
Frank G. Harris............. Newport

James F. McCusker............ Pontiac
Charles H. Handy .. .. Warren
George B. Carpenter.......... Hopkinton
John R. Hicks............. .... Tiverton

DISTRICTS.

1—Charles Fletcher .. .. Providence
  Isaac L. Goff............. Providence
2—Henry A. Stearnes........ Pawtucket
  Edward Thayer........... Pawtucket

Frank F. Olney............... Providence
Frank F. Carpenter.. .... Providence
Frank W. Tillinghast......... Johnston
James Linton......... ...... Pawtucket

SOUTH CAROLINA.

AT LARGE.

Eugene A. Webster.......... Orangeburg
William I. Crum.......... ...Darlington
Edmund H. Deas............ Darlington
Ellery M. Brayton............ Columbia

Robert Smalls.................. Beaufort
Thomas B. Johnston............ Sumter
Edward J. Dickerson............ Aiken
J. R. Tolbert................... Abbeville

DISTRICTS.

1—George I. Cunningham... Charleston
  John H. Fordham...... . Orangeburg
2—Seymour E. Smith...... .....Aiken
  Paris Simkins............... Edgefield
3—John R. Cochran............ Walhalla
  Abner S. Jamison.......... Columbia
4—John P. Scruggs............ Greenville
  Irvin J. Miller.............. Columbia
5—E. Brooks Sligh.............. Chester
  William E. Boykin........... Camden
6—Joshua E. Wilson........... Florence
  Thomas B. Johnston......... Sumter
7—John H. Ostendorff......... Berkeley
  R. H. Richardson......... Wedgefield

Robert C. Browne............ Charleston
Adam W. Johnson............ Lexington
Wesley S. Dixson........ Barnwell. C. H
Philip Riley...................... Almeda
L. C. Waller.................. Greenwood
Robert R. Talbot, jr..... ....Greenwood
Berry F Means........... ...Greenville
Pratt S. Suber. ....Laurens, C. H
Joshua F. Ensor.. .... Spartanburg
William T. Andrews............. Sumter
Edward J. Sawyer....... Bennettsville
Sylvester W. Williams......... Florence
Jonathan A. Baxter......... Georgetown
J. B. Brown................. Walterboro

SOUTH DAKOTA.

AT LARGE.

Edward C. Ericson.. ....Elk Point
Clark B. Alford................... Huron
Mahlon T. Lightner............. Roscoe
James Halley................. Fall River

Joshua Watson................ Canastota
George A. Johnston............ Mitchell
Robert E. Grimshaw .... Deadwood
Albert Sutherland.......... Mound City

DISTRICTS.

1—Joseph M. Greene ..... Chamberlain
  Nyrum E. Phillips........ Sioux Falls
2—Alexander C. Johnson.... Watertown
  Gideon C. Moody.... ... ..Deadwood

John L. Turner............. Springfield
D. William Diggs.............. Milbank
Henry C. Sessions.,............ Aberdeen
S. N. Fitch................... Custer City

TENNESSEE.

AT LARGE.

David A. Nunn................. Nashville
John C. Houk.................. Knoxville
James C. Napier.............. Nashville
H. Clay Evans............. Chattanooga

Samuel H. Haynes............. Memphis
Hugh B. Lindsay .... Knoxville
Asa H. Faulkner........... McMinnville
T. Thomas Turner............ Memphis

TENNESSEE—*Continued*.

Delegates.   *Alternates.*

DISTRICTS.

Delegates	Alternates
1—Newton Hacker .... Jonesboro	W. E. F. Milburn........ ....Greenville
H. Clay Jarvis.. ....Rogersville	George McHenderson..........Rutledge
2—J. F. Tarwater.............Rockwood	Will D. Wright ....Marlburgh
John W. Connors..........Knoxville	Samuel M. Leath...... ....Clinton
3—Thomas L. Cates.... ......Cleveland	B. W. Padgett ....Ooltewah
Edgar F. Hoyt... ......Chattanooga	Hilliard N. Willis..... ....Chattanooga
4—S. C. Brown................Lafayette	J. S. Smith.....................Lebanon
Clarence W. Garrett......Carthage	Matt Marchbanks ....Carthage
5—Sydney Houston...........Wartrace	Harlan P. Dewey............Tullahoma
John W. Overall.............Liberty	William D. Greer.........Murfreesboro
6—H. A. Hasslock.....,.....Nashville	Robert F. Boyd...............Nashville
General Quarles Boyd.....Clarsville	H. L. W. Cheatham.........Springfield
7—Archelaus M. Hughes. jr..Columbia	J. M. Puckett................Centreville
John Schade, jr. ... Lawrenceburg	Christopher C. Stribling......... Clifton
8—Samuel W. Hawkins....Huntingdon	S. Newton Williams........Huntingdon
James W. Dougherty...Decaturville	Albert Hurt.... ....Jackson
9—E. E. Bell...... ....Dresden	Robert H. McNeely.............Kenton
William F. Poston............Alamo	H. C. Rowland...........Union City
10—William J. Smith..........Memphis	Moses Stricklin.................Memphis
Josiah T. Settle.............Memphis	Granville G. Marcus.. ....Memphis

TEXAS.

AT LARGE.

N. Wright Cuney.......... ....Galveston	J. W. Burke ....Austin
John B. Rector..................Austin	Robert A. Kerr....................Bastrop
Wilbur F. Crawford... ....Cameron	D. Abner, jr.....................Seguin
Alexander Asbury ....Calvert	A. W. McKinney..............Sherman
A. J. Rosenthal................ LaGrange	R. M. Moore............. . San Antonio
Lock McDaniel...................Anderson	D. Taylor....................Navasota
Frederick C. Chase.......... ......Dallas	T. W. Troupe..................Paris
C. M. Ferguson ....Paris	George F. Wattson........Wichita Falls

DISTRICTS.

1—Waller T. Burnes...........Houston	E. J. Starks.................. Hempstead
Alexander White............Anderson	C. T. Lawson...... ....Montgomery
2—George W. Burkitt.........Palestine	....
J. N. Gillet.....................Herne	....
3—Webster Flanagan ....El Paso	J. M. Moore.. ....
J. W. Butler....................Tyler	R. A. Caldwell.................Leesburg
4—J. J. Dickerson ....Paris	W M. Johnson.................Sherman
I. J. Powell ....Sulphur Springs	E. T. Pillman ....
5—J. W. Hearne.................Dallas	S. D. Russell ....Dennison
W. H. Love. ... .McKinney	B. M. Strafford...................
6—J. M. McCormick... ....Dallas	S. W. J. Lowry..................Dallas
W. E. Davis..............Ft. Worth	S. R. Johnson ....
7—R. B. Hawley.. ....Galveston	W. H. Sinclair.............Galveston
Spencer Graves...........Richmond	H. W. Hexter..................Victoria
8—A. J. Johnson.... ......Galveston	Jesse Perrine...............Bellville
M. M. Rogers.. ....La Grange	Tom Kennedy........ ....Giddings
9—H. M. Tarver.................Gay Hill	John C. Cain................Brenham
T. A. Pope..................Cameron	E. L. Campbell......... ....Cameron
10—Harry Terrell.. ....San Antonio	C. G. Newning....... ....Austin.
J. C. DeGress,................Austin	Dave Williams ... .San Antonio
11—A. G. Malloy.................El Paso	G. B. Jackson....................San Angelo
C. W. Johnson...............Graham	M. C. Kimpson. . ...

VERMONT.

AT LARGE.

H. H. Powers................Morrisville	Albert A. Fletcher..........Middlebury
L. Downer Hazen.........St. Johnsbury	Nathan Hobson ....Island Pond
George T. Childs ....St. Albans	J. Rollin Judson ....East Arlington
Fred E. Smith................Montpelier	Osman B. Boyce..............,.......Barre

DISTRICTS.

1—William R. Page.............Rutland	Smith Wright.................Williston
Nelson W. Fiske....... Isle La Motte	Edson P. Gilson... .... Rutland
2—Adna Brown...............Springfield	Robert J. Kimball.......West Randolph
Edmund P. George......West Fairlee	Alexis B. Hewitt.................Putney

VIRGINIA.

Delegates.   *Alternates.*

AT LARGE.

Delegates	Alternates
William Mahone.............Petersburg	James S. Browning.........Pocahontas
A. W. Harris................Petersburg	Matthew C. Cardoza...Lunenburg C. H
Henry Bowen.............Tazewell C. H	Robert A. Paul...............Richmond
S. Brown Allen................Staunton	John W. Simmons....... ....Floyd C. H

DISTRICTS

1—Robert M. Mayo...............Hogue	William Voorhees...Spottsylvania C. H
Thomas C. Walker..Gloucester C. H	Josephus Trader....Matthews C. H
2—V. Despauex Groner.........Norfolk	John J. Deyer.................Handsoms
John C. Asbury...............Norfolk	Phillip C. Corrigan. ....Norfolk
3—Edmund Waddill.........Richmond	John Mitchell, jr.... ....Richmond
Edgar Allen................Richmond	C. W Harris..................Manchester
4—Benjamin S. Hooper.......Farmville	William M. Flanagan.........Powhatan
John M. Langston....... Petersburg	Andrew J. Smith............. Petersburg
5—S. J. Griggs..............Martinsville	William B. Brown........ Rocky Mount
John M. Parsons. .....Independence	Alexander Weddle.......... .....Topeco
6—Patrick H. McCaull......Lynchburg	J. C. Hanes...............Christiansburg
John H. Davis............:. Roanoke	H. Clay Harris ... .South Boston
7—Carter M. Louthan...Madison C. H.	Jacob H. Jones...............Mt. Jackson
H. M. Roundabush......Pearisburg	Charles L Pritchard. .....Front Royal
8—Minor F. Chamblin.........West End	Edward Howe..............Bristersburg
James L. Davis....Raccoon Ford	W. J. Thompson........Louisa C. H
9—Henry C. Wood...........Estellville	Henry E. McCoy..................Bristol
Philip W. Strother...... Pearisburg	William A. Hilton.........Pocahontas
10—Wm. H. Goodwin.........Afton	William Lancaster...Cumberland C. H.
E. M. Nettleton......... ..Covington	Henry W. Williams.............Staunton

WASHINGTON.

AT LARGE.

Nelson Bennett.................Tacoma	T. M. May.......................Dayton
John H. McGraw...............Seattle	Frank M. Wynship.............Sprague
Anthony M. Cannon......Spokane Falls	Henry M. Montgomery.......Cathlamet
James M. Perkins................Colfax	John T. Redman... ....Tacoma

DISTRICTS.

1—John Cleman...........North Yakima	William R. Forrest............. .Seattle
Edward Eldridge.... ....Whatcom	J. E. Gandy......... .. ..Spokane
2—William Kirkman.......Walla Walla	John S. McMillan.........Roche Harbor
L. A. Davis..................... ......Cora	Thomas Savage. ....Colville

WEST VIRGINIA.

AT LARGE.

Charles B. Hart.... ....Wheeling	Stuart F. Reed... ....Clarksburg
Thomas E. Davis........... ...Grafton	J. W. Heavener............Buckhannon
John D. Hewett...............Bramwell	Hamilton Hatter........Harper's Ferry
John A. Hutchinson ....Parkersburg	P. W. Morris.......Ritchie Court House

DISTRICTS.

1—Oliver S. Marshall..New Cumberland	Amos A. Bee......... .....West Monroe
Charles M. Hart..........Clarksburg	Casper Kronhardt ....Marshall
2—George M. Bowers. .....Martinsburg	Ellis A. Billingslea..........Fairmount
Israel C. White ....Morgantown	G. T. Goshorn................Maysville
3—Joseph L. Burey....... ....Eagle	John C. Ballard...Salt Sulphur Springs
John E. Dana ....Malden	Christopher H. Payne........Charleston
4—William N. Miller.......Parkersburg	J. E. McLaughlin ....Ravenswood
D. E. Abbott.............Huntington	B. F. Reid............. .....Port Pleasant

WISCONSIN.

AT LARGE.

John C. Spooner........ .. .. Hudson	Robert McMillen.................Oshkosh
Henry C. Payne.............Milwaukee	Henry B Smith. ....Appleton
Lucius Fairchild..............Madison	Mason A. Thayer...... ....Sparta
Isaac Stephenson.............Marinette	John Ruka...... ....Boscobel

WISCONSIN—Continued.

Delegates.   *Alternates.*

DISTRICTS.

1—William T. Lewis.............Racine | Munson Paddock..................Salem
Charles A. Booth............Monroe | John W. Blackstone.........Shullsburg
2—Andrew J. Turner..........Portage | Charles M. Dow................Madison
Jesse Stone...............Watertown | Edward Sauerherring.... ....Mayville
3—Van S. Bennett............. Rockton | John W. Gunning............Friendship
William F. Conger....Prairie du Sac | E. Whaley............. Prairie du Chien
4—Albert E. Smith..........Milwaukee | Irving M. Bean..............Milwaukee
Ferdinand Kiekhefer....Milwaukee | William Graf.................Milwaukee
5—Thomas M. Blackstock...Sheboygan | W. A. Jones............. Oconomowoc
Bruno E. Fink...........Milwaukee | J. M. LaCount.... ....Hartford
6—Samuel A. Cook............Neenah | James T. Ellarson...........Wautoma
Charles A. Galloway...Fond du Lac | G. G. Sedgewick........... Manitowoc
7—C. L. Coleman.............La Crosse | James J. McGillivray.Black River Falls
Allen H. DeGroff.....Misha Mokwa | William H. Huntington..... ....Durand
8 Thomas B. Reid............Appleton | James T. Armstrong.......Green Bay
Frederic W. Upham.....Marshfield | Alfred L. Hutchinson.....Weyauwega
9—Willis S. Reynolds............Hurley | Otto C. Davidson........Commonwealth
Cornelius S. Curtis.. ......Wausau | Cyrus C. Yawkey...........Hazelhurst
10—Frank A. Ross ......West Superior | Henry S. Comstock........Cumberland
John C. Ticknor.........Menomonee | Joel F. Nason............St. Croix Falls

WYOMING.

Stephen W. Downey.... .Laramie City | George B. McCalmont. ....Casper
Charles N. Potter............Cheyenne | Mrs. Therese A. Jenkins .....Cheyenne
Carl L. Vagner.... ...., .Carbon | John B. Okie..................Lost Cabin
Frank W. Mondell ....Newcastle | Alpha E. Hoyt.........,.......Sundance
Edward R. Dinwiddie..........Dayton | Wilbur P. Keays................Buffalo
Frank M. Foote.............. Evanston | Mrs. Cora G. Carleton. ....Hilllard

TERRITORIAL DELEGATES.

ARIZONA.

Nathan O. Murphy.............Phoenix | E. M. Sanford..................... Yuma
M. W. Stewart....................Clifton | W. G. Stewart................Flagstaff

ALASKA.

Thomas S. Nowell..................... | ....
E. T. Hatch.......... .... | ....

INDIAN TERRITORY.

Ridge Paschal............................ | F. S. Genung. ....
John S. Hammer...................... | J. W. Roberts............................

NEW MEXICO.

Thomas b. Catron.............Santa Fe | Thomas D. Burns.......Tierra Amarilla
John D. Ball..................Silver City | William A. Hawkins............. Eddy
Tranquilino Luna...........Los Lunas | Melvin W. Mills.................Springer
Jayno A. Whitmore........San Marcial | Juan Santistevan....................Taos
Miguel Antonio Otero ....Las Vegas | John H. Riley.................Las Cruces
Nicholas Galles ....Hillsborough | Juan Navarro ....Mora

OKLAHOMA.

Abraham J. Seay ....Guthrie | Charles W. McGraw..........Stillwater
Daniel W. Marquardt..........Norman | Emera E. Wilson.................El Reno
Eugene I. Sadler.............Guthrie | George L. Dobson ....Beaver
*Leo Whistler ....Chandler | G. I. Curran..................Kingfisher
*White Turkey ....Tecumseh | L. E. Wilson............Oklahoma City
John Pflaff.....................Edmond | W. P. Hackney.................Guthrie

* Indians.

UTAH.

Orange J. Salisbury .....Salt Lake City | James Sharp............Salt Lake City*
Frank J. Cannon ....Ogden | George A. Southerland....... .Provo*
C. C. Goodwin.................Salt Lake | D. B. Dolliver.................Salt Lake*
C. E. Wallen... ....Salt Lake | D. C. McLaughlin ....Park City*

* ½ vote.

DISTRICT OF COLUMBIA.

Perry H Carson.............Washington | George Holmes .... Washington
Andrew Gleason.............Washington | John W. Freeman..........Washington

Mr. WARNER MILLER, of New York. *Mr. Chairman:* I rise to make a request.

The CHAIRMAN. The gentleman from New York is recognized for the purpose of making a request.

Mr. MILLER. *Mr. Chairman:* I hold in my hand a communication from the Woman's Republican Association of the United States. A number of patriotic ladies, in a few of the last campaigns, have rendered great aid to the Republican Party. I speak especially for the party in New York. I simply desire this Convention shall recognize their work, and then give them encouragement to go on in the coming campaign. I need say nothing more, but submit this letter, and ask that it be read, and then I will move that it is the sense of this Convention that this Association should be encouraged and that the officers now present may be formally presented to the Convention.

The CHAIRMAN. Unless there is objection the communication will be read.

Reading Clerk KENYON read the communication as follows:

WOMAN'S REPUBLICAN ASSOCIATION OE THE UNITED STATES, } MINNEAPOLIS, MINN., June 6, 1892. }

Hon. Warner Miller, Chairman of the New York Delegation to the Republican National Convention:

MY DEAR SIR:—We respectfully call your attention to the work of the Republican women for the maintenance of Republican principles and the election of Republican candidates. The work of women in whatever concerns the home or the state is justified by every principle of popular government, and at the present time is made important by current political conditions. The Republican Party will be the gainer if it utilizes the social, moral and political influence of its woman sympathizers. This can only be broadly effective through organization. We earnestly ask the delegates to the Convention to seek the co-operation of women in their various localities. To aid in their co-operation we will present each delegate with a general statement of the work accomplished and plans proposed. Thus may the fireside and the schools, as well as the platform and the press, sustain the principles of the Republican Party, among which is the noble sentiment of the last National Convention, viz:

The first concern of good government is the virtue and sobriety of the citizen and the purity of the home.

Respectfully and sincerely,
J. ELLEN FOSTER,
EMILY S. CHACE, *Secretary.*   *Chairman.*

Mr. MILLER. *Mr. Chairman:* I move that it is the sense of this Convention that this organization should be used in the coming

–8

campaign, and that the officers named be now presented to the Convention.

The motion was unanimously agreed to.

The CHAIRMAN. *Gentleman of the Convention :* I have the pleasure of presenting Mrs. J. Ellen Foster, Chairman of the Woman's Republican Association of the United States. [Applause and cheers.]

MRS. FOSTER : *Mr. Chairman and Gentlemen and Lady Delegates and Alternates to this Convention :* I thank you. It is no mean honor which is given to me as a representative of many thousand Republican women to stand in this magnificent presence. It is no mean honor to be presented by the great Empire State. (Applause.) The Empire State, which in itself has to contend with the fiercest questions of civilization, and thus needs us the most. The tests of civilization which are its changed ideals, are recognized by our recognition here. A free Church and a free State are magnificent ideals, and the record of the Republican party is a record of the magnificent attainment of those ideals.

Gentlemen and Ladies, the Woman's Republican Association has prepared plans of work, with suggestions of detail which will be presented to every delegate and alternate in this Convention. We are here to help you, (Applause). And we have come to stay. (Applause). We do not seek recognition in the party in the interest of any one of the various reforms, in which, as individuals, we are interested. We believe that moral reforms should be conducted outside of party lines, (applause) in the broad field of humanitarian, philanthropic and Christian effort. Not every one who cries reform is a reformer. (Applause). When a would-be reformer declares that he will inaugurate political chaos or help enthrone political wrong because his individual convictions do not find recognition, that man is not a reformer.

A man who fails to vote or who ignores the present harm which his vote may do can find no warrant for his course in reason or in morals. (Applause). He who does not stand for the greatest present attainable good is a helper of the bad. Righteousness in government comes by evolution oftener than by revolution. When revolution is the gate through which a people emerges to large liberty, the gate is opened by the assaults of the bad, not by the hands of the good. John Brown's methods failed, and in the nature of things had to fail; John Brown's soul is marching on. [Applause.] The aggressions of slavery brought on the war; in its crimson chariot the African slave was carried to liberty.

Therefore let women weave their laurels and sing their glorias to the robust political action of the Republican party, which accepts the present as it is found, but out of it builds great boulevards of human progress. Gentlemen, in our service of Republicanism we know no personal preferences or factional strife; we wear upon our breasts the name of none of the honorable men who may be your choice; but on our hearts are carried and from prayerful lips will soon be uttered the names of your nominees. We love our States and we love the Nation. Not Cæsar less, but Rome more. I love my native State. Massachusetts is a great State; from the sands and rocks of her Atlantic coast consecrated by Plymouth's pilgrim band; through the gardens of her river valleys to the borders of the Empire State she is full of greatness; great in ideas which are the only real forces in civilization; great in power to apply those ideas in the common walks of life, in trade, in commerce, in industries, in economics, in reforms and in the science of government.

Iowa, my adopted State, thou are the beloved daughter of New England's queen, and thou dost honor thy royalty. Iowa was quick to respond to the nation's call in time of civil strife; she was first to respond to the cry of starving Russia; the sight of her corn made glad the hearts of dying men and women and little children; she even sent seven of her good women along to set the table. Iowa's corn will feed millions, but by constitutional law her people have decreed that not one kernel shall be made into poison. Massachusetts is great, Iowa is the flower of her greatness, but there sit upon this floor the representatives of a greater State, a State of rocks and rivers, of plains and mountains; a State the peer of any other in natural resources and in power of development, but peerless in the crown its civilization wears; peerless in free men and free women—Wyoming thou art the land of promise. Women of Wyoming, who gave you liberty? I hear you answer, the freemen of your own households who thought it not robbery to themselves to make you their equals before the law. [Applause.] Who placed your star in the proudest flag of the world, the most beautiful emblem that the sun shines on—except the cross of the world's Redeemer? By whose votes was Wyoming made a State? Current history answers. History—sacred and profane—will never forget. By votes of the Republicans in the Fifty-first congress, Wyoming came into the Union. The Republican party in congress was practically solid for the admission of this first free State. The Democratic party was practically solid against it. [Hisses.] God bless the Republican party in the Fifty-first congress.

Gentlemen, the Republican party is nothing if not aggressive. It is a party of action; its breath is progress; its speech is the language of the world; its dialect is the rhetoric of the home, the farm, the shop. Its shibboleths might be written on the white walls of any church. It holds within its ranks the armies of all reform; its constituencies are the living, moving, vital elements of American life. [Applause.] Why should not women rally to the support of such a party? Gentlemen, we have come; we are for service. May God keep us all wise, and true, and strong, and brave. [Applause.]

The following is a list of the National Committee as finally made up.

NATIONAL COMMITTEE.

Alabama, William Youngblood ....Birmingham
Arkansas, Powell Clayton.........................Eureka Springs
California, M. H. DeYoung..........................San Francisco
Colorado, J. F. Saunders......................................Denver
Connecticut, Samuel Fessenden..........................Stamford
Delaware, Daniel J. Layton...........................Georgetown
Florida, J. G. Long.................................St. Augustine
Georgia, W. W. Brown...Macon

Idaho, Geo. L. Shoup.....................Salmon City, U. S. Senate
Illinois, Wm. J. Campbell...............................Chicago
Indiana, James N. Huston...........................Connersville
Iowa, James S. Clarkson................................Des Moines
Kansas, Cyrus Leland Jr...Troy
Kentucky, W. O. Bradley......................... .... Lancaster
Louisiana, A. H. Leonard.......... ....New Orleans
Maine, J. H. Manley........ ....Augusta
Maryland, James A. Gary........ ....Baltimore
Massachusetts, W. Murray Crane............................Dalton
Michigan, Geo. L. Maltz.......................................Detroit
Minnesota, R. G. Evans...........................Minneapolis
Mississippi, James Hill..............................Vicksburg
Missouri, Richard C. Kerens......... ....St. Louis
Montana, Alexander C. Botkin............................Helena
Nebraska, Edward Rosewater...........................Omaha
Nevada, W. E. Sharon.... ....Virginia City
New Hampshire, Person C. Cheney.....................Concord
New Jersey, Garrett A. Hobart............................Paterson
*New York, Frank S. Witherbee.......................Port Henry
North Carolina, Henry C. Cowles.......................Statesville
North Dakota, H. C. Hansbrough........Devil's Lake, U. S. Senate
Ohio, W. M. Hahn.......................................Mansfield
Oregon, Joseph C. Simon ....Portland
Pennsylvania, David Martin........................Philadelphia
Rhode Island, Isaac M. Potter..... ....Providence
South Carolina, Ellery M. Brayton....................Columbia
South Dakota, A. B. Kittredge.....................Sioux Falls
Tennessee, Geo W. Hill................................Dandridge
Texas, N. Wright Cuney................................Galveston
Vermont, Mason S. Colburn.........................Manchester
Virginia, Wm. Mahone........ ....Petersburg
Washington, Nelson Bennett................. ....Tacoma
West Virginia, N. B. Scott..........................Wheeling
Wisconsin, Henry C. Payne...........................Milwaukee
Wyoming, Joseph M. Carey.......................U. S. Senate
Alaska, E. T. Hatch ....Sitka
Arizona, W. Griffith..
Dist. of Columbia, Perry H. Carson..............Washington City
New Mexico, Thos. B. Catron.............................Sante Fe
Oklahoma, C. M. Barnes.....................................Guthrie
Utah, O. J. Salisbury..............................Salt Lake City
Indian Territory, J. S. Hammer ....Ardmore

NOMINATIONS OF CANDIDATES FOR PRESIDENT.

The CHAIRMAN. Gentlemen of the Convention. The next order of business is the presentation of Candidates for President of the United States.

Mr. H. M. DUFFIELD, of Michigan. *Mr.Chairman:* Michigan desires unanimous consent to withdraw for fifteen minutes for conference.

*Owing to the illness of Mr. Witherbee, Mr. W. A. Southerland, of Rochester, was subsequently appointed National Committeeman by the State Committee.

Mr. J. G. CANNON, of Illinois. *Mr. Chairman:* Does that require that the Convention should wait?

The CHAIRMAN. I shall interpret that to mean that no business shall be done until the delegation returns; at least until the end of fifteen minutes.

Mr. CANNON. Would the chair call nominating speeches business?

Mr. DUFFIELD. We do not desire to delay the Convention at all

Mr. CANNON. Then I have no objection.

The CHAIRMAN. Then the understanding is that unanimous consent is given, but that we shall go on with the presentation of the names of candidates for President of the United States. That will be the next order of business.

Mr. DUFFIELD. We do desire that the Convention shall wait until we return.

The CHAIRMAN: It is the desire of the delegation from Michigan that presentation speeches should not be made for fifteen minutes, in order to give them time for conference.

A DELEGATE. *Mr. Chairman:* I have a resolution which I ask to send to the Secretary's desk to be read to the Convention.

The CHAIRMAN. Is there objection to the reading of the resolution? (Cries of "yes," "yes," "yes.") Objection is made, and the regular order of business will be proceeded with. It has been the custom in past Conventions to call the roll of States for the presentation of candidates. Is it the desire of the Convention that that should be done today? (Cries of "yes," "yes," "yes.")

The Secretary will now call the roll of States for the presentation of candidates for the office of President of the United States.

Chief Reading Clerk HANEY called the roll of states as follows:

Alabama, Arkansas, California, Colorado.

Mr. WOLCOTT, of Colorado. *Mr. Chairman—*

The CHAIRMAN. Senator Wolcott, of Colorado, will take the platform.

Mr. Wolcott came to the platform.

Mr. WOLCOTT: *Mr. Chairman, and Gentlemen of the Convention:* The Republicans of the West sometimes differ with the Republicans of the East as to what is wanted. On this occasion there is remarkable unanimity between genuine Republicans of the West and genuine Republicans of the East as to who is needed, and his name is Blaine!

It is to us a matter of comparative indifference who shall lead the Democratic hosts, but we trust they will once more renominate their prophet of tariff reform, in order that we may demonstrate how short a life have slander and calumny, that a chastened country may repair the wrong of 1884, and stamp with the seal of final disapproval a policy which could only lead to impoverishment at home and which brought only contempt and dishonor abroad.

There is practical agreement among the delegates at this Convention, certainly among the representatives of the Republican States, as to who our leader should be, (loud cheering) and its expression would find unanimous voice were there not a mistaken feeling among certain of our associates that the bestowal of office is a personal gift. The welfare of our beloved party, Mr. Chairman, is of infinitely greater importance than the vindication or nomination of any man within its ranks, and when the roll of States is called I believe it will be remembered that the obligations of office are repaid solely by faithful performance of its duties, and that manhood and independence are never bartered among good men for the emoluments and honors of public station. (Cheers.)

Our candidate, Mr. Chairman, has never been President of the United States. He will be, (Cheers. Many delegates applauding loudly) but if he has not yet occupied that office, he has, by his devotion to the party, made Republican Presidents possible, and he has enriched and guided two administrations with his sagacity and statesmanship. We are honored and respected abroad. We owe it to his statecraft. We are gathering the republics of all America together in bonds of closest friendship. It is because he devised the plan and shaped the policy. We are protecting our own people on the farm and in the workshop, and by wise concessions are inducing the nations of the world to open their gates to our products. His far seeing and discriminating vision saw the possibilities of reciprocity and induced us to foster it. (Cheers and applause.) There is no public measure since the days of reconstruction which has tended to the advancement of our country with which he is not identified, and when the history of this generation of our Republic shall be written his name will stand foremost among its statesmen. No official title or station can add to or detract from the lustre of his fame, but we may at least let history record that such as we had to give we gave with loyal and loving hearts.

The best gifts in this world are not for those who seek them. (Applause.) Our votes are to be cast for one who is almost every Republican's candidate except his own. (Applause.) For my own part I rejoice that the opportunity is given me of casting my vote for a nominee who seeks nothing for himself but everything for his country. (Cheers.) And the same devotion to the Nation's welfare which has guided him in his public life for nearly a generation insures his acceptance of any duty which this Convention may impose upon him. (Applause.) For many months there has been apprehension in the public mind respecting his health and strength. It is gratifying to be able to state that the fears which have moved us are groundless. For our country's sake and his own we could wish that he were again the young and ardent leader who has guided his party through countless battles and that his youth could be renewed like the eagle's. (Cheers and applause.)

Experience, however, Mr. Chairman, comes only with ripening years. The same unconquerable will and lofty patriotism still dominate his being, and though time has tinged his hair with white, and the years of struggle in his country's service have left their impress, he still stands for us who love him, the embodiment of all that is brightest and the best in American statesmanship, (applause) and mellowed and broadened by the creeping hours of time we thank God that he is still amply able and equipped to give to the people of these states an administration which shall protect our own citizens, and looking beyond the confines of our borders embrace the well being of all America. (Prolonged cheering.)

And so, Mr. Chairman, we turn in the hour when victory is at hand to the intrepid leader who shaped for his party the policy which has lifted it above the danger of further defeat. (Great applause and cheers.)

To those of us who belong to the younger element of the party, who are content to follow and not to lead, but who only ask to bear their share of the burden and heat of the day, he stands as our ideal, our inspiration. His name is engraved in all our hearts in loving letters that cannot fade. Brave, true hearted and great, there is no true Republican who will not follow where he leads, and with loving faith and trust that a kind Providence may long spare him to a people whose grateful love he has earned and whose affectionate devotion he possesses, we pledge our unfaltering and loyal support to James G. Blaine. (Applause and cries of Blaine! Blaine!)

The CHAIRMAN. The Secretary will proceed with the call.

Reading Clerk HANEY (continuing). Connecticut, Delaware, Georgia, Idaho, Illinois, Indiana. (Applause and cries for General Dick Thompson.)

Mr. THOMPSON, of Indiana. Mr. Chairman:

The CHAIRMAN. The gentleman from Indiana will please step forward to the platform.

Mr. Thompson came to the platform.

Mr. THOMPSON. Mr. Chairman and Gentlemen of the Convention: I do not intend to make a speech. I propose to make a nomination for the Presidency which shall strike a chord of sympathy in every true Republican heart. I propose to nominate for the presidency a man who does not seek elevation by the detraction of any other great Republican in the Republican party. [Applause.] I do not propose, however, to eulogize his history or his life before this convention, because that will be done in words of burning and breathing eloquence, which cannot be surpassed in this or any other country in the world. [Applause.] Therefore with these simple words of praise I nominate to this convention for the Presidency of the United States the warrior statesman, Benjamin Harrison, of Indiana. [Great applause.]

The CHAIRMAN.   The Secretary will proceed with the call of States.

Reading Clerk HANEY (continuing.)   Iowa, Kansas, Kentucky, Lousiana, Maine, Maryland, Massachusetts, Michigan [A Voice. "What's the matter with Alger?"], Minnesota.

Mr. WILLIAM H. EUSTIS, of Minnesota.   *Mr. Chairman:*

The CHAIRMAN.   Mr. Eustis, of Minnesota.

Mr. Eustis took the platform.

Mr. EUSTIS.   *Mr. Chairman and Gentlemen of the Convention:*   Two centuries ago when Father Hennepin first stood upon the spot where we meet, he found a beaver impaled upon a tree. It was the Indian's offering to the Spirit that dwells in the Falls of St. Anthony.   Imitating the untutored mind in the presence of nature's mighty force, may we sacrifice every selfish feeling and nonpatriotic motive to that majestic power that dwells in the people.   With them all sovereignity lies.   We are their servants, clothed for a few brief hours with trust and responsibility. They have commissioned us to name a leader for the Republican Party, and if we do so in touch with their thought, their feeling, and their love, they will crown our uncrowned leader, and make him the next President of the United States. [Applause.]

What inspirations to patriotic action fill this hour with thought. Four hundred years ago, past the hour of midnight, Columbus saw a light.   It grew.   A continent appeared.   It grew.   The Mayflower landed on Plymouth Rock.   It grew.   Freedom exiled from the old world, found in the new, a home.   It grew.   The starlit flag unfurled.   It grew.   The Republican Party came, divinely commissioned to broaden human freedom and defend that flag. Those sitting with us to-day as free men, who then were slaves, the peerless luster of the flag, and the number of stars in its azure blue, tell how well the Republican Party has kept its faith. [Applause.]   Its mission is not yet ended.   A mighty Nation, rich in all the blessings of peace, mindful of her glory and her destiny, advances with majestic step to lead the commerce, as well as the freedom, of the world. [Applause.]

Ideas, great ideas, form landmarks in the history of mankind. The great idea of the last decade is reciprocity. [Applause.]   It came to us like a discovery.   So simple in its principles, so farreaching in its consequences, we wonder that this golden rule of trade was not long ago established.   Under its magic touch soon our ships shall sail, swift as the weaver's shuttle, between our ports, and those of all the world, weaving the golden band that binds Nations together in interest and in friendship; while with our ships, and with our flag the lighted torch of freedom shall make the circuit of the globe. [Applause.]   To-day on all our farms there is not a barrel of pork or a bushel of wheat but what has a broader market and a greater purchasing power by reason of the third section of the McKinley Bill. [Applause.]

Our party stands pledged to an honest ballot, an honest dollar and protection of American industries and American labor. These epistles of the party are followed by the revelation of reciprocity.

This great revelation has demoralized free traders at home and free traders abroad. In the great commercial conflict now dawning on the world our country is armed cap-a-pie, while our great rival, in the language of her leader, is without armor and without arms. Who in this great battle is best equipped to be our leader? All honor to him whose name is a synonym for honest money; unstinted praise to the President who has upheld the flag and sustained the rights of American citizens on land and on sea; [applause] all honor and love to you, Sir, (Chairman McKinley) who stood like a rock against the floodtide of free trade, and lifted the shield of protection above the wages of the worker, and the industries of the land. [Applause.]

All honor and cheers for the gallant soldier from Michigan whose brave war record the people will not suffer Democracy to tarnish. We honor and love all these none the less, because there is one other leader whom we honor and love the more. [Cries of "Blaine, Blaine," and cheers.] For more than thirty years he has toiled for the honor of the party and the glory of the Republic. In every quadrennial contest in the history of the party, his plume has been in front of the fight.

He never for a moment has faltered in his earnest allegiance and support of the party and its nominee. He is intensely Republican as he is intensely American.

In admiration of the genius of our great Secretary of State, isle answers to isle and continent responds to continent, while a commercial linking hemisphere attests the breadth and scope of his statesmanship.

Every issue on which we must win is personified in his name.

In all the world there are three who are by common consent considered the greatest of living statesmen. The youngest and the brainiest of the three is an American.

What say the people? Shall we teach the lesson that Republics are not ungrateful, that they both produce and promote the great men of the world?

Four years ago Blaine put away the Presidency in honor prefering another. To-day he does not seek the nomination.

Such unselfish and patriotic ambition is rare in the history of the world.

Catching somewhat the same spirit, may we take one step towards a higher plane of patriotism and behold the sublime spectacle of the highest office in our gift seeking our greatest man.

Illinois: In 1876 you championed the cause of the plumed Knight in burning words of loyalty and love. During all these years that Knight has grown in admiration and love of all the States. Is this not true in Illinois? In the Indian tongue the name of your commonwealth signified a race of men. Has its meaning paled? For the past let Lincoln, Grant and Logan answer; for the present you must speak.

Illinois, with the courage of your conviction, nay more — with the courage of your love—take the hand of Minnesota and let your patriotic action this day proclaim to all the world that Illinois still means a race of men. [Applause.]

My country, it is for thee, the people cherish their best and their noblest aspirations. It is for thee, that they would exercise their godlike powers. It *was* for thee those died whose graves but yesterday we strewed with flowers.

It *is* for thee, my country, that Minnesota with loyal heart and patriotic purpose extends the hand to every sister State and seconds the nomination of James G. Blaine.

[Applause, and cheers, and cries of " Blaine ! Blaine !" lasting 30 minutes.]

The CHAIRMAN. The Secretary will proceed with the roll call.

Reading Clerk HANEY, (continuing). Mississippi.

Mr. W. E. MOLLISON of Mississippi. *Mr. Chairman:*

The CHAIRMAN. The gentleman from Mississippi is recognized'

Mr. MOLLISON came to the platform.

Mr. MOLLISON. *Mr. Chairman:* The state I hail from cast its electoral vote for Cleveland the day before yesterday. I make no promises to this Convention opposed to that election. Mississippi does not wish me to do so, and it would not be well. I come to assure the Republicans of the country that delegates from the non-suffragistStates do not always vote as a return for past favors. We come believing that New York, Wisconsin and California should tell us what candidate is dearest to the hearts of Republicans. [Applause.] We have weighed well the reasons given by our fellow Republicans who vote at elections as well as at nominating Conventions. They have told us. Winds from your great prairies bring to our ears a sound which we could not resist, if we would. Every breeze brings a name magic and charmful; it repeats a name dear to the heart of childhood as well as to the heart of age. That name is of the greatest citizen of the world. No man is jealous of him. Our greatest call him chief. Nominate him and you will render the doubtful States of the mighty East and West certain, and the certain States of the South doubtful. I ask, fellow Republicans of the great free North, with a ballot that will be counted, that you nominate that greatest living statesman of the greatest of all Republicans, James G. Blaine." [Great Applause.]

Reading Clerk HANEY.

Missouri, Montana, Nebraska, Nevada, New Jersey, New York' [Applause.]

Mr. CHANCEY M. DEPEW, of New York. *Mr. Chairman:*

The CHAIRMAN. Mr. DEPEW, of New York.

Mr. DEPEW came to the platform.

(Long continued applause.)

MR. DEPEW. *"Mr. President and Gentlemen of the Convention:* It is the peculiarity of Republican National Conventions that each one of them has a distinct and interesting history. We are here to meet conditions and solve problems which make this gathering not only no exception to the rule, but substantially a new departure. [Applause.]

That there should be strong convictions and their earnest expression as to preferences and policies is characteristic of the right of individual judgment, which is the fundamental principle of Republicanism. [Applause.] There have been occasions when the result was so sure that the delegates could freely indulge in the charming privilege of favoritism and of friendship. But the situation which now confronts us demands the exercise of dispassionate judgment and our best thought and experience. We cannot venture on uncertain ground or encounter obstacles placed in the path way of success by ourselves. The Democratic party is now divided, but the hope of the possession of power once more will make it in the final battle more aggressive, determined and unscrupulous than ever. It starts with 15 states secure without an effort, by processes which are a travesty upon popular government, and if continued long enough will paralyze institutions founded upon popular suffrage. [Applause.] It has to win four more States in a fair fight, States which in the vocabulary of politics are denominated doubtful.

"The Republican party must appeal to the conscience and the judgment of the individual voter in every State in the Union. This is in accordance with the principles upon which it was founded and the objects for which it contends. [Applause.] It has accepted this issue before and fought it out with an extraordinary continuance of success. [Applause.] The conditions of Republican victory from 1860 to 1880 were created by Abraham Lincoln and Ulysses S. Grant. [Applause.] They were, that the saved Republic should be run by its saviors [applause]; the emancipation of the slaves, the reconstruction of the States, the reception of those who had fought to destroy the Republic back into the fold, without penalities or punishments, and to an equal share with those who had fought and saved the Nation, in the solemn obligations and inestimable privileges of American citizenship. [Applause.] They were the embodiment into the constitution of the principles for which two millions of men had fought and a half million had died. [Applause.] They were the restoration of public credit, the resumption of specie payments, and the prosperous condition of solvent business. [Applause.]

"For twenty-five years there were names with which to conjure and events fresh in the public mind, which were eloquent with popular enthusiasm. It needed little else than a recital of the glorious story of its heroes and a statement of the achievements of the Republican party to retain the confidence of the people. But from the desire for change which is characteristic of free governments there came a reversal, there came a check to the progress of the Republican party, and four years of Democratic administration. These four years largely relegated to the realm of history past issues, and brought us face to face with what Democracy, its professions and its practices mean today.

"The great names which have adorned the roll of Republican statesmen and soldiers are still potent and popular. The great measures of the Republican party are still the best part of the history of the century. [Applause.] The unequaled and unexampled story of Republicanism in its promises and in its achievements stands unique in the record of parties in governments which are free. But we live in practical times, facing practical issues which affect the business, the wages, the labor and the prosperity of today.

"The campaign will be won or lost, not upon the bad record of James K. Polk or of Franklin Pierce or of James Buchanan—not upon the good record of Lincoln or of Grant or of Arthur or of Hayes or of Garfield. It will be won or lost upon the policy, foreign and domestic, the industrial measures and the administrative acts of the administration of Benjamin Harrison. [Cheers.]

Whoever receives the nomination of this Convention will run, upon the judgment of the people, as to whether they have been more prosperous and more happy, whether the country has been in a better condition at home, and stood more honorably abroad under these last four years of Harrison and Republican administration, than during the preceding four years of Cleveland and Democratic government.

"Not since Thomas Jefferson has any administration been called upon to face and solve so many or such difficult problems as those which have been exigent in our conditions. No administration since the organization of the government has ever met difficulties better, or more to the satisfaction of the American people. [Cheers.]

"Chili has been taught that no matter how small the antagonist, no community can with safety insult the flag or murder American sailors. [Cheers.] Germany and England have learned in Samoa that the United States has become one of the powers of the world, and no matter how mighty the adversary, at every sacrifice American honor will be maintained. [Cheers.] The Behring sea question, which was the insurmountable obstacle in the diplomacy of Cleveland and of Bayard, has been settled upon a basis which sustains the American position, until arbitration shall have determined our right. [Applause.]

"The dollar of the country has been placed and kept on the standard of commercial nations, and a convention has been agreed upon with foreign governments which, by making bimetallism the policy of all nations, may successfully solve all our financial problems.

"The tariff, tinkered with and trifled with to the serious disturbance of trade and disaster to business since the days of Washington, has been courageously embodied into a code—a code which has preserved the principle of the protection of American industries. To it has been added a beneficent policy, supplemented by beneficial treaties and wise diplomacy, which has opened to our farmers and manufacturers the markets of other countries. [Applause.]

"The navy has been builded upon lines which will protect American citizens and American interests and the American flag all over the world. [Applause.]

"The public debt has been reduced. The maturing bonds have been paid off. The public credit has been maintained. The burdens of taxations have been lightened. Two hundred millions of currency have been added to the people's money without disturbance of the exchanges. Unexampled prosperity has crowned wise laws and their wise administration. [Applause.]

"The main question which divides us is, to whom does the credit of all this belong? Orators may stand upon this platform, more able and more eloquent than I, who will paint in more brilliant colors, but they can not put in more earnest thought the affection and admiration of Republicans for our distinguished Secretary of State. [Cheers.]

"I yield to no Republican, no matter from what state he hails, in admiration and respect for John Sherman [applause], for Gov. McKinley [applause], for Thomas B. Reed [applause], for Iowa's great son [applause], for the favorites of Illinois, Wisconsin and

Michigan [applause]; but when I am told that the credit for the brilliant diplomacy of this administration belongs exclusively to the Secretary of State, for the administration of its finances to the Secretary of the Treasury, for the construction of its ships to the Secretary of the Navy, for the introduction of American pork in Europe to the Secretary of Agriculture, for the settlement, so far as it is settled, of the currency question to Senator John Sherman, for the formulation of the tariff laws to Governor McKinley, for the removal of the restrictions placed by foreign nations upon the introduction of American pork to our ministers at Paris and Berlin, I am tempted to seriously inquire, who, during the last four years, has been President of the United States, any how? [Cheers.]

"Cæsar, when he wrote those commentaries which were the history of the conquest of Europe under his leadership, modestly took the position of Æneas when he said, 'They are the narratives of events, the whole of which I saw, and the part of which I was.'

"Gen. Thomas, as the rock of Chickamauga, occupies a place in our history with Leonidas among the Greeks, except that he succeeded where Leonidas failed. The fight of Joe Hooker above the clouds was the poetry of battle. The resistless rush of Sheridan and his steed down the valley of the Shenandoah is the epic of our civil war. The march of Sherman from Alanta to the sea is the supreme triumph of gallantry and strategy. It detracts nothing from the splendor of the fame or the merits of the deeds of his lieutenants to say that, having selected them with marvelous sagacity and discretion, Grant still remained the supreme commander of the national army. [Cheers.]

"All the proposed acts of any administration, before they are formulated, are passed upon in cabinet council, and the measures and suggestions of the ablest Secretaries would have failed with a lesser President; but for the great good of the country and the benefit of the Republican party, they have succeeded, because of the suggestive mind, the indomitable courage, the intelligent appreciation of situations, and the grand magnanimity of Benjamin Harrison. [Cheers.]

"It is an undisputed fact that during the few months when both the Secretary of State and the Secretary of the Treasury were ill, the President personally assumed the duties of the State department and of the Treasury Department, and both with equal success. [Applause.]

"The Secretary of State, in accepting his portfolio under President Garfield wrote: 'Your administration must be made brilliantly successful and strong in the confidence and pride of the people, not at all diverting its energies for re-election, and yet compelling that result by the logic of events and by the imperious necessities of the situation.' [Applause.] Garfield fell before the bullet of the assassin, and Mr. Blaine retired to private life.

"General Harrison invited him to take up that unfinished diplomatic career, where its threads had been so tragically broken. [Cheers.] He entered the cabinet. He resumed his work, and has won a higher place in our history. [Cheers.] The prophecy he made for Garfield has been superbly fullfilled by President Harrison. In the language of Mr. Blaine 'the president has compelled a re-election by the logic of events and the imperious necessities of the situation.' [Cheers.]

"The man who is nominated here today, to win, must carry a certain well known number of the doubtful States. Patrick Henry, in the Convention which started rolling the ball of the independence of the colonies from Great Britian, said: 'I have but one lamp by which my feet are guided, and that is the lamp of experience. I know of no way of judging of the future but by the past.'

"New York was carried in 1880 by Gen. Garfield and in every important election since that time we have done our best. We have put forward our ablest, our most popular, our most brilliant leaders for Governor and State officers to suffer constant defeat. The only light which illumines with the sun of hope the dark record of those twelve years, is the fact that in 1888 the State of New York was triumphantly carried by President Harrison. [Cheers.] He carried it then as a gallant soldier, a wise senator, a statesman who inspired confidence by his public utterances in daily speech from the commencement of the canvass to its close. [Cheers.] He still has all these claims, and, in addition, an administration beyond criticism and rich with the elements of popularity with which to carry New York again. [Cheers.]

"Ancestry helps in the old world and handicaps in the new. There is but one distinguished example of a son first overcoming the limitations imposed by the pre-eminent fame of his father, and then rising above it, and that was when the younger Pitt became greater than Chatham.

"With an ancestor a signer of the Declaration of Independence, and another who saved the Northwest from savagery and gave it to civilization and empire, and who was also president of the United States, a poor and unknown lawyer of Indiana has risen by his unaided efforts to such distinction as a lawyer, orator, soldier, statesman and President that he reflects more credit upon his ancestors than they have devolved upon him, and presents in American history the parallel of the younger Pitt. [Cheers.]

"By the grand record of a wise and popular administration, by the strength gained in frequent contact with the people, in wonderfully versatile and felicitous speech, by the claims of a pure life in public, and in the simplicity of a typical American home, I nominate Benjamin Harrison." [Prolonged cheers.]

Mr. WARNER MILLER, of New York. *Mr. Chairman—*

The CHAIRMAN. Mr. Miller of New York.

Mr. Miller came to the platform. [Applause.]

Mr. MILLER. *Mr. President and Gentlemen of the Convention* You have no longer time to listen to the rehearsal of the history of the achievements of the Republican party. You have no longer time to listen to the records of our great statesmen. You have come now to the supreme hour of this Convention. Thus far it has been a Convention in which a kindly spirit has prevailed upon every side, and I have no doubt, that it is to prevail to the end, and that whatever may be the outcome of this Convention, it will be ratified by the whole Republican party of this country, and by a majority of the voters of the people. The portion of the New York delegation which I represent does not come here to make any detraction upon any man in high authority or upon the President. We indulge in nothing of this kind. We uphold the hands of the man we put in power by our votes in New York four years ago, but we come here feeling that the candidate that I shall second can do more for us in the great State of New York in enabling us to achieve victory in November than any other candidate that may be named.

Republican majorities in the State of New York are found in the interior counties north of the center of the State. Since I have been in Minneapolis, I have received hundreds of dispatches from leading citizens of those counties, and they all tell me that the idol of our people there is the idol that we have held up for twenty years, James G. Blaine. [Loud and continued cheers.] Nothing that any one could say here would add to his fame or detract from the honor belonging to him as an American statesman. His history and achievements are known to the whole world. For more than twenty years he has led the combat. Notwithstanding the variations of American politics, he has lost nothing of the affection of the great masses of the Republican party. Speaking for the majority of the delegates from the State of New York [cheers], for a vast majority of the loyal Republicans of the State, I stand here to say that if their candidate is given to them they will go into the fight confident of victory. [Applause.

(Cries of roll call.)

Reading Clerk HANEY, (continuing.)   North Carolina—

Mr. H. P. CHEATHAM, of North Carolina. *Mr. Chairman.*

The CHAIRMAN. The gentleman from North Carolina will take the platform.

Mr. CHEATHAM. *Mr. Chairman and Gentlemen:* "On behalf of the Republican party in North Carolina and the 8,000,000 negro citizens of the United States, whose progress and development in twenty-six years have surprised the world, I rise to second the nomination of the orator, gallant soldier and one of the ablest and purest statesmen who ever lived to advance the annals of the American history. This gentleman is Hôn. Benjamin Harrison, of the State of Indiana. Four years ago, Mr. President, when the flag of the grand old party was trailing in the dust and her cause had been consigned to the narrow channels of the grave of defeat, when the leaders of the party were despondent, scattered and confused—when it seemed almost impossible to find a Moses to lead the party out of the dark valley of Democracy—Gen. Benjamin Harrison came and more than triumphantly led the party to success and victory. [Applause.] Since then his record, and his acts have received the highest commendation by the people of this country, of every party. Renominate Benjamin Harrison and you will not only honor yourselves, but will insure success and victory in November next." [Applause.]

Reading Clerk HANEY:

North Dakota, Ohio, Oregon, Pennsylvania, Rhode Island South Carolina, South Dakota, Tennessee.

Mr. G. Q. BOYD, of Tennessee. *Mr. Chairman—*

The CHAIRMAN. The gentleman will come to the platform.

Mr. BOYD came to the platform.

Mr. BOYD. *Mr. Chairman and Gentlemen of the Convention:* I want to say to this Convention that we are here to do the bidding of the American people. I want to say to this Convention, if the people of this Nation, if the Republican party should gather either in the east, west, north, or south, and the names of these great men should be submitted before them, who would they demand to lead them in this contest? (Loud cries of "Blaine!" and "Harrison!") Gentlemen, and fellow-citizens, in answer to that question, I say the answer would came from a million bosoms, the name of James G. Blaine, the Plumed Knight! [Great applause.]

"Now, gentlemen of this Convention, I come to perform the will of the people, and as the gentleman from New York said he heard the noise coming from the galleries—yes, and thank God the people in the gallaries must vote for the President of the United States. [Great applause.]

"In the Sixth Congressional District of Tennessee the people met, and they said, Mr. Chairman and Gentlemen of this Convention, that with James G. Blaine out of the question then they were for Harrison, but as long as James G. Blaine stands before the American people it is our duty as citizens, and I believe I do the bidding of my constituents when I ask you to nominate that prince of parliamentarians and the matchless statesman from Maine, James G. Blaine. [Cheers.] Ladies and Gentlemen, I say ladies, because the ladies, and babies in the cradles, and everybody wants Blaine—I say to you that no words of mine could add to the record of this grand and gifted statesman. In the words of one of America's greatest statesmen, he needs not the sculptor nor the architect to perpetuate his memory, or his deeds; he needs no stately pyramid, whose towering height would pierce the stormy cloud, and rear its lofty head to heaven to tell posterity his fame. His worthy deeds alone have rendered him immortal, and when oblivion shall have swept away kingdoms, thrones, and principalities, and the last vestige of human grandeur shall have mouldered in the dust, eternity itself will treasure the name of James G. Blaine.

Chief Reading Clerk HANEY (continuing.) Texas, Virginia, Washington, West Virginia, Wisconsin. (Cries of "Spooner.")

Mr. SPOONER. *Mr. Chairman:*

The CHAIRMAN. The Gentleman from Wisconsin.

Senator Spooner came to the platform.

Mr. SPOONER. *Mr. Chairman and Gentlemen of the Convention:* The preliminaries are settled and it is a relief that we are at last face to face with the great duty which we came hither to perform. That the action of this body composed of representative men who love the Republican party and seek to promote its success, for its record and its principles will be deliberate, thoughtful and patriotic and such as to secure for it the approval of those who sent us here, can not be doubted. National Republican conventions have not been accustomed to make mistakes. That which met at Chicago in 1888 made no mistake when it entrusted the honor and responsibility of leadership to Benjamin Harrison of Indiana, and Benjamin Harrison made no mistakes. He quickly proved himself an ideal candidate and a leader who

led. Millions of hostile and eager eyes searched his whole life in
vain for spot or blemish. Calm, dignified and wise, every day
brought from his lips a declaration, in itself a perfect platform,
unexcelled for grace of diction, power of epigrammatic statement
and the spirit of true eloquence. He imbued the party with
renewed vigor and strength and intrepidly led it to victory. His
friends bring his name into this convention proudly conscious
that the record which he has made need not be supplemented by
words of advocacy. He has been from the day of his inaugura-
tion what the people elected him to be—President of the United
States. He has given to the country an administration which for
ability, efficiency, purity and patriotism, challenges without fear
of comparison any which has preceded it since the foundation
of the government. He has been free from "variableness or
shadow of turning" in his devotion to the principles of the
Republican party and to the redemption of the pledges made
by it to the people. He has stood firm for the interests of Americans and placed the stamp of his approval upon the great
tariff bill of the Fifty-first congress, which has outridden
the flood of misrepresentation which swept over it as did the
ark the deluge of old and now rests upon a foundation as solid as
Mount Ararat. He championed and promoted by every means in
harmony with the dignity of his great office the adoption of the
scheme of reciprocity which was enacted in favor of our people;
not limiting to the South American republics or bartering the
interests of one industry for the benefit of another by the free
admission of competitive products, but compelling fair treatment
by all governments of our people and our products under penalty
of commercial retaliation.

Openly friendly to the use of silver as one of the coin metals of
the country, under conditions which shall maintain it at a parity
with gold, by international agreement, the existence of those
conditions stand nevertheless firm as the granite which underlies
the continent against a policy which would debase the currency
of the people. Nor did he forget or disregard the solemn pledge
of the Republican party that "every citizen, rich or poor, native
or foreign born, white or black, is entitled at every public election
to cast one free ballot, and to have that ballot honestly counted
and faithfully returned."

With a skill, dignity and courage which has commanded the
admiration of political friend and foe alike he has caused it to be
understood throughout the world that the American flag represents a growth which has the power and will to protect the
American uniform and interests at all hazards everywhere,
whether assailed by peppery neighbors to the southward of us or
by the diplomacy or power of Great Britain. Every interest of
the people has had his best care and his best thought, and he
stands before the country to-day well approved and universally
acknowledged to be a man of transcendent ability, of extraordinary capacity for the discharge of executive duty, of exalted patriotism and lofty purpose, who would not for an unanimous
re-nomination by this Convention and a re-election by the people
swerve one hair's breadth in any matter of duty, great or small,
from what he believed to be just and right. This Convention will
not mistake the lamentations of the disappointed for the voice of
the "plain people." This argument against him overestimates
the individual and underestimates the intelligence of the masses.

—9

They do not demand of a President that he shall be able to please every one. They want good government, they demand honesty and ability and industry and purity in public and private life, and all this they have in Benjamin Harrison, and they know it. We place him before the Convention as one who can bear his full share in the great contest which is to-day to begin. The Republicans of every State save one have assembled and endorsed with enthusiasm his administration. Upon that administration and its record of efficiency and achievement the party is to win if at all in the coming campaign. Place again in his hand the banner of Republicanism and he will carry it aggressively all the time at the front; and he will lead us again to victory. There will be irresistible power and inspiration in the knowledge which pervades the people that so long as he is a President there is one at the helm who, whatever betides us at home or abroad, will bring to the solution of every question and to the performance of every duty a splendid and disciplined intelligence, an absolutely unfaltering desire to improve every interest of every section, and a patriotism which never has wavered either in war or in peace. [Applause and cheers.]

Mr. BRUNO E. FINK, of Wisconsin. *Mr. Chairman:*

The CHAIRMAN. Mr. Fink of Wisconsin.

Mr. Fink came to the platform.

Mr. FINK. *Gentlemen of this Convention:* Doubly handicapped by the eloquent address of the senior of our delegation, young and inexperienced as I am in the domain of practical politics, it is with a considerable degree of diffidence that I venture to arise to my feet on this occasion, to raise my voice in the midst of this august assembly. But this diffidence is overcome and dissipated in the contemplation of the fact and of the proud privilege, that, thanks to Republican principles and institutions we dwell in a land where the citizen is the sovereign. [Applause.] Where we have freedom of speech and thought, and where the humblest and the lowliest born among us may at all times have a chance given for the expression of his opinion free and untrammeled. [Applause.] Mr. Chairman, willingly, gracefully, cheerfully will the young Republicans of this broad land bow to the judgment of this Convention. [Applause.] They have subscribed with alacrity to the truism, "Old men for council, but young men for war." [Applause.] So unswerving is their devotion to the tenets of Republicanism, so unlimited is their confidence in the eternal righteousness of our cause, so implicitly do they believe that you, my fellow delegates here assembled, you who represent the leading spirits of our party, will in these your deliberations always endeavor to administer for the greatest good to the greatest number, that it makes no difference whom you nominate, whether it be the worthy, fearless, independent and aggressive son of Old Tippecanoe, Benjamin Harrison, [great applause] or whether it be your will that the mantle of the highest office in sight of the civilized world shall descend upon the honored shoulders of our worthy president [prolonged cheers and cries of "McKinley"] the Napoleon of the tariff, William McKinley, jr., [cries of "hear, hear" and long continued applause] or whether it should be your will that the party should honor him who from a position of obscurity in the pine forests of Michigan arose to be a favorite son of that State, General Alger [applause]; or whether, last but not least, you should decide that the sword of commander-in-chief be placed in the hands of the evergreen from Maine, brainy James G. Blaine. Upon whomsoever may rest your choice, around his flag will the young men of this country, the young Republicans of this land, deem it their bounden duty to rally and they will follow him with a will in the fight from this hour forth, until the sun shall have set on the day of election in next November [applause and cries of "good"].

"But Mr. Chairman and fellow delegates, since the cardinal issues of this campaign—protection and free trade relate to the commercial expansion of this, our country, you will pardon me as one who like many hundreds among your good selves have been reared in the domain of commercial activity, to give to this meeting my opinion, yes, my conviction, that if Benjamin Harrison, instead of occupying the executive chair at the head of this nation, had for the last four years been acting manager of a private enterprise and corporation in which we are the stockholders; and had he during that term of office displayed that signal and singular fitness for an office; had he brought to his work that keenness of judgment and correctness of foresight, and above all things that absolute certainty of mind and purpose which he has shown us in his administration of the executive office; and were we sitting here today, not as delegates in a Republican Convention, but as stockholders in a commercial enterprise with the duty in hand to select a manager for another term, there would not, aye, there could not be a division of sentiment but what we would promptly and gladly re-elect Benjamin Harrison. If you would have—[cries of "Time, time."]—if you would have the judgment and decision of this convention to be an object lesson to the rising generation of this land, and above all if you would afford to the young Republicans an incentive for learning to know the right and for battling for it; if you would have them understand that above all else this broad land of ours, this generous people of ours is a thankful and appreciative people [cries of "Time, time."] ready at all times [cries of "Time, time, sit down."]—ready at all times to reward with highest trust duty faithfully performed, then cast your ballots by all means for Benjamin Harrison. [Applause.]

Reading Clerk HANEY. Wyoming.

Mr. STEPHEN W. DOWNEY, of Wyoming. *Mr. Chairman:*

The CHAIRMAN. The gentleman from Wyoming, Mr. Downey.

Mr. Downey came to the platform.

Mr. DOWNEY. *Mr. Chairman and Gentlemen of the Convention:* I come from one of the far off states, a state many miles from here. [Applause.] We have come here to have a voice in this Convention, and to say who shall be nominated by the Republican party for the Presidency of the United States. When I listened to the distinguished gentleman from New York, the Hon. Chauncey M. Depew, as he referred in such eloquent terms to the orator from Colorado, (Senator Wolcott), and said that he had drawn down upon himself the genius of oratory and that he had tipped his tongue with the silver of the state of Colorado, I thought that in the person of the distinguished gentleman from New York (Mr. Depew), that I saw once more in this great convention, as in ancient times, a Demosthenes. [Laughter, and confusion.]

You say, "Gentlemen, nominate Benjamin Harrison." On behalf of the other contingent, I say we will show you a better man, James G. Blaine. [Cheers.] I represent the hardy frontiersmen, the miners, the ranchmen, the farmers, and I say to you that the name of James G. Blaine will bring us votes by the thousands, (laughter and cheers) and he is the man to be nominated.

Why, gentlemen of the Convention—[Cries of "time," "time."] He is the man who was honored by that grand man of history, James A. Garfield. Let the sound go forth, and let the facts be known. [Applause, and confusion.]

Gentlemen of the Convention, the youngest State in the Nation demands a hearing at your hands. We are here, and though I am not a distinguished Senator of the United States, not a member of Congress, I demand in the name of the common people that I be heard in this Convention. [Applause and cries of "good."]

The CHAIRMAN: The Chairman desires to state that there is no limit to this debate, and until a limit is put upon it, it is due any gentleman who rises to speak that he shall have a hearing.

Mr. DOWNEY. I recognize in the distinguished chairman here, one who is all fairness, and I want to say now to him, in view of what I have said here about others: make no pledges, and when four years more roll around, we will (turning to McKinley) make you President of the United States. [Great applause.]

Mr Chairman, when General Garfield organized his cabinet, who was the distinguished American citizen who was called to fill the first place in the cabinet? It was the distinguished gentleman whose name was presented here so eloquently by the gentleman from Colorado. We have no fight with Mr. Harrison. We are here simply to determine which is the better man, and who can best serve the interests of this great country. [Cries of "Blaine" and "Harrison."] Aye, James G. Blaine was fit to be made a cabinet officer. He was Secretary of State in the Garfield administration. He was called upon to the highest position in the cabinet of President Harrison, and yet his name has been villified and abused by the grossest slander that was ever promulgated on the face of the earth. [Cries of "no," "no."] I say to you in all earnestness, whatever we have to meet in this campaign, whatever issues we have— [Great confusion.]

The CHAIRMAN. The Chair insists that order must be maintained.

Mr. DOWNEY. The issues of this campaign will be the issues which were made by our distinguished permanent Chairman, and that is protection, reciprocity and free ballot. Show us a man in the Republican party who has done more to advance these things than the honored statesman, the illustrious man whose nomination I am here to second, James G. Blaine. [Applause.]

The PRESIDENT. Gentlemen of the Convention I desire to make a statement. The friends of both candidates have announced to the Chair that there are gentlemen from five or six States who failed to respond when their States were called, who desire to be heard. [Cries of "no," "no," and "ballot."]

THE BALLOT FOR PRESIDENT.

Mr. SEWELL, of New Jersey. *Mr. President:* I move that the Convention proceed to ballot for a candidate for President of the United States.

The motion prevailed unanimously. [Applause.]

The CHAIRMAN. *Gentlemen of the Convention:* There is a matter of very considerable moment that should be disposed of before we proceed to ballot. The question has been raised, whether the delegates from Alaska and Indian Territories are entitled to vote in this Convention. The understanding of the Chair was that a motion was first made by the delegates respectively from those two Territories, that they be admitted into this Convention. That motion was passed, and then the question of credentials went to the Committee on Credentials, and the gentleman from Massachusetts, the Chairman of the Committee, (Mr. Cogswell) reported the names of the delegates who were entitled to have their seats in this Convention, and so that there may be no confusion hereafter, I submit to the Convention whether the understanding which I have stated is the understanding of the Convention. [Cries of "yes" and "call the roll."] The question is whether it was your understanding by that action this morning, that the delegates from those two Territories are entitled to vote. [Cries "yes."]

A DELEGATE, from Iowa. I move you that the delegates admitted to this hall from Alaska and from the Indian Territory be permitted to cast their vote in this Convention.

A DELEGATE, from Indiana. We do not understand the question. Put the question. [Cries "call the roll."]

The CHAIRMAN. The gentleman from Iowa submits a motion that the delegates from Alaska and the Indian Territory be permitted to vote in this Convention.

The question being put to a vote was unanimously carried.

Mr. ELLERY M. BRAYTON, of South Carolina. *Mr. Chairman* I rise to a question of privilege. My question of privilege is that

I ascertain from an inspection of the roll of this Convention that there has been a mistake in the Fifth District of South Carolina, and the name of Joshua F. Ensor is named as a delegate instead of that of E. Brooks Sligh. The facts are these—

The CHAIRMAN. Is there any dispute about that?

Mr. BRAYTON. Yes, sir. The facts are these: There was a contest with regard to that District. The sub-Committee reported in favor of seating E. Brooks Sligh in place of Joshua F. Ensor, and made Joshua F. Ensor the alternate. It was adopted by the Committee and became incorporated in the permanent roll.

The CHAIRMAN. I am informed by the Chairman of the Committee on Credentials that the delegate seated by the National Committee is the delegate.

Mr. BRAYTON. Will the gentleman please have the roll corrected, and have Mr. Sligh's name corrected, and Mr. Ensor's name taken off?

Mr. JOHN H. OSTENDORF, of South Carolina. *Mr. Chairman:* As a member of the Committee on Credentials I beg to state to this Convention that the roll in possession of the Secretary of the Committee on Credentials will show that the name of Dr. Joshua F. Ensor appears upon that roll, and it can be testified and certified to by the Secretary of the Committee on Credentials. [Cries "regular order" and "call the roll."]

The CHAIRMAN. I can only repeat what I stated before, that the Chairman of the Committee informs me that the roll which the Secretary has contains the name of the delegate whom they seated by their report.

Mr. OSTENDORF of South Carolina. Then, Mr. Chairman, I hope that this Convention will call upon the Secretary of the Committee on Credentials and let him state to the Convention what name is on that roll from the Fifth South Carolina District. [Cries "vote, vote."]

The CHAIRMAN. The Secretary will call the roll of the States and Territories.

Mr. ROBBINS of Illinois. *Mr. Chairman:* May I ask that the rule applicable to the manner of voting be read before the vote is taken?

The CHAIRMAN. The Secretary will read Rule 9.

The SECRETARY. "RULE 9. In the record of the votes by States, the vote of each State, Territory and District of Columbia shall be announced by the Chairman, and in case the vote of any State, Territory or District of Columbia, shall be divided, the Chairman shall announce the number of votes cast for any candidate, or for or against any proposition; but, if exception is taken by any delegate to the correctness of such announcement by the Chairman of his delegation, the President of the Convention shall direct the roll of members of such delegation to be called, and the result shall be recorded in accordance with the votes individually given."

Reading Clerk HANEY called the roll of States and Territories, which was responded to by the various delegations as follows:

Alabama—Harrison, 15; William McKinley, Jr., 7.
Arkansas—Harrison, 15; Mc Kinley, 11.   .
California—Harrison, 8; Blaine, 9; McKinley, 1.

A member of the California delegation called for the poll of the State, which was ordered by the Chair with the following results:

M. H. DeYoung, Blaine; Charles N. Felton, Harrison; E. F. Spence, Harrison; N. D. Rideout, Harrison; D. T. Cole, Harrison; E. V. Spencer, Harrison; J. F. Kidder, Blaine; A. J. Rhoads, Blaine; Eli Dennison, Blaine; R. D. Robbins, Blaine; E. S. Pillsbury, Harrison; Joseph S. Speer, Jr., McKinley; O. A. Hale, Blaine; George A. Knight, Blaine; E. P. Johnson, Harrison; R. E. Jack, Blaine; P. Y. Baker, Blaine; R. W. Button, Harrison.

Reading Clerk HANEY:

California—Harrison, 8; Blaine, 9; McKinley, 1.
Colorado—Blaine, 8.
Connecticut—Harrison, 4; McKinley, 8.
Delaware—Harrison, 4; Blaine, 1; McKinley, 1.
Florida—Harrison, 8.
Georgia—Harrison, 26.
Idaho—Blaine, 6.
Illinois—Harrison, 33; Blaine, 15.

Mr. CULLOM. As a delegate from our Delegation challenges the correctness of the count, we ask for a roll call.

The CHAIRMAN. Who questions the correctness of the vote.

Mr. KERR. I question the accuracy of the vote?

The CHAIRMAN. The gentleman from Illinois questions the accuracy of the announcement. The Secretary will call the roll of the delegates.

The roll was called with the following result:

For Harrison—S. M. Cullom, R. J. Oglesby, J. G. Cannon, Joseph Robbins, J. H. Gilbert, Miles Kehoe, George B. Swift, Herman H. Kohlsaat, Solomon H. Bethea, A. C. Stanley, N. M. Steward, W. N. Hannah, E. A. Wilcox, W. A. Rankin, O. F. Price, John A. Gray, Morris Rosenfield, William A. Lorimer, Edward A. Crandall, John

W. Kitchell, Joseph V. Graff, David S. Shellaberger, John Kirby, Patrick Richards, Horace Dollarhide, P. W. Barnes, D. H. Zepp, James A. Gregory, James T. McCasland, Louis Krughoff, T. S. Ridgway, J. Shoemaker, J. P. Roberts, S. L. Taylor.

For Blaine—Samuel B. Raymond, W. R. Kerr, E. J. Magerstadt, William Lorimer, R. L. Martin, F. S. Baird, Henry Wulff, Arthur W. Pulver, I. L. Ellwood, James B. Lane, W. S. Cowan, J. N. Sharp, Joseph F. Durant, T. J. Golden.

Reading Clerk HANEY:

Illinois—Harrison, 34; Blaine, 14. (Continuing the call.)

Indiana—Harrison, 30.

Iowa—William McKinley, 1; James G. Blaine, 5; Benjamin Harrison, 20.

Kansas—Benjamin Harrison, 11; William McKinley, Jr, 9.

Kentucky—Benjamin Harrison, 22; James G. Blaine, 2; William McKinley, 1; Absent, 1.

Louisiana—James G. Blaine, 8; Benjamin Harrison, 8.

Maine—James G. Blaine, 12.

Maryland—Benjamin Harrison, 14; William McKinley, 2.

Massachusetts—Harrison, 18; McKinley, 11; Blaine, 1.

Michigan—Blaine, 2; Harrison, 7; McKinley, 19.

Minnesota—McKinley, 1; Harrison, 8; Blaine, 9.

Mississippi—Blaine, $4\frac{1}{2}$; Harrison, $13\frac{1}{2}$.

Missouri—McKinley, 2; Blaine, 4; Harrison, 28.

Montana—Blaine, 1; Harrison, 5.

Nebraska—Harrison, 15; McKinley, 1.

Nevada—Blaine, 6.

New Hampshire—Harrison, 4; Blaine, 2; Thomas B. Reed, 1; Robert T. Lincoln, 1.

New Jersey—Blaine, 2; Harrison, 18.

New York—Blaine, 35; Harrison, 27; McKinley, 10.

North Carolina—Harrison, $18\frac{2}{3}$; Blaine, $2\frac{1}{3}$; McKinley, 1.

Mr. YOUNG, of North Carolina.

Mr. CHAIRMAN: I challenge the vote of North Carolina.

The CHAIRMAN. The Secretary will call the roll of that State.

The roll was called resulting as follows:
Jeter C. Pritchard, Harrison; Elihu A. White, Harrison; H. P. Cheatham, Harrison; John C. Dancy, Harrison; Claude M. Bernard, Harrison; Hugh Cale, Harrison; John H. Hannon, McKinley; Charles A. Cook, Harrison; A. R. Middleton, Harrison; George C. Scurlock, Harrison; John Nichols, Harrison; Edward A. Johnson, Harrison; Thomas B. Keogh, Harrison; James A. Cheek, Blaine; Archibald Brady, Harrison; James H. Young, Harrison; J. J. Mott, Blaine, $\frac{2}{3}$ vote; Zebulon A. Walser, Harrison, $\frac{2}{3}$ vote; William A. Bailey, Blaine, $\frac{2}{3}$ vote; L. L. Jenkins, Harrison; J. O. Wilcox, Harrison; C. J. Harris, absent; William W. Rollins, alternate, absent; R. W. Logan, Harrison.

Reading Clerk HANEY:

North Carolina—Harrison, $17\frac{2}{3}$; Blaine, $2\frac{1}{3}$; McKinley, 1.

(Roll call continued.)

North Dakota—Harrison, 2; Blaine, 4.

Ohio.

Mr. FORAKER. *Mr. Chairman:* Ohio asks time for consultation.

Mr. NASH. (After a pause.) *Mr. Chairman:* The vote of our delegation shows:

Harrison—2 votes; William McKinley, 44 votes.

Chairman MCKINLEY. I challenge the vote of Ohio.

Mr. FORAKER. The gentleman is not a member of this delegation at present.

Chairman MCKINLEY. I am a member of that delegation.

Mr. AMBLER. The gentleman has left the delegation, to assume a higher position, and has substituted an alternate.

Mr. FORAKER. The gentleman's alternate has taken his place in the delegation and the gentleman is not recognized as a member of the delegation now, and we make that point of order.

The CHAIRMAN. The Chair overrules the point of order, and asks the Secretary to call the roll of Ohio.

Reading Clerk HANEY called the roll which resulted as follows:

William McKinley, Jr., Harrison; Joseph B. Foraker, William McKinley, Jr.; Asa S. Bushell, McKinley; William M. Hahn, McKinley; George B. Cox, McKinley; Charles Fleischman, McKinley; Norman G. Kenan, McKinley; George B. Fox, McKinley; W. E. Crume, McKinley; R. C. McKinney, McKinley; Levi S. Jamison, McKinley; James I. Allread, McKinley; G. L. Marble, McKinley; Oscar C. Eaton, McKinley; Erskine Carson, McKinley; G. W. Stanley, McKinley; Oliver S. Kelly, McKinley; D. I. Worthington, McKinley; C. C. Harris, McKinley; Isaac N. Zearing, McKinley; William H. Tucker, McKinley; John P. Wilson, McKinley; Lucian J. Fenton, McKinley; Samuel Llewellyn, McKinley; John C. Entriken, McKinley; Charles E. Spencer, McKinley; George K. Nash, McKinley; Cyrus Huling, McKinley; George C. Gormley, McKinley; Wilbur C. Brown, McKinley; W. C. Cooper, Harrison; Harry Griffith, McKinley; John H. Riley, McKinley; Wm. A. Johnson, McKinley; Isaac H. Taylor, McKinley; G. A. Keepers, McKinley; M. Luther Smyser, McKinley; William C. Lyon, McKinley; Jacob A. Ambler, McKinley; George E. Baldwin, McKinley; Charles W. F. Dick, McKinley; William Ritezel, McKinley Isaac P. Lamson, McKinley; James A. Allen McKinley; Louis Black, McKinley; Amos Dennison, McKinley

Mr. COOPER, of Ohio. I announced my vote as for Harrison. I wish to have it changed to William McKinley, Jr. [Cheers.]

Mr. NEVIN, of Ohio. That there may be no mistake about it, I want to say that as the alternate for William McKinley, Jr and at his request I originally voted for Benjamin Harrison.

Reading Clerk STONE.

Ohio—McKinley, 45; Harrison, 1.

Reading Clerk HANEY (continuing.)

Oregon—McKinley, 7; Harrison, 1.

Pennsylvania.

Mr. QUAY. Mr. Chairman, there is a difference of opinion in the Pennsylvania delegation and we ask a poll of the vote.

The CHAIRMAN. On account of a misunderstanding in the Pennsylvania delegation, a poll of the vote is asked, and the roll will be called.

Reading Clerk HANEY called the roll resulting as follows:

Hamilton Disston, Harrison; William L. Elkins, Harrison; William Flinn, McKinley; Henry W. Oliver, McKinley; Frank Reeder, McKinley; Samuel A. Davenport, McKinley; H. C. McCormick, McKinley; Lyman D. Gilbert, McKinley; Henry H. Bingham, William McKinley, Jr.; Oliver Wilson, Wm. McKinley, Jr.; David H. Lane, McKinley; Jacob Wildemore, William McKinley, Jr.; Theodore B. Stulb, William McKinley, Jr.; James B. Anderson, William McKinley, Jr.; George S. Graham, Benjamin Harrison [cheers]; A. S. L. Shields, McKinley; David Martin, William McKinley, Jr.; Wilbur F. Short, alternate for John S. McKinlay, William McKinley; Enos Verlenden, McKinley; Thomas S. Butler, James G. Blaine; Jacob A. Strassberger [a voice "call the alternate"] Daniel S. Shiffert (alternate), Benjamin Harrison; E. Wesley Keeler, Benjamin Harrison; M. C. Luckenbach, McKinley; William H. Stroh, Harrison; Augustus M. High, James G. Blaine; James Thomas, McKinley; Dr. John P. Miller, Benjamin Harrison; George R. Sensenige, Benjamin Harrison; Edward N. Willard, Benjamin Harrison; Benjamin Hughes, Benjamin Harrison; Alex. Farnham, Benjamin Harrison; William J. Scott, James G. Blaine; Alexander Scott, Harrison; Christian Lenker, Benjamin Harrison; John E, Fox, William McKinley, Jr.; Jacob H. Grove, Wm. McKinley, Jr.; Galusha A. Grow, (not responding to his name first alternate Martin B. Allen was called and he not responding, second alternate, J. W. Hearst cast one vote for William McKinley, Jr.;) Fred. I. Wheelock, McKinley; Albert M. Bennett, McKinley; William I. Lewis, William McKinley, Jr.; William C. McConnell, Benjamin Harrison; William L. Gouger, Benjamin Harrison; Karl F. Espenshade, William McKinley, Jr.; J. J. Cromer, McKinley; J. C. Lower, McKinley; C. H. Mullen, McKinley; Henry W. Storey, William McKinley; John H. Jardon, absent; alternate, Jasper Augustine, absent; second alternate, John R. Scott, William McKinley, Jr.; J. Owen Edelblute, William McKinley, Jr.; Norman K. Coller, William McKinley, Jr.; Joseph O. Brown, William McKinley, Jr.; Christopher L. Magee, Benjamin Harrison; William Witherow, McKinley; Joseph N. Davidson, William McKinley, Jr.; Frank M. Fuller, William McKinley, Jr.; George M. Von Bonnhorst, Harrison; Matthew S. Quay, William McKinley, Jr.; David W. Pearson, McKinley; Charles M. Reed, McKinley; John J. Carter, Harrison; William W. Brown, Harrison; Thomas B. Simpson, McKinley; Daniel C. Oyster, McKinley; A. Wayne Cook, McKinley.

The secretary announced the vote as follows: McKinley, 42; Harrison, 19; Blaine, 3. [Applause.]

Reading Clerk HANEY.

Rhode Island—Harrison, 5; Blaine, 1; McKinley, 1; Thomas B Reed, 1.

South Carolina—Harrison, 13; Blaine, 3; McKinley, 2.

Mr. E. H. DEAS. *Mr. Chairman:* I call for a call of the roll.

The roll was called resulting as follows:

E. A. Webster, Harrison; W. D. Crum, Harrison; E. H. Deas, Harrison; T. M. Brayton, Blaine; George I. Cunningham, Harrison; John H. Fordham, Harrison; S. E. Smith, McKinley; Paris Simpkins, Harrison; John R. Cochran, Harrison; Abner J. Jamison, Blaine; John P. Scruggs, Harrison; Irving J. Miller, McKinley; J. F. Ensor, no response; E. B. Sligh, [Mr. Ensor's alternate] Blaine; William E. Boykin, Harrison; J. E. Wilson, D. D., Harrison; T. B. Johnston, Harrison; John H. Ostendorff, Harrison; R. H. Richardson, Harrison.

Reading Clerk HANEY.

South Carolina—Harrison, 13; Blaine, 3; McKinley, 2.

Reading Clerk HANEY (continuing):

South Dakota—Harrison, 8.
Tennessee—McKinley, 3; Blaine, 4; Harrison, 17.

[Great confusion.]

Texas—Harrison, 22.

[Loud continued applause and great confusion.]

Chairman MCKINLEY invited Mr. Elliott F. Shepard of New York to the chair, and taking the floor addressed the convention.

Mr. MCKINLEY. *Mr. President and Gentlemen of the Convention:* I move that the rules be suspended and that Benjamin Harrison be nominated for President of the United States by acclamation.

Mr. CLARKSON, of Iowa. *Mr. Chairman:* I second the motion.

Mr. WOLCOTT, of Colorado. *Mr. Chairman:* I rise to a point of order, that we are on the call of the States and nobody has a right to make a motion while the roll call is in progress. There are many here who are not willing to let the judgment of the States before them stand as their judgment in this ballot.

Governor MCKINLEY. In reply to that I desire to say that you can suspend any rule you have by a two-thirds majority and let us do it now.

The CHAIRMAN. All in favor of that motion of Governor McKinley to suspend the rules, seconded by Gen. Clarkson, of Iowa—

Mr. C. B. HART, of West Virginia. *Mr. Chairman:* I make a point of order, that the motion is not in order pending a roll call. Every delegate on this floor has a right to vote, and desires to do so.

The CHAIRMAN. The rules of the Fifty-first Congress are in vogue, and an eminent interpreter of those rules says that we may suspend the rules at any point by a two-thirds vote.

Mr. HART. During the roll call, never.

The CHAIRMAN. This is the ruling of a most distinguished parliamentarian.

Governor McKINLEY. Let me say one word. There are States as I understand that have not been reached that desire to record their vote. And their desire is to record their vote in the direction of my motion, and I therefore, to enable them to do that, withdraw my motion.

Governor McKINLEY again resumed the chair.

Reading Clerk HANEY (continuing the roll call):

Texas—Harrison, 22; Blaine, 6; T. B. Reed, 2.
Vermont—Harrison, 8.
Virginia—Harrison, 9; McKinley, 2; Blaine, 13.
Washington—Blaine, 8.
West Virginia—Harrison, 12.
Wisconsin—Harrison, 19; Blaine, 2; McKinley, 3.
Wyoming—Harrison, 4; Blaine, 2.
Arizona—Harrison, 1; Blaine, 1.
District of Columbia—Blaine, 2.
New Mexico—Harrison, 6.
Oklahoma—Harrison, 2.
Utah—Harrison, 2.
Alaska—Harrison, 2.
Indian Territory—Harrison, 1; Blaine, 1.

The CHAIRMAN: The State of Washington, the Chairman informs me, made an error in the announcement, and he desires to have the correction made, and he has sent the corrected statement to the desk. By unanimous consent we will make change in the count. [Great confusion and cheers.]

The vote of Washington was then announced, giving McKinley 1; Harrison 1; Blaine 6.

(Cries of " Give the vote.")

The CHAIRMAN: The Secretary will announce the result of the vote.

Secretary JOHNSON: Whole number of votes cast 904⅓. Necessary for a choice 453. Benjamin Harrison receives 535 1-6 votes.

James G. Blaine receives 182 1-6 votes. William McKinley receives 182 votes. Robert Lincoln receives 1 vote. Thomas B. Reed receives 4 votes. [Great applause and cheering.]

The CHAIRMAN: President Harrison having received a majority of all the votes cast, shall his nomination be made unanimous? Those favoring such action say "aye." Those opposed, "no."

The nomination is made unanimous. [Great applause.]

The following is the result of the first ballot.

STATES AND TERRITORIES.	Harrison.	Blaine.	McKinley.	Reed.	Lincoln.
Alabama	15	....	7	......	......
Arkansas	15	......	1	....	....
California	8	9	1	......	......
Colorado	...	8	....	......	......
Connecticut	4	....	8	......	....
Delaware	4	1	1	......	....
Florida	8	....	....	......	......
Georgia	26	....	....	......	......
Idaho	....	6	....	....	....
Illinois	34	14	....	......	....
Indiana	30	....	......	......	....
Iowa	20	5	1	......	....
Kansas	11	....	9	......	......
Kentucky	22	2	1	......	......
Louisiana	8	8	....	......	......
Maine	......	12	....	...	...
Maryland	14	....	2	......	....
Massachusetts	18	1	11	......	....
Michigan	7	2	19	......	....
Minnesota	8	9	1	......	....
Mississippi	13½	4½	....	......	....
Missouri	28	4	2	......	....
Montana	5	1	......	......	....
Nebraska	15	....	1	......	....
Nevada	....	6	....	....	....
New Hampshire	4	2	......	1	1
New Jersey	18	2	......	....	...
New York	27	35	10	......	....
North Carolina	17⅔	2⅔	1	....	....
North Dakota	2	4	......	....	....
Ohio	1	......	45	....	...
Oregon	1	......	7	......	....
Pennsylvania	19	3	42	......	....
Rhode Island	5	1	1	1	......
South Carolina	13	3	2	......	....
South Dakota	8	....	....	....	....
Tennessee	17	4	3	...	....
Texas	22	6	......	2	....
Vermont	8	....	....	......	....
Virginia	9	13	2	......	....
Washington	1	6	1	......	....
West Virginia	12	....	....	......	...
Wisconsin	19	2	3	......	....
Wyoming	4	2	....	......	....
Alaska	2	....	......	......	....
Arizona	1	1	......	....	....
Indian Territory	1	1	......	...	...
New Mexico	6	....	......	....	....
Oklahoma	2	......	....	....	....
Utah	2	......	....	....	....
District of Columbia	......	2	......	...	....
Totals	535 1-6	182 1-6	182	4	1

Mr. INGALLS, of Kansas. *Mr. Chairman:* I send to the desk a resolution which I wish read and unamious consent that it be passed.

The CHAIRMAN. Senator Ingalls offers the following resolution which I think should pass. The Reading Clerk will read the resolution.

The Reading Clerk read the following resolution:

"RESOLVED: That the Secretary of the Convention prepare a full report of the National Republican Conventions of 1856, 1860 and 1864, and cause them to be sold at the cost of printing; and a similar arrangement shall also be made for the publication of the proceedings of this Convention.
Resolution adopted unanimously.

Mr. DEPEW, of New York. *Mr. Chairman:* I move that this Convention take a recess until 8 o'clock this evening.

The CHAIRMAN. The gentleman from New York, Mr. Depew, moves that this Convention take a recess until 8 o'clock this evening. Those in favor will say "aye." Those opposed, "no." The ayes have it.

Then at 4:44 P. M. the Convention took a recess until 8 o'clock.

EVENING SESSION.

FRIDAY, June 10th, 1892.

CHAIRMAN McKINLEY called the Convention to order at 8:55 P.M.

The CHAIRMAN. The Convention will come to order. The next order of business is the presentation of candidates for Vice-President. The Secretary will call the roll of States.

Mr. BAIRD, of Illinois. If it is in order I would like to make a motion at this time. There are a great many seats in the galleries that are empty and there are a great many people outside who have no tickets. I would move that the sergeant-at-arms be directed to open the galleries and admit the people who are now outside.

The CHAIR—The sergeant-at-arms informs me that an order of that kind has already been made.

Chief Reading Clerk HANEY.

Alabama, Arkansas, California, Colorado, Connecticut, Delaware, Florida, Georgia, Idaho, Illinois, Indiana, Iowa, Kansas, Kentucky, Louisiana, Maine, Maryland, Massachusets, Michigan Minnesota, Mississippi, Missouri, Montana, Nebraska, Nevada, New Hampshire, New Jersey, New York.

EDMUND O'CONOR, of New York. *Mr. Chairman :*

The CHAIRMAN. The gentleman from New York.

Mr. O'CONOR came to the platform.

Mr. CHAIRMAN : At a meeting of the New York delegation regularly called, in the absence of Senator Miller I was designated its Chairman and instructed by the unanimous voice of the delegation to present the name of a distinguished citizen of the State New York in nomination for vice-President. As you all know, the great majority of the delegation, since the opening of the Convention, have been working very strenuously for the nomination of a candidate that this Convention in its wisdom did not see fit to sanction ; but we want to notify the Republican delegates from every part of the United States that that large majority subordinate their personal views and acquiesce in the wisdom of this Convention. We want to assure you that in our opposition to the nomination of the successful candidate there was nothing of a personal nature, and we now recognize the duty of every Republican to bow loyally to the judgment of this Convention. We believe, however, that New York State ought to be aided in the great struggle it will have to make to land that State in the Republican column ; and I believe the gentleman whom I shall name will aid us materially in accomplishing that purpose. I will not detain this Convention. Gen. Horace Porter of the city of New York will tell this Convention the distinguished claims of the gentleman I shall nominate. I therefore will conclude my labors in behalf of the New York State delegation by placing in nomination for the Vice-Presidency of the United States Hon. Whitelaw Reid, of New York.

Mr. HORACE PORTER, of New York. *Mr. Chairman :*

The CHAIRMAN. I have the pleasure of presenting Gen. Horace Porter of New York.

Gen. PORTER. *Mr. Chairman, and Gentlemen of the Convention:* I rise on behalf of the New York delegation to commend to you the distinguished gentleman whose name has just been pronounced as a candidate for the vice-Presidency by the Chairman of that delegation. This gentleman, by his private worth and public services, has well commended himself, not only to the people of the Empire State, but to the people of all the States throughout the Union. His name, his character, his services will give an assurance that he will carry out the policy of the party; that he will stand strong in the affections of his fellow citizens ; that he will command the unqualified respect of all the civilized globe. He is pre-eminently to-day New York's favorite son. On our side of politics we have not been as prolific in favorite sons as the Democracy. New York has given birth to two favorite sons. There we have twins, but unlike other twins, even the parents who begat them, cannot trace any marked resemblance between them. Mr. Reid began his career and continued his service in the broad and instructive field of American journalism. He became the legitimate and worthy successor to that great creator of modern journalism, Horace Greeley. So broad were Mr. Reid's views, so thoroughly was he informed in everything pertaining to the country's history and the country's success that the people demanded, and in recognition of their wish, the appointing power selected him as minister to France at a very important crisis in the diplomatic relations of our two countries.

We were glad to see him serve as minister from the oldest Republic of the new world to the newest Republic of the old world. Scarcely was he installed in office when there fell upon him for solution the most complicated, the most intricate questions that had ever arisen in diplomacy between the two countries. That he solved them successfully, met them boldly, is a matter of inexpressible pride to every one who honors the American name. In the exhibits at the French exposition he brought order out of chaos. He negotiated a most important extradition treaty. He succeeded in securing France as the first nation to accept our Nation's invitation to the International Columbian fair. He secured France as the first nation to give her assent to the terms of our international copyright. He negotiated there an important reciprocity treaty. And last he achieved his greatest triumph in that warfare of intellectual giants in securing the repeal of the prohibitory duties upon American pork. In that he showed himself the master of modern diplomacy. Throughout those complicated transactions he retained the absolute confidence of his own government and secured the sympathy and respect of the great government to which he was accredited. His duty done, he resigned the office which he never sought, and made manifest his feeling that the post of honor is the private station. When he returned to our shores all the honors in the land were heaped upon him. He was made an honorary member of the chamber of commerce and of many important societies. He was everywhere given banquets in his honor. His name is one which stands without reproach. There is no blotch on his escutcheon. He has not had to learn that reproach is a concomitant of greatness. He is an eminently practical man. He has always tried to perform not what he knows, but what he can do. He has been a loyal party man. He has always placed loyalty to party next only to loyalty to his Nation. He believes, as you, Mr. Chairman, and as every delegate, I think, on this floor believes, in the necessity of party; believes that the end of party is the origin of faction; the abandonment of party is the beginning of anarchy. It is said that Mr. Reid has had difficulties with the Typographical Union. That has all been amicably settled. We have that statement from the president of that organization, who is here present today and has placed it in writing. Give us Mr. Reid and his name and his services will do more than those of any other in assisting in the campaign there. Give us him and we will give you a victory next November. Bring forth the banners, inscribe them with Harrison and Reid. With those two marshals in the van we shall enter upon that campaign with no doubts to shake our purposes; with no ill-advised measures to dampen the ardor of the campaign. We shall have no deserters from our ranks. We shall have recruits flocking to our standard from every quarter. With all our battalions in the field, with all our columns on the march, with our banners inscribed with the proud record of past successes, we shall move on to final triumph and fall not until our banners sound the glad notes of victory.

Mr. BUCKLEY, of Connecticut. *Mr. Chairman:*

The CHAIRMAN. Governor Buckley, of Connecticut, is recognized.

Governor Buckley came to the platform.

Mr. BUCKLEY. *Mr. Chairman and Gentlemen of the Convention*: As a sister State and closely allied to the State of New York, at the request of the Connecticut delegation I am here to second the nomination of Whitelaw Reid, and I am pleased to say as I stand here, although we are not in Connecticut always pleased to be classed as a doubtful State, to assure the Republicans assembled here in this great Convention, that while we appeared here on this floor to-day in favor of another candidate then the one you have selected for the President of the United States, you will find in the Republicans of Connecticut the same loyalty and the same energetic endeavor for success which we gave to Benjamin Harrison four years ago. And I am also proud to stand here as a representative of one of the old thirteen states, and the State which gave to the country and to the world the first written constitution under which a free people ever lived, and on the construction of which was largely modeled the constitution under which the great and prosperous people of this country live to-day. The Republicans of Connecticut acquiesce heartily and warmly in the decision of this Convention, and we shall acquiesce as warmly and well if you add to the ticket the name of Whitelaw Reid. It is a gratification to me to meet this grand Convention representing a party so grand and which has exercised so great an influence and accomplished so much good for this grand country in which we live.

I am satisfied that if the nomination which New York asks of this convention is granted to-night, and the ticket under which we shall march from now till November next is Harrison and Reid, [applause,] the success, not only of our candidates, but of the grand principles for which we fight always and loyally, will be achieved, and for a generation to come the country will live and prosper under the principles enunciated in the platform which you have formulated and adopted in this Convention.

The CHAIRMAN. Are there any further nominations?

Mr. JOHN A. HUTCHINSON, of West Virginia. *Mr. Chairman :* I move that the nomination of Mr. Reid be made by acclamation.

The motion was seconded.

Mr. J. T. SETTLE, of Tennessee. *Mr. Chairman:* I think I had the floor before the gentleman over at the other end of the building arose to his feet, and in obedience to the request of the delegation from Tennessee I desire to make a nomination.

The CHAIRMAN. The gentleman from Tennsssee is recognized.

Mr. SETTLE. *Mr. Chairman:* Under ordinary circumstances we who live in the far off South land do not have much to say about nominating candidates for President and for vice-president. We prefer rather to let you gentlemen who live in the Republican States in the North to make the nominations and then do what we can to help you elect them. But Tennessee to-day feels that she has a right to ask this Convention to nominate a man for vice-President who is as intensely American as any man who breathes air upon the American continent—a man who

—10

has demonstrated to the American people his ability at all times and under all circumstances to make American citizenship respected all over this broad land, a man who was able to and who did stop the Democratic party in the halls of the American Congress from fillibustering and who succeeded in giving us a business government. A man who believes that citizenship in Tennessee or in Louisiana is entitled to the same protection that it has in New York or Connecticut. Tennessee, Mr. Chairman, places in nomination for the vice-President of the United States one of the grandest characters in American politics, Thomas B. Reid of Maine. [Applause, and cries for Reid.]

The CHAIRMAN. Are there any further nominations? Shall we dispense with the further call of the roll?

Mr. C. M. LOUTHAN, of Virginia. *Mr. Chairman:*

The CHAIRMAN. The gentleman from Virginia.

Mr. LOUTHAN. *Mr. Chairman and Gentlemen of the Convention:* The name of Thomas B. Reed, of Maine, ought to be sacred not only to the consideration of every Southern man, but to the consideration of every citizen of this great country of ours. I have the honor to say to this Convention that there is no name that by any possibility can be named from Maine to Texas, from Oregon to Florida, which would excite grander or wilder enthusiasm in the Republican ranks than that of Thomas B. Reed, of Maine. As I sat in my seat as a member of the Virginia delegation, when that name was mentioned, it struck as by the power of magic; and if Mr. Reed be nominated by this Convention as a candidate for Vice-President, I am satisfied that he will give great strength to the Republican ticket. And why do I say so?

We have heard much said about the tariff question, and that is a question of great importance. We have heard much said about the question of silver, and that, too, is a question of grand importance to this people; but there is a question which rides above every other one, and that involves the rights, the freedom of American citizens. What we want in the far South land is a free ballot and a fair count. What we want above and beyond every other consideration is that every man's vote may be cast and that it may be counted as cast. Let us pause upon the threshold. I know not which of these gentlemen may be nominated by this Convention. I know it to be true that the name of Whitelaw Reid is one that will excite enthusiasm wherever it is mentioned, but I am satisfied that the name of Thomas B. Reed, of Maine, is one that will thrill this nation wherever heard. I say to you, gentlemen of the Convention, that grand as is the name of William McKinley, than which there is none grander in all this galaxy of States, grand as is the name of John Sherman, than which there is none grander in all this galaxy of States, grand as is the name of Benjamin Harrison, whom we have just nominated and whom in November we will elect, grand as is the name of the plumed knight who excites admiration and the very wonder and the gratitude and affection of his followers all over this land, there is none to whom the American people owe a higher debt of gratitude than to Thomas B. Reed, of Maine. And I second the nomination of Mr. Reed, not in behalf of the Virginia delegation, not in behalf of the delegation from Tennessee, not in behalf of the delegation from Georgia, not in behalf of the delegation from Pennsylvania, or New York, or Indiana, or Ohio, but in behalf of the great Republican party of this great Nation. [Applause.]

Mr. LITTLEFIELD, of Maine. *Mr. Chairman :*

The CHAIRMAN. General Littlefield, of Maine.

Mr. LITTLEFIELD. *Mr. President :* In behalf of the Maine delegation, I ask the delegates to this Convention to decline to cast any votes for the Hon. Thomas B. Reed, of Maine, for the office of Vice President until they can be assured that the gentlemen have authority to present his name to this Convention. I say to you, Mr. Chairman and gentlemen of the Convention, that it is the opinion of the Maine delegation that Mr. Reed would decline the nomination if tendered to him by this convention; and, therefore, I request the delegates not to vote for Thomas B. Reed until they are assured that it is by his authority that his name is used in this Convention.

Mr. SETTLE. I have had no conference with Mr. Reed. I do not know the gentleman; I would not know him if I should meet him on the road [laughter], but I only voice the sentiment of the people of this country from one end to the other. I do not insist upon it. I have been glad of an opportunity to present to this convention the idea, the thought, that, whilst assembled here in the midst of this grand deliberative body, there should be at least a tribute to the exalted genius of this greatest of Republicans in this great land of ours.

Mr. LOUTHAN. It was at the request of the delegation from Tennessee that I had the honor of placing the distinguished gentleman from Maine before this Convention. We had not seen him nor had we consulted with the delegation from Maine, but we placed him in nomination because he was grand and great enough to excite our admiration and love. [Applause.] But while we do delight to honor Mr. Reed, because we do think that he is one of the grandest heroes in American politics today— while we do think that he would be a tower of strength to the ticket—while we do think that he could do more, perhaps, in the South—no, not more than any other great American, but as much —still, in deference to the opinion of the gentleman from Maine I withdraw his name.

Mr. KEARNEY, of Iowa. I move you that the nomination of Whitelaw Reid for Vice President of the United States be now made by acclamation. I move to suspend the rules and make the nomination by acclamation.

The CHAIRMAN. The gentleman from West Virginia earlier moved that the rules be suspended and that the Hon. Whitelaw Reid be declared nominated by acclamation. Are you ready for the question?

The question being put to a vote and the ayes and noes being taken the Chairman said:

The Chairman. In the opinion of the Chair more than two-thirds have voted in the affirmative, and the rules are suspended and the nomination is made. Shall it be unanimous? Those favoring it will say it aye.

The motion was carried unanimously.

[Three cheers were given for Whitelaw Reid.]

The Chairman. The next order of business is the appointment of Committees, to notify the nominees of their nomination.

Reading Clerk Haney, read the following announcement:

The new National Committee will meet immediately after the adjournment of this Convention at the rooms of the National Committee in the West Hotel.

Mr. Depew. *Mr. Chairman:* I beg leave to introduce the following resolution.

Reading Clerk Stone read the resolution as follows:

"Resolved, that in the organization of the American Republican College league, an event significant in American politics, the young Republicans of the colleges and universities of the Nation have merited our congratulation and highest commendation, and we welcome them to the ranks of the party in an active participation in the affairs of State."

The resolution was carried unanimously.

Mr Shepard, of New York. *Mr. Chairman:*

I wish to offer a resolution, and beg that Senator Cullom of Illinois may be invited to take the chair.

Senator Cullom was invited to the chair.

Reading Clerk Stone read the resolution.

Resolved, That the thanks of this Convention and of the whole Republican party are due and tendered to Hon. William McKinley, Jr., of Ohio, for the splendid, impartial and courteous way in which he has discharged his duties as the presiding officer of this Convention. We wish Gov. McKinley a prosperous administration in Ohio, health and happiness in his private life, and an increasing usefulness in the service of his country.

Chairman Cullom. *Gentlemen:* You have heard the resolution just read. All those in favor of its adoption will say aye.

The motion was carried unanimously, and three cheers were given for Gov. McKinley.

Chairman Cullom. If the Convention will allow it, the present occupant of the chair will put the motion in another form. Those in favor of the resolution read will rise and stand until you are counted.

The entire Convention stood up and cheered again for Gov·
McKinley.

Chairman CULLOM.   There are 960 delegates standing, and there
is no necessity of a further count.

Reading Clerk STONE read the following resolution :

RESOLVED, That the thanks of this Convention are also extended
to the Secretary, Charles W. Johnson, to Col. C. F. Meek, the
Sergeant-at-arms, and to all the other officers of this Convention
for the manner in which they have discharged their respective
responsibilities devolved upon them by the Convention.

RESOLVED, That the members of this Convention extend their
hearty thanks to the patriotic citizens of Minneapolis for their
liberality in their provision for the accommodation and comfort
of all the delegates, their families and friends ; and we wish them
to see that their broad, populous and fertile State shall cast its
electoral vote for Harrison and the Republican National ticket
nominated within this magnificent hall.

Chairman CULLOM.   The Chair will take occasion to divide the
resolution, first voting upon the resolution of thanks to the subordinate officers of the Convention-

The first clause of the resolution was unamiously carried.

Chairman CULLOM.   The Chair will now put that portion of the
resolution thanking the citizens of Minneapolis for their splendid
entertainment of the Convention throughout the session.   All
those who are in favor of the resolution will rise to their feet.

Mr. SHEPARD (New York)—Cannot the galleries join in this vote ?

The CHAIRMAN.   Yes.   Let all stand up.

The resolution was unanimously adopted by a rising vote of
every delegate and the 10,000 spectators, who greeted its passage
with tremendous applause and three cheers for the resolution.

Chairman MCKINLEY resumed the chair.

Mr. CLARKSON, of Iowa.   *Mr. Chairman:*

The CHAIRMAN.   The Gentleman from Iowa, Gen. CLARKSON.

Mr. CLARKSON.   I offer the following resolutions :

Reading Clerk HANEY read the resolution as follows:

Resolved, That the   thanks   of this   body   are hereby   expressed to the people of the City of Minneapolis, for the complete
and superior accomodations that they have provided for the
national Convention; the unequaled and commodious hall and the
generous and adequate provision for the entertainment of visitors;
the unusual hospitality of the city and its people have been
worthy of all commendations.   The labors devolving upon the
executive committee, led by the Hon. George A. Brackett, have
been large and exacting, but have been performed alike with
thoroughness and fidelity.   This convention and the great

assemblage of people attending it, have proved that Minneapolis as a Convention City is equal to any demands which may hereafter be made upon its generosity or capacity.

Chairman McKINLEY. Similar resolutions have been sent to the desk from very many delegates and from very many of the States represented in this Convention. Those agreeing to the resolution just read will manifest it by rising to their feet.

The convention arose in a body.

The CHAIRMAN. We have several invitations extended to the Convention which will be read and placed on file. One is from' the Zenith City of the unsalted sea.

The invitations were read as follows:

To the Delegates and Alternates of the National Republican Convention; The comercial organizations of Duluth extend a cordial invitation to you to visit our city and be our guests. A special train will leave the Union depot tomorrow morning at 10 o'clock. Full information will be given at Duluth Headquarters, Room 425, Lumber Exchange, which will be open until midnight.
Signed by the Duluth Chamber of Commerce, the Duluth Jobbers, the Union Real Estate Exchange and Stock Exchange.

WINONA, Minn., June 10, 1892.—The people of the City of Winona send greeting to the Chairman, Officers, Delegates and Alternates to the National Republican Convention now in session at Minneapolis, and to all other persons in attendance there, and cordially invite them to the celebration of our 116th anniversary of the National Independence on July 4, 1892, at Winona, on the occasion of the dedication and opening of the high steel bridge which is to bind in still closer and more fraternal bonds the great States of Wisconsin and Minnesota.

M. LOYE,
Mayor of the City of Winona.

FRANK L. RANDALL, Chairman, ⎫
O. H. CLARK, Secretary,   ⎬ Committtee on Invitations.

The CHAIRMAN. We have also a telegram which will be read.

Reading Clerk KENYON read the following:

"Oregon has indorsed Republican principles by 8,000 'majority [cheers] and will give President Harrison 10,000 in November. [Cheers.] Legislature Republican in both branches. [Cheers.]
E. T. McCORMICK, Secretary.
W. BOYCE,
Chairman State Central Committee."

Mr. M. H. DEYOUNG. *Mr. Chairman:*

The CHAIRMAN. The gentleman from California.

Mr. DEYOUNG. In behalf of the members of the press in this city I desire to offer the following resolution:

The CHAIRMAN. The Secretary will read the resolution.

The Reading CLERK read the resolution as follows:

Resolved, That the thanks of this Convention be tendered to the Press Committee for the excellent facilities and arrangements provided for newspaper correspondents; particularly to Col. Pierce, Mr. Nind, Mr. Harris and Maj. Brackett, of the Executive Committee.

The resolution was unanimously adopted.

Mr. CULLOM. *Mr. Chairman:*

The CHAIRMAN. The gentleman from Illinois.

Mr. CULLOM. I desire the Secretary to read the following resolution.

The Reading CLERK read the resolution:

Resolved, That the President of this Convention, Hon. William McKinley, Jr., be appointed Chairman of the Committee to notify the nominee for President, and that such Chairman be requested to call the Committee together and give notice of the time and place of their meeting.

Mr. CANNON. I will state to the Convention that this is the usual resolution, and I move its adoption. For the moment I will assume the Presidency of the Convention and put the motion. All those in favor of the adoption of this resolution say aye.

The resolution was unanimously adopted.

The CHAIRMAN. Immediately upon the adjournment of this Convention the Committee to notify the President of the United States will meet on this platform.

Mr. MAGEE, of Pennsylvania. *Mr. Chairman:*

The CHAIRMAN. The gentleman from Pennsylvania.

Mr. MAGEE. I offer the following resolution:

Reading CLERK:

Resolved, That the services of the retiring National Committee in the campaign of 1888 entitles the members to the thanks of the Republican party of the Nation.

(Carried unanimously.)

The CHAIRMAN. The Secretary will now call the roll of States to receive the report from delegations of the names of the members of the Committees to notify the nominees for President and Vice President of the United States.

Reading Clerk STONE called the roll, and the following is the list of members of such committees as designated by the several States and Territories.

Secretary JOHNSON announced a special meeting of National and State Republican League officers at the rooms of the Republican National Committee in the West Hotel to-morrow morning at 10 o'clock.

The CHAIRMAN. Is there any further business before this Convention?

Mr. LORIMER (Illinois). *Mr. President:* I move we now adjourn.

The CHAIRMAN. The gentleman from Illinois, Mr. Lorimer, moves that this Convention do now adjourn.

The motion was carried unanimously, and the Chairman announced that the Convention now stands adjourned *sine die.*

COMMITTEE TO NOTIFY THE PRESIDENT.

Alabama ....Chas. O. Harris ....Montgomery.
Arkansas ....L. Altheimer.............Pine Bluff.
California .... Chas. N. Felton..........San Mateo, U.S. Senate
Colorado...........Hon. Hosea Townsend..Silver Cliff.
Connecticut ......Hon. Morgan G.Bulkley.Hartford.
Delaware ....Geo. W. Marshall........Milford.
Florida ....Jas. A. Spann............Pensacola.
Georgia............ ....
Idaho ....Hon. Fred T. DuBois....U. S. Senate.
Illinois ....Jas. H. Gilbert........ ..Chicago.
Indiana............J. B. Homan...... .....Danville.
Iowa ....C. W. Mullan ....Waterloo.
Kansas ....Calvin Hood............Emporia.
Kentucky......... L. P. Tarlton............Frankfort.
Louisiana ....A. Hero, Jr..............New Orleans.
Maine ....E. B. Mallette, Jr........Freeport.
Maryland ....Maj. Alexander Shaw...Baltimore.
Massachusetts.....Wm. Cogswell...... ....Salem.
Michigan ....Dexter M. Ferry........Detroit.
Minnesota.........D. S. Hall .... Stewart.
Mississippi ....S. S. Mathews.......... Winona.
Missouri ....Hon. Chas. C. Bell.......Booneville.
Montana ....A. B. Hammond....... Missoula.
Nebraska ....Axlee Hart ....Dakota City.
Nevada ....
New Hampshire...Geo. T. Cruft............Bethlehem.
New Jersey ....Alexander Gilbert......Plainfield.
New York.........Elliott F. Shepard.......New York City.
North Carolina....Hon. H. P. Cheatham...Littleboro.
North Dakota......Col. W. H. Robinson ....Mayville.
Ohio ....Hon. Jos. B. Foraker....Cincinnati.
Oregon ....C. M. Donaldson.........Baker City.
Pennsylvania .....Alexander Farnham....Wilkesbarre.
Rhode Island......Sam'l P. Colt ....Bristol.
South Carolina....E. H. Deas.... ....Darlington.
South Dakota......Alex. C. Johnson ....Watertown.
Tennessee ....E. F. Hoyt..............Chattanooga.
Texas ....W. F. Crawford.........Cameron.
Vermont..........W. R. Page.............Rutland.
Virginia ....
Washington ....William Kirkman.......Walla Walla.
West Virginia.....George M. Bowers.......Martinsburg.
Wisconsin ....Thomas M. Blackstock..Sheboygan.
Wyoming..........S. W. Downey...........Laramee City.
Alaska ....
Arizona ....M. W. Stewart....,......Wilcox.
Dist. of Columbia.Perry H. Carson.........Washington, D. C.
New Mexico........Miguel A. Otero.........Los Vegas.
Oklahoma ....A. J. Seay..............Guthrie.
Utah......C. C. Goodwin...........Ogden.
Indian Territory ..Frank S. Genung........Muscogee.

COMMITTEE TO NOTIFY THE VICE-PRESIDENT.

Alabama	A. N. McEwan	Mobile
Arkansas		
California	R. E. Jack	San Louis Obispo
Colorado	Judd L. Brush	Greeley
Connecticut	Hon. James P. Platt	Meriden
Delaware	George W. Marshall	Milford
Florida	John F. Hart	Key West
Georgia		
Idaho	Hon. Fred T. Dubois	U. S. Senate
Illinois	Isaac L. Ellwood	DeKalb
Indiana	W. T. Durbin	Anderson
Iowa	J. L. Carney	Marshalltown
Kansas	C. W. Little	Alma
Kentucky	Dan'l Davis	Parrettsville
Louisiana	J. W. Booth	Point a la Hache
Maine	E. F. Webb	Waterville
Maryland	John T. Ensor	Baltimore
Massachusetts	Walter Clifford	New Bedford
Michigan	Fred E. Lee	Dowagiac
Minnesota	Dan'l Schell	Worthington
Mississippi	A. T. Wimberly	Mayersville
Missouri	Hon. Joseph E. Black	Richmond
Montana	Thomas Couch	Butte City
Nebraska	L. E. Walker	Beatrice
Nevada		
New Hampshire	Charles T. Means	Manchester
New Jersey	Dr. H. C. H. Herald	Newark
New York	Hon. H. H. Warner	Rochester
North Carolina	James H. Young	Wilmington
North Dakota	John A. Percival	Devils Lake
Ohio	W. C. Lyon	Newark
Oregon	C. M. Donaldson	Baker City
Pennsylvania	Hon. H. H. Bingham	Philadelphia
Rhode Island	Henry A. Stearns	Lincoln
South Carolina	J. H. Fordham	Orangeburg
South Dakota	James Halley	Rapid City
Tennessee	G. Q. Boyd	Clarksville
Texas	W. E. Davis	Fort Worth
Vermont	W. R. Page	Rutland
Virginia		
Washington	William Kirkman	Walla Walla
West Virginia	J. E. Dana	Charleston
Wisconsin	T. B. Reid	Appleton
Wyoming	F. W. Mondell	New Castle
Arizona	Gov. N. O. Murphy	Phoenix
Dist. of Columbia	Andrew Gleason	Washington
New Mexico	T. B. Catron	Santa Fe
Oklahoma	A. W. Marquardt	Norman
Utah	James T. Hammond	Salt Lake City
Indian Territory	Frank S. Genung	Muscogee

NOTIFICATION OF THE CANDIDATES.

BENJAMIN HARRISON NOTIFIED.

The committee to notify the Nominee for President, assembled under the call of their Chairman, Gov. Wm. McKinley, Jr., at the Ebbitt House, Washington, on the 20th day of June. The following is the list of Committeemen on hand:

Charles O. Harris, Alabama; Louis Altheimer, Arkansas; C. N. Felton, California; Hosea Townsend, Colorado; M. C. Buckley, Connecticut; J. A. Spann, Florida; C. C. Wimbish, Georgia; F. T. Dubois, Idaho; James M. Gilbert, Illinois; J. B. Homan, Indiana; C. W. Mullan, Iowa; L. B. Tarlton, Kentucky; Andrew Hero, Louisiana; Alex. Shaw, Maryland; Wm. Cogswell, Massachusetts; Dexter M. Ferry, Michigan; Samuel Schell, Minnesota; S. S. Matthews, Mississippi; Charles C. Bell, Missouri; O. B. Hammond, Montana; Andrew Gleason, District of Columbia; M. W. Stewart, Arizona; Axlee Hart, Nebraska; Alex. Ebert, New Jersey; E. F. Shepard, New York; Henry Cheatham, North Carolina; William H. Robinson, North Dakota; J. B. Foraker, Ohio; Charles M. Donaldson, Oregon; Alex. Farnham, Pennsylvania; J. W. Case, Rhode Island; E. H. Deas, South Carolina; E. F. Hoyt, Tennessee; Wilbur F. Crawford, Texas; William R. Page, Vermont; Edgar Allen, Virginia; William Kirkman, Washington; George M. Bowers, West Virginia; Thomas M. Blacklock, Wisconsin; Miguel A. Otero, New Mexico.

At one o'clock the Committee proceeded to the Executive Mansion, where they were met by about two hundred other guests and friends of President Harrison. The East Room was beautifully decorated when the Committee entered and ranged themselves in a semicircle, Governor McKinley being the keystone of the arch. A few moments later the President, leaning on the arm of Secretary Foster, and followed by the other members of his Cabinet, entered, and without any preliminaries Governor McKinley made his brief speech officially informing the President of his nomination. It was as follows:

President Harrison: This Committee, representing every State and Territory in the Union, are here to perform the trust committed to them by the National Republican Convention, which convened at Minneapolis on June 7, 1892, of bringing you official notification of your nomination as the Republican candidate for President of the United States.

We need hardly assure you of the pleasure it gives us to convey this message from the Republicans of the country to their chosen leader. Your nomination was but the registering by the Convention of the will of the majority of the Republicans of the United

States, and has been received in every quarter with profound satisfaction.

In 1888 you were nominated, after a somewhat prolonged struggle upon a platform which declared with clearness the purposes and policies of the party if entrusted with power, and upon that platform you were elected President. You have had the good fortune to witness the execution of most of those purposes and policies during the Administration of which you have been the head, and in which you have borne a most conspicuous part. If there has been failure to embody into law any one of those purposes or policies, it has been no fault of yours.

Your administration has more than justified your nomination four years ago, and the confidence of the people implied by your election. After one of the most careful, successful and brilliant Administrations in our history, you receive a renomination, furnishing an approval of your work which must bring to you the keenest gratification. To be nominated for a second term upon the merits of his Administration is the highest distinction which can come to an American President. The difficult and embarrassing questions which confronted your Administration have been met with an ability, with a fidelity to duty and with a lofty patriotism which fill the American heart with glowing pride. Your domestic policy has been wise, broad and statesmanlike; your foreign policy firm, just and truly American. Those have won the commendation of the thoughtful and conservative, and the confidence of your countrymen, irrecspetive of party, and will, we believe, insure your triumphant election in November.

We beg to hand to you the platform of principles unanimously adopted by the Convention which placed you in nomination. It is an American document. Protection, which shall serve the highest interests of American labor and American development; reciprocity, which, while seeking the world's markets for our surplus products, shall not destroy American wages or surrender American markets for products which can be made at home; honest money, which shall rightly measure the labor and exchanges of the people and cheat nobody; honest elections, which are the true foundation of all public authority—these principles constitute for the most part the platform—principles to which you have already by word and deed given your earnest approval, and of which you stand to-day the exponent and representative. Other matters treated of in the platform will have your careful consideration.

I am bidden by my associates, who come from every section of the Nation, to assure you of the cordial and hearty support of a harmonious and united Republican party.

In conclusion we desire to extend to you our personal congratulations, and to express our gratification at the rare honor paid you by a renomination, with a firm faith that the destinies of this great people will be confided to your care and keeping for another four years.

The speech excited the enthusiasm of those present to a remarkable degree, almost every sentence being received with hearty applause, and at its close the demonstrations of approval were earnest and long continued.

The President in accepting the nomination said:

Governor McKinley and Gentlemen of the Committee: When four years ago, on the anniversary of the declaration of our National independence, a Committee designated by the Republican National Convention held in Chicago came to my home in Indianapolis to notify me of my nomination for the Presidency, my sense of gratitude, great as it was, was forced into the far background by an overwhelming sense of the responsibility of leadership in a civil contest that involved so much to my country and to my fellow citizens. I could not hope that much would be found when the record of a quiet life had been brought under the strong light of public criticism to enthuse my party followers, or upon which an assurance of adequacy for the highest civil affairs might be rested. No one so much as I realized that the strength of the campaign must be found in Republican principles; and my hope was that nothing in life or word of mine might weaken the appeal of our American policies to the American heart. That appeal did not fail. A Republican President and Vice-President and a Republican Congress were chosen.

The record has been made, and we are now to submit it to the judgment of a patriotic people. Of my own relation to the great transactions in legislation and in administration which must be the basis of this judgment, it does not become me to speak.

I gratefully accept, sir, the assurance given by the Republican State Conventions and by the National Convention, through you, that no charge of inadequacy or delinquency to principle has been lodged against the Administration. The faithful and highly successful work done by the able heads of the executive departments, and by our representatives abroad, I desire most cordially to acknowledge and commend. The work of the LIst Congress, in which you, sir, bore so conspicuous and useful a part, will strongly and most beneficially influence the National prosperity for generations to come.

The general results of three years of Republican control have, I believe, been highly beneficial to all classes of our people. The home market for farm products has been retained and enlarged by the establishment of great manufacturing industries; while new markets abroad of large and increasing value, long obstinately closed to us, have been opened on favored terms to our meats and breadstuffs, by the removal of unjust discriminating restrictions and by numerous reciprocal trade agreements under section 3 of the McKinley bill. These acts of administration and legislation can now fortunately be judged by their fruits. In 1890 it was a conflict of predictions; now our adversaries must face trade statistics and prices current.

But it is not appropriate that I should at this time discuss these public questions. I hope before long to be able by letter to convey to you a more formal acceptance of the nomination which the National Republican Convention has tendered me, and to give briefly my reasons for adhering to the declaration of principles adopted by the Convention, and which you have so admirably summarized.

Will you accept, sir, for yourself and your associates upon the Committee, and for the whole body of the great Convention whose delegates you are, my profound thanks for this great honor? And will you, sir, allow me to express my most sincere appreciation of the gracious and cordial terms in which you have conveyed this message?

The President's speech was also received with enthusiasm, hearty applauses following every point. At its close the members of the Committee pressed forward and congratulated him on his nomination. Those not already known to him were introduced by Governor McKinley. He shook hands cordially with each member of the Committee, and when all had been received, invited them to luncheon. As the party were about leaving the East room, E. F. Shepard, of New York, mounted a chair and proposed three cheers "for the President of the United States." They were given with a will, Mr. Shepard leading. He next proposed three more for "Benjamin Harrison, who will be re-elected President by a larger majority of votes than he received in 1888." Again the applause rang out and continued while the party proceeded to the State dining room, the President leading with Governor McKinley. Other invited guests to a considerable number followed. The luncheon consisted of sweetbreads, with peas, cold ham, tongue, chicken, lobster and chicken salads, creams, ices and fruits of all kinds. Lemonade and apollinaris water were the only beverages served. An arrangement of red lilies, white magnolias and blue larkspurs gave the table a patriotic appearance. Among those present, in addition to the Committeemen, were Justice and Mrs. Harlan, Mrs. McKee, Mrs. Dimmick, Mrs. Parker, Senator Hawley, Senator and Mrs. Platt, Senator and Mrs. McMillan, Senator and Mrs. Cullom, Senators Proctor, Sawyer, Sherman and Aldrich, Miss Sherman, Representative Hitt, Representative and Mrs. and Miss Dalzell, Representative and Mrs. Huff, Mrs. Logan, Mrs. Noble, Miss Halstead, Mrs. Dunn, Mr. and Mrs. David R. McKee, Representative Curtis, of New York; General and Mrs. Breckinridge, Miss Breckinridge, Major and Mrs. Parker, Representative Burrows, Senator Hiscock, Senator and Mrs. Manderson, Col. Chas. W. Johnson, Secretary of the National Convention, Assistant Secretaries Spaulding, Nettleton and Crounse, Assistant Postmaster-General Whitfield, Auditors Hart and Lynch, Mr. Leech, Director of the Mint; Commissioner Mason and others.

WHITELAW REID NOTIFIED.

Hon. W. T. Durbin, of Indiana, Chairman of the Committee to notify the Candidate for Vice-President, called that Committee together at the Fifth Avenue Hotel, New York City, on the 21st day of June. The Committee was to meet Mr. Reid, at his country home, Ophir Farm, in Westchester County, New York.

The Committee was called to order in Parlor I, of the Fifth Avenue Hotel about 9:30 o'clock, by Chairman Durbin.

The Secretary of the Committee, General E. Brown Allen, of Virginia, called the roll, and the following members answered to their names.

J. O. Beocraft, California; James P. Platt, Meriden, Conn; J. F. Horr, Key West, Fla.; C. C. Wichlish, Atlanta, Ga.; United States Senator Fred T. Dubois, Idaho; Isaac L. Ellwood, Dekalb, Ill.; W. T. Durbin, Anderson, Ind.; J. L. Carney, Marshalltown, Iowa; Walter Clifford, Massachusetts; Fred E. Lee, Dowagiac, Mich.; Daniel Schell, Worthington, Minn.; C. C. Bell, Missouri; S. S. Matthews, Mississippi; Joseph E. Black, Richmond, Mo.; C. M. Donaldson, Baker City, Oregon; Thomas C. Walker, Virginia; General Edgar Allen, Richmond, Va.; George M. Bowers, West Virginia; Frank S. Genung, Muscogee, I. T.; Thomas M. Blackstock, Wisconsin; D. M. Ferry, Michigan, and E. H. Deas, South Carolina.

When the roll had been called, red, white and blue badges were distributed among the delegates. Each badge had the familiar features of President Harrison upon it. Some of the members of the delegation were not content with this outward display of Republicanism alone, for they produced the badges which they had worn at the National Convention. Under the leadership of Chairman Durbin and Senator Dubois, the delegation marched in a body out of the Twenty-third street entrance of the hotel to the Madison avenue surface cars at Twenty-third street and Fourth avenue. As the delegation walked through the street it received much attention from people, many of whom raised their hats. Two drawing-room cars had been provided for the delegates. They were attached to the regular train on the New-York and Harlem Railroad for White Plains, leaving the Grand Central Station at 10:30 o'clock. Most of those in the party had never been in New-York State before, and after the tunnel had been passed and the open country was reached much interest was shown in the scenery.

The train reached White Plains about 11:30 o'clock. Several hundred persons were at the station to meet the committeemen, and they received an extremely warm welcome. Ex-Judge Robertson, of Katonah, and Edward B. Long, the Editor of "The Westchester News," were at the head of the local committee appointed to receive the members of the Committee. Carriages gayly decorated with flags and bunting were in readiness, and they were soon rolling through the shaded streets in the direction of Ophir Farm. In the village itself most of the houses along the route were trimmed with flags and bunting, and in front of one large building hung large paintings of Harrison and Reid. The structure itself was almost covered with bunting. The drive through the woods to the farm, where Mr. Reid was awaiting the coming of his guests, was enjoyed by all. A large flag waved from the staff on the tower, and it could be seen for some time before the house came into view.

As the head of the long line of carriages reached the house, the Portchester band, which was stationed on the broad piazza, struck up a familiar air. Mr. and Mrs. Reid and D. O. Mills were waiting at the entrance to the main hall, and as each member of the party reached the door he received a cordial welcome. Some of those present were old acquaintances of Mr. Reid, and they shook him vigorously by the hand, while offering their congratulations on his nomination. Then Senator Dubois and the Chairman of the Committee, on each side of Mr. Reid, entered the large reception room. They were followed by Mrs. Reid and her father, Mr. Mills. Then came the rest of the members of the Committee.

Chairman Durbin faced Mr. Reid and said:

Mr. Reid: I have the honor to present the Committee appointed by the Republican National Convention to inform you of your nomination for the second place upon the Republican National ticket. The duty is a pleasant and agreeable one. I now introduce to you United States Senator Fred T. Dubois, of Idaho.

Senator Dubois advanced a few steps toward Mr. Reid and said:

Mr. Reid: The National Republican Convention recently held in Minneapolis selected a representative from each State and Territory from among its delegates to notify you that the great Republican party of the Nation had selected you as its candidate for Vice-President of the United States. Speaking for them, it is now my pleasing duty to give you that formal notification.

This honor, one of the highest which a free and thoughtful people can bestow, came to you unsought and with a unanimity rarely witnessed.

Your constant, consistent and effective advocacy of Republican measures for many years, and the honor and dignity with which you represented our country abroad, have merited for you this distinction.

The American people appreciated the patient and skillful diplomacy by which you opened the markets of France to the product of the American farmer. The market is the ultimate object of all nations in modern politics, and your success in that great field will command for you the hearty approval of the producers of the United States. [Loud applause.]

We believe that the people will sustain Republican principles, will indorse the personality of our standard bearers, and that the wisdom of our action at Minneapolis will be fully demonstrated by your triumphant election at the polls in November next.

Every one listened attentively to the young Senator's speech, and they applauded it with much earnestness and enthusiasm Mr. Reid's reply was as follows:

Mr. Chairman and Gentlemen: Your visit at my home and this formal statement deepen on my mind the impression which the known act of the Convention had already produced. The occasion is too great for the expression of merely personal feelings. Even my natural and heartfelt .sense of gratitude, for the confidence shown and the high trust devolved, seems in this case too unimportant to those you represent for more than a word.

The party which has guided this country on its path of unparalleled prosperity with but four years' interval since 1860 gives official notice through its duly authorized representatives, in forty-four independent States and five Territories, of its choice for the second office within the gift of sixty-five millions of freemen who cover a continent and are soon also to possess once more the seas. A profound sense of responsibility and a most earnest desire to discharge the trust you have reposed, to the satisfaction now of those you represent, and if successful, for the best interests of the country afterwards, are the overmastering emotions of the hour.

Not having sought the great honor you confer, as you have justly stated, I am the more prompt in saying that as a citizen and Republican, I shall not shrink from the duty you impose.

There will be a more convenient opportunity for such expression of political convictions as may be thought appropriate to the times and to the actual issues. But having already carefully considered the statement of our party principles put forth by your convention, I may say at once that I accept and adopt them in full. They are the principles and the party under the sway of which the country has.attained its phenomenal growth and prosperity; under which the plain people have ruled; labor has been freed, honored and better rewarded than elsewhere; the largest example of equality before the law the world has yet seen has been secured, and education, morality and the general welfare have been promoted. To reject these principles and this party would be to indict the glorious history of the Nation for almost the past third of a century.

You find a natural leader in the eminent public servant, the substantial results of whose wise and faithful Administration furnish such inspiration for the canvass. I had expected to find associated with him my distinguished friend who now adorns the office of Vice-President. As the delegation of my State and with it, the representatives of the party at large, have thought it politically wise to adhere here to the doctrine of rotation in office it gives me the right to claim, not merely the earnest support of a united party, of which we are sure, but the best counsel and the most watchful personal assistance of all its faithful and experianced leaders without exception, to the end that this great Commonwealth may again throw its decisive vote, as it did four years ago, and indisputably can do again on the Republican side.

I cannot suppress on this occasion, in which he would have taken such a cordial interest, one word of affectionate recollection for my friend in so many Presidential campaigns, the great statesman, whose present cruel bereavement, following

−1 1

hard upon two similar blows, has touched the tenderest sympathy of all, not merely of his political associates, but of both parties and of the whole country.

My State, and I think I may venture to add, my profession will appreciate the manner in which this nomination has been made and announced—deriving an added grace as it does from the unanimous vote, and from the character of this body of representative men from every section of our country.

The political sky is bright with promise. It seems a Republican year; and invoking the favor of Almighty God upon a cause which we profoundly believe just, we may courageously face the contest with the confident hope of victory at the end.

Close attention was paid to the reply, and vigorous hand-clapping followed each point in it. At its close some one proposed three cheers for Whitelaw Reid, "the next Vice-President of the United States." They were given with a will; the band struck up "Hail to the Chief," and the formal part of the presentation was over. Then introductions followed, and the members of the committee, at Mr. Reid's request, wrote their names in an album. An inspection of the house and grounds followed. C. C. Bell, of Missouri, went out into the grounds and gathered a bunch of wheat, rye, clover and apples. Returning to the reception room, he found Mr. Reid and said to him:

"Mr. Reid, I always thought that your energies all tended in one direction, the journalistic field, but I am glad to see that you are a succesful farmer as well. I propose three cheers for 'Farmer' Reid." The cheers were given heartily.

Luncheon followed, and a happy hour was spent at the table. Mrs. Reid presided, the Rev. Dr. Bushnell, of Rye, who offered grace before the meal, and Chairman Durbin sitting at each side of her. Mr. Reid and Senator Dubois had seats at the other side of the table. Ex-Judge Robertson and D. O. Mills sat next to each other. During the luncheon the band played popular and patriotic airs. While the committeemen were waiting to return to the station, photographers took pictures of them, with Mr. and Mrs. Reid sitting in the center of the group, and of the newspaper men, with Mr. Reid also in this group. From where the picture was taken the white spire of a Connecticut church could be seen.

"This is a good omen," said one delegate, "we are looking to Connecticut, and we will carry it!"

Just before the visitors left the house three cheers were given, first for Mr. Reid and then for Mrs. Reid. The station was reached in time to catch the 4:22 o'clock train for the city. The members of the committee returned to the Fifth Avenue Hotel in time to attend the mass-meeting in the Carnegie Music Hall last night.

The following letter was sent to Mr. Durbin by O. W. Little, Editor of "The Alma Enterprise," of Alma, Kansas:

I very much regret my inability to be with you as a member of the committee to notify the Hon. Whitelaw Reid of his nomination. Please be kind enough to convey to him my highest respects, and assure him in my name of the electoral vote of the Sunflower State. By doing so you will confer a lasting favor upon and receive the thanks of your humble servant in the grand cause of Republicanism. Very truly yours,   O. W. LITTLE.

This letter came from William C. Lyon, Editor of "The American," of Newark, Ohio:

Owing to pressing business engagements I am compelled to forego the pleasure and appreciated honor of meeting at the Fifth Avenue Hotel, New-York, on Tuesday next, for the purpose of formally notifying the Hon. Whitelaw Reid of his nomination to the place of Vice-Presidential candidate on our ticket. You will express my regrets at my inability at not being able to be with you in this laudable work. The ticket as nominated is the strongest that could have been selected, and Ohio will roll up a splendid majority in November for the two Ohio men at its head and for protection and honest dollars. Yours very truly,

WILLIAM C. LYON.

The Letters of Acceptance.

FROM BENJAMIN HARRISON, CANDIDATE FOR PRESIDENT.

Washington, Sept. 6.—President Harrison's letter accepting the nomination for President is as follows:

Washington, Sept. 3, 1892.

Hon. William McKinley, Jr., and Others, Colleagues, Etc.— GENTLEMEN: I now avail myself of the first period of relief from public duties, to respond to the notification, which you brought to me on June 20, of my nomination for the office of President of the United States by the Republican Convention recently held at Minneapolis. I accept the nomination, and am grateful for the approval expressed by the Convention of the acts of the administration. I have endeavored without wavering or weariness, so far as the direction of public affairs was committed to me, to carry out the pledges made to the people in 1888. If the policies of the administration have not been distinctively and progressively American and Republican policies, the fault has not been in the purpose, but in the execution. I shall speak frankly of the legislation of Congress, and of the work of the Executive Department, for the credit of any success that has been attained is in such measure due to others—senators and representatives, and to the efficient heads of the several Executive Departments,—I may do so without impropriety. A vote of want of confidence is asked by our adversaries, and this challenging to a review of what has been done we promptly and gladly accept.

The great work of the Fifty-first Congress has been subjected to the revision of a Democratic House of Representatives, and the acts of the Executive Departments to its scrutiny and investigation. The Democratic national administration was succeeded by a Republican administration, and the freshness of the events gives unusual facilities for fair comparison and judgment. There has seldom been a time, I think, when a change from the declared policies of the Republican to the declared policies of the Democratic party involved such serious results to the business interests of the country. A brief review of what has been done and of what the Democratic party proposes to undo will justify this opinion.

OUR CURRENCY SYSTEM.

The Republican party, during the civil war, devised a national currency, consisting of United States notes, issued and redeemable by the government, and of national bank notes, based upon the security of United States bonds. The tax was levied upon the issues of state banks, and the intended result, that all such issues should be withdrawn, was realized. There are men among us now who never saw a state bank note. The notes furnished directly or indirectly by the United States, have been the only safe and acceptable paper currency of the people. Bank failures have brought no fright, delay or loss to the bill holders. The note of an insolvent bank is as good and as current as a treasury note, for the credit of the United States is behind it. Our money is all National money—I might almost say International, for their bills are not only equally and indiscriminately accepted at par in all the States, but in some foreign countries. The Democratic party, if intrusted with the control of the government, is now pledged to repeal the law on state bank issues, with a view of putting into circulation again, under such diverse legislation as the States may adopt, a flood of local bank issues. Only those who in the years before the war experienced the inconveniences and loss attendant upon such money, can appreciate what a return to that system involves. The denomination of a bill was then often no indication of its value. The banking directory of yesterday was not a safe guide to-day as to credit of values. Merchants deposited several times during the day, lest the hour for bank closing should show a depreciation of the money taken in the morning. The traveler could not use in a journey to the East the issues of the most solvent banks of the West, and in consequence a money changer's office was the familiar neighbor of the ticket office and the lunch counter. The farmer and the laborer found the money received for their products or their labor depreciated when they came to make their purchases, and the whole business of the country was hindered and burdened. Changes may become necessary, but a national system of currency—safe and acceptable throughout the whole country—is the fruit of bitter experience, and I am sure our people will not consent to the reactionary proposal made by the Democratic party.

THE OCEAN CARRYING TRADE.

Few subjects have elicited more discussion or excited more general interest than that of a recovery by the United States of its appropriate share of the ocean carrying trade. This subject touches not only our pockets, but our national pride. Practically all the freight transportation to Europe, the enormous annual supplies of provisions furnished by this country and for the large return of manufactured products have for many years been paid to foreign ship owners. Thousands of immigrants annually seeking homes under our flag have been denied a sight of it until they entered Sandyhook, while increasing thousands of American citizens bent on European travel have each year stepped into a foreign jurisdiction at the New York docks. The merchandise balance of trade, which the treasury books show, is largely reduced by the annual tribute which we pay for freight and passage moneys. The great ships—the fastest upon the sea—which are now in peace profiting by our trade, are in a secondary sense, war ships of their respective governments, and in case of war would, under existing contracts with those governments, speedily take on the guns for which their decks are already prepared and enter with efficiency upon the work of destruction. The undisputed fact is that the great steamship lines of Europe were built up and are today partly sustained by direct or indirect government aid, the latter taking the form of liberal pay for carrying the mails or of annual bonus given in consideration of agreements to construct ships so as to adapt them for carrying an armament and to turn them over to the government on demand, upon specified terms. It was plain to every intelligent American that if the United States would have such lines a similar policy must be entered upon. The Fifty-first Congress enacted such a law, and under its beneficent influence sixteen American steamships, of an aggregate tonnage of 57,400 tons and costing $7,400,000, have been built or contracted to be built in American ship yards. In addition to this it is now practically certain that we shall soon have, under the American flag, one of the finest steamship lines sailing out of New York for any European port. This contract will result in the construction in American yards of four new passenger steamships of 10,000 tons each, costing about $8,000,000, and will add to our naval reserve six steamships, the fastest upon the sea.

A special interest has been taken by the establishment of a steamship line from our South Atlantic and gulf ports, and, though my expectations have not yet been realized, attention has been called to the advantages possessed by these ports, and when their people are more fully alive to their interests, I do not doubt that they will be able to secure the capital needed to enable them to profit by their great natural advantages. The Democratic party has found no place in its platform for any reference to this subject, and has shown its hostility to the general public by refusing to expend an appropriation made during the last administration, for contracts with American lines. The practical people, the workmen in our shops, the capitalists seeking new enterprises, must decide whether the great ships owned by Americans, which have sought American registry, shall again humbly ask a place in the English naval reserve, the great ships now on the designers' tables go to foreign seipbuilders for construction and the United States lose the now brightening opportunity of recovering a place commensurate with its wealth, the skill of its constructors and the courage of its sailors in the carrying trade of all the seas.

RECIPROCITY.

Another related measure, as furnishing an increased ocean traffic for our ships, and of great and permanent benefit to the farmers and manufacturers as well, is the reciprocity declared by Section 3 of the tariff of 1890, and now in practical operation with five of the nations of Central and South America, San Domingo, the Spanish and British West India islands, and with Germany and Austria, under special trade arrangements with each. The renewal of the duty on sugar, and the continuance of coffee and tea upon the free list, while giving great relief to our own people by cheapening articles used increasingly in every household, was also of such enormous advantage to the countries exporting these articles as to suggest that in consideration thereof, reciprocal factors should be shown in their tariffs to articles exported from the United States to their markets. Great credit is due to Mr. Blaine for the vigor with which he pressed this view upon the country. We have only begun to realize the benefit of these trade arranegments. The work of creating new agencies and of adapting our goods to new markets has necessarily taken time; but the results already attained are such, I am sure, as to establish in public favor the policy of reciprocal trade, based upon the free importations of such articles as do injuriously compete with the products of our farms or factories, in exchange for the free or favored introduction of our products in other countries. The obvious efficacy of this policy so increased the trade of the United States that it at once attracted the attention of European trade journals and boards of trade. The British board of trade has presented to the government a memorial asking for the appointment of a commission to consider the best means of counteracting what is called the "commercial crusade of the United States." At a meeting held in March last of the associated chambers of commerce of Great Britain the President held that exports from Great Britain to the Latin-American countries during the last year had decreased £23,750,000, and that this was not due to temporary causes, but directly to the reciprocity policy of the United States. Germany and France have also shqwn their startled appreciation of the fact that a new and vigorous contestant has appeared in the markets and has already secured important advantages. The most convincing evidence of the tremendous commercial strength of our position is found in the fact that Great Britian and Spain have found it necessary to make recipocal trade agreements with us for their West Indian colonies, and that Germany and Austria have the continued free importation of their beet sugar. A few details only as to the increase of our trade can be given here. Taking all the countries with which arrangements have been made, our trade to June 30, 1892, has increased 23.78 per cent. With Cuba during the first ten months our exports increased $5,702,193, or 54.86 per cent, and with Porto Rico $590,599, or 34 per cent.

The liberal participation of our farmers in the benefits of this policy is shown from the following report from our consul general at Havana under date of July 26 last:

"During the last half of the year 1891 Havana received 140,056 bags of flour from Spain, and other ports of the island about an equal amount, or approximately 280,112 bags. During the same period Havana received 13,976 bags of American flour and other ports an equal amount, making about 28,000 bags. But for the first half of this year Spain has sent less than 1,000 bags to the whole island, and the United States has sent to Havana alone 168,487 bags and about an equal amount to other ports of the island, making approximately 337,000 for the first half of 1892."

Partly by reason of the reciprocal trade agreement, but more largely by reason of the removal of the sanitary restrictions upon American pork, our export of pork products to Germany increased during the ten months ending June 30 last $2,025,074, or about 32 per cent. The British Trade Journal of London, in a recent issue, speaking of the increase of American coal exports and of the falling off of the English coal exports to Cuba says:

"It is another case of American competition. The United States now supply Cuba with about 150,000 tons of coal annually, and there is every prospect of this trade increasing as the forests of the island become exhausted, and the use of steam machinery on the sugar estates is developed. Alabama coal especially is securing a reputation in the Spanish West Indies, and the river and rail improvements of the Southern States will undoubtedly create an important gulf trade. The new reciprocity policy by which the United States are enabled to import Cuban sugar will, of course, assist the American coal exporters even more effectively than the new lines of railway." The Democratic platform promises a repeal of the tariff law containing this provision, and especially denounces as a sham reciprocity that section of the law under which these trade arrangements have been made. If no other issue were involved in the campaign, this alone would give it momentous importance. Are the farmers of the great grain-growing States willing to surrender these new, large and increasing markets for their surplus? Are we to have nothing in exchange for free importation of sugar and coffee and at the same time to destroy the sugar planters of the South and the beet-sugar industry of the Northwest and the Pacific coast, or are we to have the taxed sugar and coffee which a "tariff for revenue only" necessarily involves, with the added loss of the new markets which have been opened? As I have shown, our commercial rivals in Europe do not regard this reciprocity policy as a "sham," but as a serious threat to a trade supremacy they have long enjoyed. They would rejoice—would illuminate their depressed manufacturing cities over the news that the United States had abandoned its system of protection and reciprocity. They see very clearly that restriction of American products and trade, and a corresponding increase of European production and trade, would follow; and I will not believe that what is so plain to them can be hidden from our own people.

THE TARIFF.

The declaration of the platform in favor of the "American doctrine of protection" meets my most hearty approbation. The Convention did not adopt a schedule, but a principle that is to control all tariff schedules. There will be differences of opinion among protectionists as to the rate upon particular articles necessary to effect an equalization between wages abroad and and at home. In some not remote National Campaigns the issue has been—or more correctly has been made to appear to be— between a high and a low protective tariff; both parties expressing some solicitous regard for the wages of our working people and for the prosperity of our domestic industries. But, under a more courageous leadership, the Democratic party has now practically declared that, if given power, it will enact a tariff law without any regard to its effect upon wages or upon the capital invested in our great industries. The majority report of the committee on platform to the Democratic National Convention at Chicago contained this clause:

"That when custom house taxation is levied upon articles of any kind produced in this country the difference between the cost of labor here and abroad, when such a difference exists, fully assures any possible benefits to labor and the enormous additional impositions of the existing tariff fall with crushing force upon our farmers and workingmen."

Here we have a distinct admission of the Republican contention that American workmen are advantaged by a tariff rate equal to the difference between home and foreign wages, and a declaration only against the alleged "additional impositions" of the existing tariff law. Again, this majority report further declared:

"But in making a reduction in taxes, it is not proposed to injure any domestic industries, but rather to promote their healthy growth. Moreover, many industries have come to rely upon legislation for successful continuance, so that any change of law must be at every step regardful of the labor and the capital thus involved."

Here we have an admission that many of our industries depend upon protective duties "for their successful continuance" and a declaration that tariff changes should be regardful of the workmen in such industries and of the invested capital. The overwhelming rejection of these propositions, which had before received the sanction of Democratic National Conventions, was not more indicative of the new and more courageous leadership to which the party has now committed itself than the substitute which was adopted. This substitute declares that protective duties are unconstitutional-high protection-all unconstitu low protction tional. A Democratic Congress holding this view cannot enact or approve any tariff schedule, the purpose or effect of which is to limit importations or to give any advantage to an American workman or producer. A bounty might, I judge, be given to the importer under this view of the condition in order to increase the importations, and so this revenue for "revenue only," is the limitation. Reciprocity of course falls under this denunciation, for its object and effect are not revenue but the promotion of commercial exchanges, the profits of which go wholly to our producers. This destructive, un-American doctrine was not held or taught by the historic Democratic statesmen whose fame as American patriots has reached this generation—certainly not by Jefferson or Jackson. This mad crusade against American shops, the epithets applied to American manufacturers, the persistent disbelief of every report of the opening of a tin plate mill or of an increase of our foreign trade by reciprocity are as surprising as they are discreditable. There is not a thoughtful business man who does not know that the enactment into law of the declaration of the Chicago Convention on the subject of the tariff would at once plunge the country into a business convulsion such as it has never seen; and there is not a thoughtful workman who does not know that it would at once reduce the amount of work to be done in this country by the increase of importations that would follow and necessitate a reduction of his wages to the European standard. If any suggest that this radical policy will not be executed if the Democratic party attains power, what shall be thought of a party that is capable of thus trifling with great interests? The threat of such legislation would be only less hurtful than the fact. A distinguished Democrat rightly described this movement as a challenge to the protected industries to a fight of extermination, and another such rightly expressed the logic of the situation when he interpreted the Chicago platform to be an invitation to all Democrats holding even the most moderate protectionist views to go into the Republican party.

THE M'KINLEY BILL.

And now a few words in regard to the existing tariff laws. We are fortunately able to judge of their influence upon production and prices by the market reports. The day of the prophet of calamity has been succeeded by that of the trade report. An examination into the effect of the law upon the prices of protected products and of the cost of such articles as enter into the living of people of small means has been made by a Senate Committee, composed of leading Senators of both parties, with the aid of the best statisticians, and the report signed by all the members of the Committee, has been given to the public. No such wide and careful inquiry has ever before been made. These facts appear from the report:

First—The cost of articles entering into the use of those earning less than $1,000 per annum has decreased up to May 1892, ¾ per cent, while in farm products there has been an increase in prices, owing in part to an increased foreign demand and the opening of new markets. In England during the same period the cost of living increased 1-9 per cent. Tested by their power to purchase articles of necessity the earnings of our working people have never been as great as they are now.

Second—There has been an average advance in the rate of wages of 1.79 per cent.

Third—There has been an advance in the price of all farm products of 18.67 per cent and of all cereals 33.59 per cent.

The ninth annual report of the chief of the bureau of labor statistics of the State of New York, a Democratic officer, very recently issued, generally corroborates as to that State the facts found by the Senate Committee. His extended inquiry shows that in the year immediately following the passage of the tariff act of 1890 the aggregate sum paid in wages in that State was $6,377,925 in excess, and the aggregate production $31,315,130 in excess of the preceding year. In view of this showing of an increase in wages, a reduction in the cost of articles of common necessity and of the advance in the prices in agricultural products, it is plain that this tariff law has not imposed burdens, but has conferred benefits upon the farmer and the workingman. Some special effects of them could be noticed. It was a courageous attempt to rid our people of a long maintained foreign monopoly in the production of tin plate, pearl buttons, silk plush, linens, lace, etc. Once or twice in our history the production of tin plate had been attempted, and the prices obtained by the Welsh makers would have enabled our makers to produce it at a profit. But the Welsh makers at once cut prices to a point that drove the American beginners out of the business, and when this was accomplished again made their own prices. A correspondent of the Industrial World, the official organ of the Welsh tin plate workers, published at Swansea, in the issue of June 10, 1892, advises a new trial of these methods. He says:

"Do not be deceived. The victory of the Republicans at the polls means the retention of the McKinley bill and means the rapidly accruing loss of the 80 per cent. of the export American trade. Had there been no Democratic victory in 1890 the spread of the tin plate manufacture in the United States would have been both rapid and bona fide. * * * It is not yet too late to do something to reduce the price of plates. Put them down to 11s per box of 100, 14x20, full weight basis. Let the workmen take half pay for a few months and turn out more, then let the masters forgo profits for the same time."

And again that paper says: "It is clearly the interest of both (employer and workmen) to produce tin plates, tariff or no tariff, at a price that will drive all competitors from the field."

But, in spite of the doubts raised by the elections of 1890 and of the machinations of foreign producers to maintain their monopoly, the tin plate industry has been established in the United

States notwithstanding the alliance between the Welsh producers and the Democratic party.

The official returns to the treasury department of the product of tin and terne plates in the United States during the last fiscal year show a total production of 13,240,830 pounds, and a comparison of the first quarter, 826,922 pounds, with the last, 18,000,000 pounds, shows the rapid development of the industry. Over 5,000,000 pounds during the last quarter were made from American black plates, the remainder from foreign plates. Mr. Ayer, the treasury agent in charge, estimates as the result of careful inquiry that the production of the current year will be 100,000,000 pounds, and that by the end of the year our production will be at the rate of 200,000,000 pounds per annum.

Another industry that has been practically created by the McKinley bill is the making of pearl buttons. Few articles coming to us from abroad were so distinctly the product of starvation wages.

But, without unduly extending this letter, I cannot follow in detail the influences of the tariff law of 1890. It has transplanted several important industries and established them here and has revived or enlarged all others. The act gives to the miners protection against foreign silver bearing lead ores the free introduction of which threatened the great mining industries of the Rocky mountain states, and to the wool growers protection for their fleeces and flocks, which has saved them from a further and disastrous decline. The House of Representatives at its last session passed bills placing these ores and wools upon the free list. The people of the West will know how destructive to their prosperity measures would be. This tariff law has given employment to these many thousands of American men and women, and will each year given employment to increasing thousands. Its repeal would throw thousands out of employment and give work to others only at reduced wages. The appeals of the free traders to the workingman are largely addressed to his prejudices or to his passions, and not infrequently are pronouncedly communistic. The new Democratic leadership rages at the employer, and seeks to communicate his rage to the employee. I greatly regret that all classes of labor are not just and considerate and that capital sometimes takes too large a share of the profits. But I do not see that these evils will be ameliorated by a tariff policy, the first necessary effect of which is a severe wage cut, and the second a large diminution of the aggregate amount of work to be done in this country. If the injustice of his employer tempts the workman to strike back, he should be sure that his blow does not fall upon his own head or upon his wife and children. The workmen in our great industries are as a body remarkably intelligent, and lovers of home and country. They may be roused by injustice, or what seems to them to be such, or to be led for the moment by others into acts of passion ; but they will settle the tariff contest in the calm light of their November firesides and with sole reference to the prosperity of the country of which they are citizens and of the homes they have founded for their wives and children. No intelligent advocate of a protective tariff claims that it is able of itself to maintain a uniform rate of wages without regard to fluctuations in the supply of and demand for the products of labor—but it is confidently claimed that protective duties strongly tend to hold up wages, and are the only barrier against a reduction to the European scale. The Southern States have had a liberal participation in the benefits of the tariff law, and, though their Representatives have generally opposed the protection policy, I rejoice that their sugar, coal, ores, corn, fruits, cotton cloths and other products have not been left to the fate which the votes of their Representatives would have brought upon them. In the construction of the Nicaragua canal in Central America, in the establishment of American steamship lines, these States have also special interests, and all these interests will not always consent to be without representation at Washington. Shrewdly, but not quite fairly, our adversaries speak only of the increased duties imposed upon tin, pearl buttons and other articles by the McKinley bill, and omit altogether any reference to the great and beneficial enlargement of the free list. During the last fiscal year $438,000,772 worth of merchandise, or 55.35 per cent. of our total importations, came in free (the largest precentage in our history) while in 1889 the per cent. of free importations was only 34.02. The placing of sugar upon the free list has saved to the country in duties in 15 months, after paying the bounties provided for, $87,000,000, This relief has been substantally felt in every household, upon every Saturday's purchase of the workingmen.

One of the favorite arguments against a protective tariff is that it shuts us out from a participation in what is called with swelling emphasis "the markets of the world." If this view is not a false one how does it happen that our commercial competitors are not able to bear with more serenity our supposed surrender to them of the "the markets of the world," and how does it happen that the partial loss of our market closes foreign tin plate mills and plush factories that still have all other markets? Our natural advantages, our protective tariff and the reciprocity policy make it possible for us to have a large participation in the "markets of the world" without opening our own to competition that would destroy the comfort of our people.

BIMETALLISM.

The resolution of the Convention in favor of bimetallism declares, I think, the true and necessary condition of a movement that has upon these lines my cordial adherence and support. I am thoroughly convinced that the free coinage of silver at such a ratio to gold as will maintain the equality in their commercial uses of the two coined dollars would conduce to the prosperity of all the great producing and commercial nations of the world. The one essential condition is that these dollars shall have and retain an equal acceptability and value in all commercial transactions. They are not only a medium of exchange, but a measure of values, and when unequal measures are called in law by the same name, commerce is unsettled and confused and the unwary and ignorant are cheated. Dollars of unequal commercial value will not circulate together. The better dollars are withdrawn and become merchandise. The true interests of our people and especially of the farmers and working people, who cannot closely observe the money market, is that every dollar, paper or coin, issued or authorized by the government, shall at all times and in all its uses be the equivalent, not only in debt paying but in purchasing power, of any other dollar. I am quite sure that if we now act on this subject independent of other nations we would greatly promote their interests and injure our own. The monetary conditions in Europe within the last two years tended very much to develope a sentiment in favor of a larger use of silver, and I was much pleased and encouraged by the cordiality, promise and unanimity with which the invitation of this government for an international conference upon this subject was accepted by all the powers. We may not only hope for, but expect some highly beneficial results from this conference, which will now soon assemble. When the results of this conference is know we shall then be able intelligently to readjust our financial legislation to any new conditions.

FAIR APPORTIONMENTS AND FREE ELECTIONS.

In my last annual message to Congress I said: "I must yet entertain the hope that it is possible to secure a calm, patriotic consideration of such constitutional or statutory changes as may be necessary to secure the choice of the officers of the government to the people by fair apportionments and free elections. I believe it would be possible to constitute a commission, non-partisan in its membership and composed of patriotic, wise and impartial men, to whom a consideration of the questions of the evils connected with our elections system and method might be committed with a good prospect of securing unanimity in some plan for removing or mitigating those evils. The constitution would permit the selection of the commission, to be vested in the Supreme Court, if that method would give the guaranty of impartiality. This commission should be charged with the duty of inquiring into the whole subject of the law of elections as related to the choice of officers of the national government, with a view to securing to every elector a free and unmolested exercise of the suffrage and as near an approach to an equality of value in each ballot cast as is attainable."

The demand that the limitations of suffrage shall be found in the laws only was a just demand and no just man should resent or resist it. It seemed to me that an appeal to our people to consider the question of readjusting our legislation upon absolutely fair non-partisan lines might find responsive effect—many times I have occasion to say that laws and elections methods, designed to give unfair advantages to the party making them would some time be used to perpetuate in power a tradition of a party against the will of the majority of the people. Of this we seem to have an illustration in the recent State elections in Alabama. There was no Republican ticket in the field. The contest was between white Democrats. The Kolb party say they were refused the representation guaranteed by law upon the Election Boards; and that when the courts by mandamus attempted to right this wrong, an appeal that could not be heard until after the election made the writs ineffectual. Ballot boxes were thrown out for alleged irregularities or destroyed, and it is asserted on behalf of one-half, at least, of the white voters of Alabama, that the officers to whom certificates have been given were not honestly elected. There is no security for personal or political rights. The power of the States over the question of the qualification of electors is simply to protect them against the dangers of an ignorant or depraved suffrage and the demand that every man found to be qualified under the law should be made secure in the right to cast a free ballot and have that vote honestly counted cannot be abated. Our old Republican battle cry, "a free ballot and a fair count," comes back to us not only from Alabama, but from other States and from men who, while differing from us widely in opinion, have come to see that parties and political debate are but a mockery if, when the debate is ended, judgment of honest majorities are to be reversed by ballot box frauds and tally sheet manipulations in the interests of the party, or party faction, in power. These new political movements in the States and the conditions of some of the State courts against unfair apportionment laws encourage the hope that the arbitrary and partisan election laws and practices which have prevailed may be corrected by the States, the law made equal and non-partisan, and the elections free and honest. The Republican party would rejoice at such a solution—as a healthy and patriotic local sentiment is the best assurance of free and honest elections. I shall again urge upon congress that provision be made for the appointment of a non-partisan commission to consider the subject of apportionments and elections in their relation to the choice of federal officers.

THE CIVIL SERVICE.

The civil service system has been extended and the law enforced with vigor and impartiality. There has been no party juggling with the law in any of the departments or bureaus, as had before happened, but appointments to the classified service have been made impartially from the legal lists. The system, now in force in all the departments for the first time, has been placed in prominence on the basis of merit, as ascertained by a daily record, and the efficiency of the force thereby greatly increased.

The approval so heartily given by the Convention to all those agencies which contribute to the education of the children of the land was worthily bestowed, and meets my hearty approval, as does also the declaration as to liberty of thought and conscience, and the separation of church and State. This republic in intelligent citizenship and the increased interest manifested in the States in education, the cheerfulness with which the necessary taxes are paid by all classes and the renewed interest manifested by the children in National affairs are hopeful indications that the coming generations will direct public affairs with increased prudence and patriotism. Our interest in free public schools open to children of suitable age is supreme and our care for them will be jealous and constant. The public school system, however, was not intended to restrain the natural right of the parent, after contributing to the public school fund, to choose other educational agencies for his children. I favored aid by the general government to the public schools, with a special view to the necessities of some of the Southern States. But it is gratifying to notice that many of the States are with commendable liberality developing their school systems and increasing their school revenues to the great advantage of the children of both races.

AGRICULTURE.

The considerate attention of the farmers of the whole country is invited to the work done through the State and Agricultural Departments in the interest of agriculture. Our pork products had for ten years been not only excluded by the great continental nations of Europe, but their value discredited by the reasons given for this exclusion. All previous efforts to secure the removal of these restrictions had failed, but the wise legislation of the Fifty-first Congress, providing for the inspection and official certification of our meats and giving the President power to forbid the introduction into this country of selected products of such countries as should continue to refuse our inspected meats, enable us to open all the markets of Europe to our products. The result has been not only to sustain prices by providing new markets for our surplus, but to add 50 cents per hundred pounds to the market value of the inspected meats. Under the reciprocity agreements special favors have been secured for agricultural products and our exports of such products have been greatly increased with a sure prospect of a further and rapid increase. The Agricultural Department has maintained in Europe an agent whose special duty it is to introduce their various preparations of corn as articles of food, and his work has been very successful.

The Department has also sent skilled veterinarians to Liverpool to examine, in connection with the British veterinarians, the live cattle from the United States landed at that port ; and the result, in connection with the sanitary methods adopted at home, has been that we hear no more about our cattle being infected with pleuro-pneumonia. The judicious system of quarantine lines has prevented the infection of northern cattle with the Texas fever. The tariff bill of 1890 gives better protection to farm products subject to foreign competition than ever before, and the markets for such products have been enlarged by the establishment of new industries and the development of others. We may confidently submit to the intelligent and candid judgment of the American farmer whether in any corresponding period so much has been done to promote his interests, and whether in a continuance and extension of these methods there is not a better prospect of good to him than in the invitation of the Democratic party to give our home market to foreign manufacturers and to abandon the reciprocity policy; and better also than the radical and untried methods of relief proposed by other parties which are soliciting his support.

THE NICARAGUA CANAL.

I have often expressed my strong conviction of the value of the Nicaragua Ship Canal to our commerce and to our navy. The project is not one of convenience, but of necessity. It is quite possible, I believe, if the United States will support the enterprise, to secure the speedy completion of the canal without taxing the treasury for any direct contribution, and at the same time to secure to the United States that influence in its management which is imperative.

OUR FOREIGN POLICY.

It has been the purpose of the Administration to make its foreign policy not a matter of partisan policy, but of patriotism and National honor ; and I have very great satisfaction in being able to state that the Democratic members of the Committees of foreign affairs responded in a true American spirit. I have not hesitated to consult freely with them about the most confidential and delicate affairs, and I frankly confess my obligation for needed co-operation. They did not regard a patient but firm insistence upon immunity from insult and injury for our citizens and sailors in foreign ports as a policy of "irritation and bluster." It would seem that to be a Democrat one must take the foreign side of every international question if a Republican Administrator is conducting the American side. I could not believe that the same submission to insult and outrage by any Nation at the hands of any other can ever form the basis of assisting friendship—the necessary element of mutual respect will be wanting.

The Chilian incident, now so happily and honorably adjusted, will, I do not doubt, place our relations with that brave people upon a more friendly basis than before. In our relations with the great European powers, the rights of the United States and her citizens have been insisted upon with firmness. The strength of our cause and not the strength of our adversary, has given tone to our correspondence. The Samoan question and the Behring sea question which came from the preceding Administration, have been, the one settled and the other submitted to arbitration. Never before, I think, in a like period, have so many important treaties and commercial agreements been concluded, and never before, I am sure, have the honor and influence, national and commerical, of the United States, been held in higher estimation in both hemispheres:

THE VETERAN SOLDIER.

The Union soldiers and sailors are now veterans of time as well as of war. The parallels of age have apporached close to the citadels of life, and the end, for each, of a brave and honorable career is not remote. Increasing infirmity and cares give the minor tone of sadness to the appeal of service and suffering. The ear that does not listen with sympathy and the heart that does not respond with generosity are the eart and heart of an alien and not the heart of an American. Now soon again the surviving veterans are to parade upon the great avenues of the National' Capital, and every tribute of honor and love should attend the march. A comarde in the column of the victors' parade in 1865, I am not less a comarde now.

IMMIGRATION.

I have used every suitable occasion to urge upon the people of all sections the consideration that no good cause can be promoted upon the lines of lawlessness. The punishment inflicted by them have no salutary influence; on the contrary, they perpetuate feuds. It is practically the duty of the educated and influential to help the ignorant and weak when possible. The moral sentiment of the country should be aroused and brought to bear for the suppression of these offenses against the law and social order.

The necessity of a careful discrimination among the emigrants seeking our shore becomes every day more apparent. We do not want and should not receive those who, by reason of bad character, are not wanted at home. The industrious and self-respecting, the lovers of law and liberty, should be discriminated from the pauper, the criminal and the anarchist, who come only to burden and disturb our communities. Every effort has been made to enforce the laws and some convictions have been secured under the contract labor law.

OUR PROSPERITY.

The general condition of our country is one of great prosperity. The blessing of God has rested upon our fields and upon our people. The annual value of our foreign commerce has increased more than $400,000,000 over the average for the preceding 10 years and more than $210,000,000 over 1890, the last year unaffected by the new tariff. Our exports in 1892 exceeded those of 1890 by more than $172,000,000, and the annual average for 10 years by $265,000,-000. Our exports of breadstuffs increased over those of 1890 more than $144,000,000; of provisions over $4,000,000, and of manufactures over $8,000,000. The merchandise balance of trade in our favor in 1892 was $202,944,342. No other Nation can match the commercial progress which those figures disclose. Our compassion may well go out to those whose party necessities and habits still compel them to declare that our people are oppressed and our trade restricted by a protective tariff. It is not possible for me to refer even in the briefest way to many of the topics presented in the resolutions adopted by the Convention. Upon all that have not been discussed I have before publicly expressed my views. A change in the personnel of a National Administration is comparatively of little moment if those exercising public functions are able, honest, dilligent and faithful. Others possessing all these qualities may be found to take their places, but changes in the laws and in administrative policies are of great moment. When public affairs have been given a direction and business has adjusted itself to those lines, any sudden change involves a stoppage and new business adjustments. If the change of direction is so radical as to bring the commercial turntable into use the business changes involved are not readjustments but reconstructions. The Democratic party offers a program of demolition. The protective policy—to which all business, even that of the importer, is now adjusted—the reciprocity policy the new merchant marine, are all to be demolished –not gradually, nor taken down, but blown up. To this program of destruction it has added one constructive feature, the re-establishment of state banks of issue. The policy of the Republican party is, on the other hand, distinctively a policy of safe progression and development—of new factories, new markets and new ships. It will subject business to no perilous changes, but offers attractive opportunities for expansion upon familiar lines.

Very respectfully yours,

BENJAMIN HARRISON.

FROM WHITELAW REID, CANDIDATE FOR VICE PRESIDENT.

Hon. W. T. Durbin, Anderson, Ind.:

DEAR SIR—When the nomination with which the National Convention had honored me was formally announced by your committee, I accepted it at once. In doing so, I accepted also, the principles set forth in the resolutions adopted by the Convention as the basis of the appeal to the popular suffrage.

To do other or less than this, is, to any honorable man, an impossibility. A political party is an association of citizens seeking to have the government conducted in accordance with its views and presenting candidates whom it strives to elect for that purpose. To accept its nomination without intending to carry out its principles would be as dishonorable and as criminal as to procure goods under false pretenses.

There will be no misunderstanding as to the purposes of the Republican party in this contest, and no doubt as to the attitude of its candidates. What it intends it has set forth in language that cannot be mistaken; and they will strive by all the lawful means in their power to enforce its plainly expressed will. Since my interview with your committee further reflection and careful attention to the arguments on both sides in the current public discussion have confirmed my belief in the wisdom of the Republican declarations, as well as in the lucid candor with which they have been presented.

THE PARTY PLATFORMS.

The party platforms, so-called, are more important this year than usual. Both the leading candidates have once commanded the approval of the American people in its highest form of expression. Attention is therefore concentrated less on the men themselves, and more on the principles each is put forward to represent, and would, in case of election, be required to carry out. The declarations of our opponents demand a still closer scrutiny, since their victory now would give them the first opportunity they have had since 1859 to put in practice their policy. Never, since that date, have they had control at once both in the executive and legislative departments of the government. This year the election of a President clearly carries with it majorities in both houses of congress.

It is obvious that, in the common judgment of the people in all parts of the country, the really vital issues which this year divide the parties, and demand a popular decision, are those relating to the tariff and currency. Fortunately both sides have stated their positions on the subjects with directness, simplicity and frankness. The issues thus made between the rival candidates for the popular suffrage are specially sharp and distinct. We favor a protective tariff, and when in full power, made the present one. Our opponents favor a tariff for revenue only and promise the repeal of the present one.

We maintain that the tariff should cover the difference in the cost of the home and foreign product, caused by the difference in the home and foreign wages for the labor employed upon it. Our opponents distinctly repudiated the proposition that American wages should be considered in the matter, and insisted instead that a tariff levied for anything but revenue only was unconstitutional. As the London Times of Sept. 28 very naturally remarked, "this policy, if fairly and logically carried out, is not to be distinguished from free trade, in the practical form in which we are familiar with it."

If protective duties are unconstitutional, as was asserted at Chicago, no financial legerdemain can produce any other "readjustment" than that which would naturally follow the removal of all imposts tending to bolster up particular branches of industry and commerce.

Should the American people now choose the Republican candidates the present tariff would stand, or when amended, would only be so changed as to secure a closer conformity in practice to the principles on which it was made. If our opponents should be chosen, their congress is pledged to the repeal of the present tariff and to the adoption of one arranged for revenue only, and their executive is pledged to the doctrine that a tariff having regard also for American wages is also unconstitutional, so that the only new one that could escape the presidential veto must be of the kind which the London Times considers equivalent to free trade. We maintain that the present tariff has worked well; that it has developed American manufactories, steadied and increased American wages and promoted the general prosperity. Our opponents deny that there has been any increase of prosperity under the present tariff, declare that wages have been reduced, and denounce Republican policy, which, as they say, fosters no other industry so much as that of the sheriff.

We favor the system by which, when we think the country ready for the reduction or abolition of duties, we insist upon getting corresponding and reciprocal advantages from foreign countries as the condition of their enjoying these advantages in our own markets. Our opponents denounce this reciprocity as a sham, and therefore inferentially pledge themselves to its repeal.

The sharp issues thus presented for the decision of the American people cover more comprehensively and more specifically than ever before the whole range of considerations relating to the protective tariff, its constitutionality, its expediency, its relation to wages, its practical workings, and the question whether, as it is from time to time reduced, we should throw away the advantages thus extended to foreign nations or should get something in return for them.

The constitutionality of the protective tariff has heretofore been thought established. A tariff bill avowedly for "the encouragement and protection of manufacturers," was carried through the first congress by James Madison and was signed by George Washington. A third of a century later, Andrew Jackson, in a message to congress, (Dec. 7. 1830) maintaining the constitutional protective system said: "In this conclusion I am confirmed as well by the opinions of Presidents Washington, Jefferson, Madison and Monroe, who have each repeatedly recommended the exercise of this right under the constitution, as by the uniform practice of congress, the continued acquiescence of the states and the great understanding of the people."

To this testimony from the men who made the constitution, and from the father of the modern Democratic party, may be added that of the latest high authority of that party on constitu-

tional law, the Hon. George Ticknor Curtis, who has recently
said: "In common with many other Democrats I cannot sub-
scribe to the doctrine that a protective tariff is unconstitutional.
In drafting and voting for this resolution the members either
showed dense ignorance of American political history, or they
manifested a purpose to win votes by deceiving the voters. I
cannot, at the bidding of these gentlemen, unlearn the lessons of
my whole life. If I cannot claim to be an authority on the subject, I can point out to others the true sources from which to de-
rive interpretations of the constitution. They are to be found in
the interpretations given by the first congress, by Washington's
administration, and by the succeeding administrations of Jefferson, Madison, John Quincy Adams and Jackson."

The expediency of a protective tariff has been vindicated by the
experience of the last 30 years- the most wonderful period of
financial success over unheard-of difficulties in the record of
modern civilization. Under it and by its aid the Republican
management of our finances has resulted in the largest payment
of a National debt in the shortest time known to history, and in
the simultaneous development of the industries of the country
and the prosperity of the people on a scale without a parallel.
Eight years ago, in a masterly public paper, James G. Blaine
called attention to the revelations of the United States census as
to the net results of the labor and savings of the American people under the tax system of a protective tariff. The "true value"
of all the property in the United States, excluding slaves, was set
down in the census of 1860 as fourteen thousand million of dollars
-that being what there was to show for the toil of 250 years.
With the success of the Republican party that year the Republican protective policy which has since prevailed was introduced.
In the census of 1880 the true value of the property in the United
States was set down at $44,000,000,000, making an increase in these
20 years of Republican protection of $30,000,000,000, or over double
the entire growth of the previous 250 years. We are now able to
carry the comparison 10 years further, through the disclosures of
another decennial census. It appears that the property of the
United States has been still further increased in the last 10 years
by $14,000,000,000, making a total increase in the 30 years of Repub-
lican rule and a Republican protective tariff of $44,000,000,000.
against the $14,000,000,000 earned in the previous 250 years.

Our opponents join issues with us directly and positively on
the effects of the present tariff. They deny that there has been
any increase of prosperity under it, declare that wages have
been reduced, and denounce our policy, saying with a sneer, it
fosters no industry so much as that of the sheriff. It has been a
fortunate circumstance for an impartial public, which desires
above all, to ascertain the exact facts in regard to such an asser-
tion, that in the course of their official duty a number of Democratic officers have since been required to report the statistics in
their several departments, bearing upon this subject. Such
reports have been made successively by the commissioner of
labor statistics, the bank commissioner and the board of equalization of the state of New York, by the chairman of the savings
bank commission and the chief of the bureau of labor statistics
of Massachusetts, by the commission of bureau of statistics
of New Jersey, and by others. All these reports tend to
show an increase during the year 1891 under the present tariff,

in wages, in the value of products, in the deposits in savings banks, or in building and loan associations, and in the value of real and personal property as fixed for purposes, not of speculation, but of taxation. In the state of New York alone these Democratic reports, all presented since the adoption of the Democratic platform, show the following results: Net increase of wages, $6,377,920.09; net increase of product, $31,315,130.68; increase of savings bank deposits, $18,755,448.27; net sum invested during the year in building and loan associations, $18,789,720; increase in the valuation of the real and personal property of the state, $152,374,753.

These official Democratic refutations of the Democratic denial that the country is prosperous are confirmed by the personal experience and observation of the people at large. They know that their own regions are not suffering from general calamities and in their communities other industries are more prosperous than that of the sheriff; and that they may be left to form their own opinions of the degree of trust and power they should now give to a party thus eager to calumniate the country.

The market of the United States is the largest and best in the world, because our people, in proportion to their means and numbers, are the largest purchasers. The reciprocity policy so far adopted by the Republican party simply provides that where we now take off duties, and give foreign products free access to this market, we shall stipulate for corresponding advantages to our products on their markets. How an intelligent and candid American can object to this is incomprehensible, but the Democratic party has formally denounced it as a sham. At the close of the fiscal year, June last, it had been in operation but a few months, and under all the disadvantages attending the opening of new lines of trade in foreign countries. Yet even then it had increased our trade with the foreign countries to which it had been applied, nearly one-fourth. The exact increase was 23.78 per cent. Since then there has been a still greater increase, amounting, on Sept. 1, the latest date to which the official statistics are yet available, to 27.6 per cent. The total values of our domestic exports to the countries with which we have reciprocity treaties since these have been in force down to Aug. 31, 1892, amount to $104,406,516. The total values of our domestic exports to the same countries for the corresponding period of the year before these reciprocity treaties, amounted to $81,837,752. The net value of sham reciprocity, therefore, to the United States in this brief time, and during its infancy, was $22,569,284. It is obvious that the new trade thus opened, particularly with our neighbors in Central and South America, is far reaching. This trade lies at our doors and is with people naturally inclined to friendly commercial relations with us through kindred interests and political aspirations. It involves largely the exchange of products peculiar to each country and needed by the other; it opens new markets for our cereals and vast fields for the use of our machinery and manufactures, and it must naturally bring with it also an annual increase of miscellaneous business between us and them, outside the articles directly affected by the treaties. In short, it reclaims American business which should belong to us, but has heretofore crossed the Atlantic, and brings it to our ports. To abandon this system, which is absolutely equitable to both sides, which costs us nothing and which brings such results, would be madness; while to denounce it as a sham is an untruth. It is for the people who are so generally benefited by it already, and who must see its promise of the future, to decide whether they should now intrust the care of it to the party which threatens the one and does the other.

THE CURRENCY.

On the subject of currency the issue between the Republican party and its opponents is almost as sharply defined as the one of tariff. We demand that every dollar, paper, silver or gold, shall be made and kept as good as any other dollar. Our opponents, while professing the same desire, demand that the national bank currency shall be broken down by the repeal of the 10 per cent tax on the issues of state banks. The lamented Garfield proudly claimed, in 1880, that our paper currency is now as national as the flag and everywhere equal to coin. The proposal of our opponents is to sectionalize it again and thus return to the state bank system, under which it was rarely equal to coin, was often at a ruinous discount and often worthless. No human being ever lost a dollar or a cent by the note of a national bank, solvent or otherwise. Losses by state bank notes have been counted by tens of millions, have touched all classes and reached every corner of the country. It is true that the gradual payment of the government bonds may require some change in the securities demanded as a guarantee for national bank notes. The party which devised the system and made it a magnificent success may be depended upon to meet that emergency when it arises; and the one party assured that they could not be relied upon in the matter is the party which has now formally proposed, as its remedy for the difficulty, a return to the semi-barbarous condition of the heterogeneous bank issues before the war. There is good reason to hope for some practical union of effort for common solution of the silver problem with an increased use of silver, through the renewed international silver conference, which the wise policy of the present Administration has secured from the leading commercial nations of the world, but in any event the country has learned in all such questions to trust the financial skill and integrity of the Republican party and to distrust its opponents. The Republican party, in raising the funds for prosecuting the war for the Union, in devising the national banking system, in resuming specie payments, in paying the debt, in providing the great sums required for giving just pensions to the soldiers and in its whole policy of the last thirty years, has shown the greatest financial ability and achieved the greatest financial successes attained during the century in any part of the world, and has, therefore, a right to claim the popular confidence now. The Democratic party has opposed in whole or in part at every one of the successful steps, and has encouraged in turn every financial heresy of the same period from fiat money and the payment of bonds in greenbacks to the substitution of state for national bank notes; and it has therefore no right to claim the popular confidence now on this subject. It is a statement which no candid and competent business authority, whatever its political tendencies, can deny that the adoption now of the policy pursued by our opponents in their declaration of principles as to the repeal of the present tariff, the passage of a tariff for revenue only and the substitution of state bank for national currency, would give an immediate and disastrous shock to business. But we are sometimes told that they do not mean what they say. If so, could the people wisely intrust power to a party which does not mean to keep its promises, and appeals for popular support with an admitted lie upon its lips?

At other times we are told that their candidate neither believes their platform nor would dream of carrying it out, and that therefore there is no danger.

We put no such aspersion upon their candidate. To hold the nomination under such circumstances would be an act not only of treachery to the party whose standard he bears, but of folly besides—since the country could not help seeing that an effort was in progress to deceive it, as to either the policy of the party or the purpose of the candidate. Above all things the American people like plain dealing, despise men who have not the courage of their convictions, and repudiate those who try to deceive them. It is impossible that any candidate in this contest can for one instant have intended to occupy a position so unworthy.

Furthermore, the duty of carrying out the plain purpose decided by an overwhelming majority in the highest Democratic tribunal would devolve, not only upon the President, but upon the congress to be elected by this party, which promises the repeal of the present tariff, which demands a tariff for revenue only and pronounces any other unconstitutional and proposes to abandon the national bank currency in favor of the issue by the state banks.

The danger has never before been so great. The Democratic party has threatened the peace or prosperity of the country but within the memory of this generation it has never had the power to carry out its purposes. As has been already remarked, when it had a President he was held in check by a Republican congress; and when a Democratic house of representatives was elected it was still held in check by a Republican senate. Not for one hour since March, 1859, has the Democratic party had the power to control the legislation and direct the policy of the United States government. On the comparatively recent occasion, when it elected the only President it has chosen since James Buchanan, it did not succeed in securing a majority in the senate, and was, therefore unable to enact such legislation as is now proposed. It has been sometimes said: You predicted all manner of disasters when Mr. Cleveland was elected, but nothing happened.

A good many regrettable things did happen; though the worst could not, because the hands of the party were tied in congress. But the present political situation makes it plain to everyone that a Democratic victory in the states which they must now carry in order to elect a President, would also insure them enough new senators to reverse the present slender majority in the senate. If they elect a President this time, they will certainly have both the house and the senate too and the United States will be placed in their absolute control for the first time since 1859, with nothing to prevent their carrying out the threats they have made against both the present tariff and the present currency. It is as idle, therefore, as it is slanderous to say that there is no danger from the triumph of our opponents since their candidate will refuse to carry out their principles. He could not, with credit, and he could not anyway, because the power would rest not with him but with congress.

These questions of tariff and the currency are of vital and instant importance to the whole country and to all its people. The radical change, amounting to an absolute reversal of policy urged in this time of great prosperity and general contentment would affect the earnings of every factory, the wages or employment of every operative, the markets of every farmer, the transactions of every business man, the well-being of every citizen of the republic. The attempt to change this issue and divert attention from these pressing questions of the hour to an alleged force bill scarcely calls for notice. The very title of the bill referred to proclaimed its object to be to prevent the use of force at elections. It failed lately anyway, and the Southern white men who were its chief, as they were its most interested opponents, now begin to wish it revived to protect them from being themselves counted out of elections they have fairly won—as the other day in Alabama—by their own white fellow Democrats. It is well, however, to say that the denunciation in the Democratic platform of the principle that the federal government may supervise the election of federal officers is grotesque. That principle has been long recognized; and it has been sustained by the courts, it now stands undisputed on the statute books, and it was enforced at recent elections by Grover Cleveland, then President of the United States, through his order of Oct. 5, 1886, to Mr. Garland, his attorney-general. But it is not to be disguised that the recent clamor against the principle, if it means anything, means a purpose to nullify the XIV. and XV. articles of the constitution of the United States.

AMERICAN SHIPPING.

The revival of American shipping is a subject of great and growing importance. The Republican party has taken successful steps to this end; and the resolutions of its Convention confirm its devotion to a principle on which its practice has already been wise and efficient. The Democratic resolutions say nothing on the subject, and it is fair to say that the Democratic party takes no interest in it. Its only desire is that we should buy our ships abroad—just as through the whole tariff contests, it wished us to buy our iron and clothes and cotton goods and glassware and pottery and tin abroad.

In addressing to you, in accordance with usage, these observations, I have preferred to confine them to the questions of policy, of present and commanding importance, on which the position of the two parties are absolutely antagonistic. But I take this opportunity to repeat my adhesion to the resolutions of our Convention as a whole.

The Administration of President Harrison has been generally recognized, honest, able and safe. Considering the number of important subjects, of both foreign and domestic policy, it has been compelled to deal with and the satisfaction that has attended the results, it may, indeed, be pronounced brilliantly successful. Abroad it has adjusted difficult questions with consideration for weak nations and with courteous but resolute firmness to the most powerful. It has protected the honor of the flag, and the rights of our citizens; has preserved the peace and secured the further application of its principles of international arbitration; has removed the long standing prohibitions on unjust charges of unhealthfulness against our food products; has opened new markets with our neighbors and promoted a closer intercourse. At home it has refunded a portion of the remaining debt at the lowest rates recommended by any nation in the civilized world; has largely strengthened and improved our navy; has greatly enlarged the free list at our custom house and remitted over $100,000,000 of duties on a single article in admitting sugar free. Not to enumerate further, it may be fairly said that the present condition of the country and the general public confidence in the administration combine to form the strongest protest against subjecting the people to the shock and needless risk inevitable in such a change.

A sudden reversal of policy is not what either the suggestions of ordinary business prudence or the other obvious and general contentment of the people call for.

I believe your declaration of principles and your renomination of a prudent, spotless and skillful President will command the popular approval at the polls, and will, under God, inure to the continued benefit of our country.

Very respectfully yours,

WHITELAW REID.

Ophir Farm, New York, Oct. 18, 1892.

APPENDIX.

GOV. PILLSBURY'S RESOLUTION LIMITING THE PRESIDENTIAL TERM.

Resolved, that the Republican Party, in National Convention assembled, most earnestly and emphatically urge the adoption of an amendment to the National Constitution, extending the term of office of the President of the United States to six years; and providing, that no person who has been President of the United States shall thereafter be eligible to the same office.

We therefore respectfully request the Congress now in session to propose an amendment to the National Constitution that will speedily accomplish this end.

INDEX.

PILLSBURY'S

FLOUR

MAKES

More Bread
Better Bread
Whiter Bread

THAN ANY OTHER
FLOUR.

Daily Product
of the
Pillsbury Mills,
15,500 BARRELS.

Sold by all Grocers

BETWEEN
CHICAGO, PEORIA, ST. LOUIS

AND

ST. PAUL,	MINNEAPOLIS,	COUNCIL BLUFFS,
OMAHA,	ST. JOSEPH,	KANSAS CITY,
ATCHISON,	LINCOLN,	DEADWOOD,
	CHEYENNE,	DENVER.

THE SAFEST WAY
THE QUICKEST WAY
THE EASIEST WAY
THE ONE WAY

IS VIA THE GREAT

MAGNIFICENT VESTIBULED TRAINS OF

PULLMAN SLEEPING CARS
RECLINING CHAIR CARS
PEERLESS DINING CARS
Run Every Day in the Year.

Any information desired as to Rates of Fare, Time of Trains and Choice of Routes can be obtained by addressing any of the following representative of the Burlington Route:

P. S. EUSTIS, G. P. & T. A.,	A. C. DAWES, G. P. & T. A.,
CHICAGO, ILL.	ST. LOUIS, MO.
J. FRANCIS, G. P. & T. A.,	W. J. C. KENYON, G. P. A.
OMAHA, NEB.	ST. PAUL, MINN.

The New York Tribune.

A GREAT REPUBLICAN, HIGH CLASS NEWSPAPER.

The Daily averages more than 12 pages a day. Large Type. Broad columns. The easiest paper in the United States to read. Foreign letters; admirable market and Wall street reports; the best reviews and criticisms; and all other features of a great metropolitan Daily.

The Sunday Tribune averages not less than 24 pages and is less political than the week-day issues. To the news, editorials, and other regular features of the Daily, are added a great mass of brilliant special features, reviews, society news, illustrated special articles, foreign letters, Fashions, Home Decoration, etc.

The Semi-Weekly is a most charming and complete newspaper for those living beyond the range of the Daily and who want a low-priced compilation of all the news of the week and the best features of both the Daily and Weekly.

The Weekly is printed every Wednesday. It contains a page for old soldiers, two for farmers, and a collection of all the best that appears in the Daily. Like the Semi-Weekly it is distinguished by nearly a page a week of the entertaining and masterly writings of Roswell G. Horr on the Tariff, the Currency, Coinage, and other great questions of the day.

The Monthly includes the great "Extras" published by The Tribune every year.

Postage prepaid by Tribune, except on Daily and Sunday paper for mail subscribers in New York City, and on Daily, Semi-Weekly and Weekly to foreign countries, in which case extra postage will be paid by subscribers.

Remit by Postal Order, Express Order, Check, Draft or Registered Letter. Cash or Postal Note if sent in an unregistered letter, will be at owner's risk. When sending by Express, be particular to buy an Express Money Order.

RATES BY MAIL.

	1 year.	6 mos.	3 mos.	1 mo.
Daily, 7 days a week....................	$10 00	$5 00	$2 50	$1 00
Daily, without Sunday...................	8 00	4 00	2 00	90
Sunday Tribune.........................	2 00	1 00	50	— —
Weekly Tribune	1 00	—	—	—
Semi-Weekly Tribune....................	2 00	—	—	—
Monthly Tribune, 12 numbers a year.....	2 00	—	—	— —

www.ingramcontent.com/pod-product-compliance
Lightning Source LLC
Chambersburg PA
CBHW030840270326
41928CB00007B/1145